D1369538

J. Ranade Workstation Series

To order, or to receive additional information on these or any other McGraw-Hill titles, please call 1-800-822-8158 in the United States. In other countries, please contact your local McGraw-Hill office. **BC14BCZ**

Solaris 2.x

**System Administrator's
Guide**

S. Lee Henry
*Johns Hopkins University
Baltimore, Maryland*

John R. Graham
*Catalina Consulting Group
Baltimore, Maryland*

McGraw-Hill, Inc.

New York   San Francisco   Washington, D.C.   Auckland   Bogotá
Caracas   Lisbon   London   Madrid   Mexico City   Milan
Montreal   New Delhi   San Juan   Singapore
Sydney   Tokyo   Toronto

Library of Congress Cataloging-in-Publication Data

Henry, S. Lee.
    Solaris 2.x system administrator's guide / S. Lee Henry, John R.
Graham.
        p.   cm.
    Includes index.
    ISBN 0-07-029368-6
    1. Operating systems (Computers)   2. Solaris (Computer file)
I. Graham, John R.   II. Title.
QA76.76.063H475   1995
005.4′469—dc20   94-28036
                                                                        CIP

    4 5 6 7 8 9 10 11 12 13 14 BKMBKM 9 9 8 7

ISBN 0-07-029368-6

*The sponsoring editor for this book was Jerry Papke, the editing supervisor was
Caroline R. Levine, and the production supervisor was Suzanne W. Babeuf. This
book was set in Century Schoolbook by McGraw-Hill's Professional Book Group
composition unit.*

Contents

Part 5   Theory of Operation

Chapter 14. The Solaris Kernel   257

Chapter 15. Multithread Architecture   269

Chapter 16. Scheduling   277

Preface

This book is about how to do Solaris 2.x system administration. This is a simple statement with far-reaching implications. The problem with writing a book of this nature is that there are literally millions of UNIX users in the world, each with a particular way of doing things, each with a particular experience level, and each, at least in a small way, affecting the system administrator's job. To offer something substantive to this menagerie of users and system administrators requires a special approach. What we have sought to do in this book is to provide insight into how Solaris 2.x works and how to most easily manage it.

Organization of the Book

This book is organized to tackle two very large issues. First, we are attempting to appeal to all levels of administrators and, in a sense, all users. Second, we have attempted to sift through mounds of documentation and provide a one-stop reference to get you started on almost any task. This is not to say that we have provided an end-all book of this genre, but we believe that we have a design that offers something for everyone.

To get the most value from this book, we suggest that you identify your own level of expertise and use the chart we've prepared to guide you to the most appropriate reading path. The levels that we pictured while writing this book are

- *Novice*: Level I. The beginning system administrator and users familiar with the basic UNIX command set who are curious about what it is like to manage Solaris 2.x systems. Some knowledge of shell environments is assumed.

- *Intermediate*: Level II. The intermediate system administrator or system-savvy user. This individual understands the concepts of file systems, knows how to manage user accounts, has a handle on UNIX security basics, and has some experience with backups and software installation.

- *Advanced*: Level III. The advanced system administrator develops plans and strategies for system administration, including overall network and system security, naming services, system tuning, and optimization.

- *Migrating*: Levels II and III.   Someone who has been working on UNIX-based systems at the intermediate or advanced level who wishes to apply the knowledge gained from this work to the Solaris 2.x environment.

We have divided the book into five major parts. Look under your experience levels in the chart below for the sections we think you should read.

		Level	
Section	I	II	III
Part 1 Introduction	x		
Part 2 Installation	x	x	x
Part 3 Basic Administration Tasks	x	x	x
Part 4 Advanced Administration		x	x
Part 5 Theory of Operation			x

Additional Reading

This book is not intended to replace any documentation provided by Sun. Rather, it is intended to supplement it. Our hope is that it will serve as a desktop reference for most system administration tasks and will provide a place to go to help you sort through the "standard" UNIX documentation.

Many would consider essential to system administration several topics not covered in this book, such as UUCP and sendmail. These topics and others have remained unchanged from previous releases and are extremely well documented in other places. In some cases, we have included sources for additional or related material in summary sections and bibliographies.

Brave New World

There is a portion of this book which we believe is unique to system administration texts: Part V—Theory of Operation. With the introduction of Solaris 2.x, the system has exposed many previously hidden features of the kernel. At least they were hidden to all but the most advanced users and hackers who dared to brave the world of adb. Now, there are literally hundreds of kernel variables which are tunable, rather than the handful you could change under SunOS 4.x. This feature is a double-edged sword. Used properly, tuning kernel variables will improve the performance of many operations. Without proper guidance, however, the results can be disastrous. The intent of Part 5 is to give some insight into the inner workings of the Solaris kernel and allow very fine tuning of the system. Be aware, however, that kernel tuning is still very much an art form and use caution!

S. Lee Henry
John R. Graham

Acknowledgments

John and I wrote this book because we had to. Although we joke that we did it for money and fame, we really did it because we are part of the Sun user community. That community is undergoing a major transition. We had to play a part in this—even above and beyond our normal jobs.

I was originally inspired by the dedication of SunSoft's Norman Eaglestone. His campaign to guide Sun users through to being successful and self-confident with Solaris 2.x was deployed with considerable technical content rather than "marketing fluff." As a long-time Sun systems manager, a columnist, and a board member of the Sun User Group, I felt I needed to join the pilgrimage. It wasn't easy. After taking a leave of absence from a federal job, I found myself cut off from any support or resources. Simply getting what I needed to do the book became a challenge—until a number of people came through for me. From a top executive to Calvin Fox (my favorite field engineer), a number of Sun people (and a couple of non-Sun people) helped me to get what I needed and encouraged me to keep writing. Then John climbed on board and with him, the assurance that the book would be that much better.

I have more people to thank than I will be able to mention. For helping me stay afloat equipmentwise: Jan Hauser (Sun) and Mike Sheffield (HDSi). For timely "marketing support": Bev Burge and Jay Koontz (both Sun). And for encouragement and understanding when times were rough: Anna Easley (IDA). I would also like to thank Patrick Bernhardt for the CD "Solaris Universalis"; not every author gets to have theme music.

I would like to thank Johns Hopkins University for giving me a job (and income!) even when I was still somewhat preoccupied with completing the book. And Alan, Geir, Gyula, Julian, Kavan, Eric, Steve, and a whole lot of others for helping me to feel at home and keeping my spirits up.

I would also like to thank the staff and members of the Sun User Group (SUG) both for the opportunity to "field test" some of this material at one of the SUG conferences and for all the insights and support that I've garnered from being a SUG member for so many years.

I can't thank enough my husband, Fred, and our daughters, Danielle, Vail, and Onowa Nicole, for allowing me this opportunity to do something that I felt was important even though it was a financial challenge and, at times, I neglected them terribly.

S. Lee Henry

Introduction

1

The Role of Systems Administration

"It's a dirty job, but somebody has to do it." We've all heard these words, mostly said in jest when the "poor" marketing rep has booth duty for two weeks in Hawaii. Applied to systems administration, however, it may be close to the truth. It's a dirty job. It's also a job that you may be able to shape to your personality and interests. If you get a kick out of helping people (regardless of whether they're grateful) and if you're compulsive enough to take care of dozens of problems all at the same time, ranging from the tedious to the terrifying, you might have what it takes to live and thrive as a systems administrator.

Systems administrators run the gamut in both skills and responsibilities. Some are unwilling "volunteers" from other ranks in their organizations— clerks or data analysts who didn't seem quite busy enough in spite of frenzied work schedules and, all of a sudden, "Hey, you can manage the systems, too" comes out of their bosses' mouths. For others, systems administration is their chosen profession and they have worked and studied hard to be very good at it. For most of us, however, we "kinda got here" almost by accident. Starting out as programmers, engineers, even mathematicians and scientists, we first got involved in administering systems because it was needed and, eventually, we got hooked. The excitement of managing networks of sophisticated systems hypnotized us, and the continuing challenge of keeping these networks humming smoothly has kept us hooked.

Systems administrators do everything from repairing cables to designing networks, from installing systems to debugging complex applications, from helping users who've forgotten their passwords to setting the computing directions for large organizations. For the most part, they are overworked and underappreciated. This truth is further complicated by the fact that the role that systems administrators play in most organizations is poorly defined. They generally have a lot of responsibility for the productivity of many other people, yet inadequate control over those people and resources needed to do their jobs properly. In addition, the better they do their jobs, the more they are taken for granted. When computer networks run smoothly, no one notices "the person behind the curtain."

To a large degree, the jobs of systems administrators are tightly linked to the sophistication of their users. Organizations in the business of building sophisticated software or hardware will be populated by people who can, independently, manage their own systems. This fact, however, doesn't necessarily spell a cushy job. It simply poses different problems for the system administrator who needs to track the configuration of all these "independently" managed systems.

Another important factor that shapes the job is the size and focus of the organization. Some systems administrators do "everything" for a small group of users, while others play a more limited role within a much larger organizational structure.

The politics of systems administration are wrought with difficulty as well. For one thing, systems administrators are almost never part of the mainstream of their organizations; they provide support to the organization's focus, whether that focus is commercial, educational, or governmental. As such, they often suffer from "second-class citizen" syndrome. They rarely own or control the resources that they administer and often have to petition to get the tools that they need to meet their responsibilities.

1.1 Routine Responsibilities

When most people think of systems administration, they imagine someone standing by a nine-track tape drive feeding it tapes while it backs up users' files. They think about someone setting up accounts for new users and, if they're lucky, being informed so that they can remove them when people quit or retire.

These two images are certainly realistic but paint only a cartoonlike picture of what systems administration is about. Besides the more obvious responsibilities, systems administrators are network sleuths, application drill sergeants, and fair-usage diplomats.

Backing up file systems is certainly one of the more important tasks of systems administration. Safeguarding their users' productivity is the single most critical thing that systems administrators do; backups are one important aspect of this. Routine backups can be time-consuming and troublesome or relatively painless depending on the hardware and software that is available and the sophistication of the administrator; those who manually enter dump commands and spend hours each week changing tapes have quite a bit to learn when it comes to making their jobs manageable.

Another aspect of safeguarding systems and their data is systems security. In most organizations, the system administrator is responsible for establishing and implementing network security policy and monitoring network security in practice.

Administering user accounts is a responsibility that some administrators handle with fairly rigid policies and centralized controls while others simply get their users off the ground by creating a login account and then leave them on their own to use and manage it.

Managing mail systems is a very important task in most organizations since electronic mail is becoming more and more important as a standard means of communication within large organizations. Organizations which are connected to the Internet are especially attuned to the opportunities and risks of global communications.

Managing network naming services involves managing hostnames and addresses, information about network users, mail addresses, and network services. With tools like NIS and NIS+, much of this work has been automated. Still, there is much that administrators need to understand and do to provide proper and up-to-date network information across their networks.

Managing printers is one of the responsibilities that most systems administrators come to dislike. This is because Murphy's rules apply to printers more than just about any other piece of networking equipment. Printers are always getting jammed, exhausting toner cartridges, and frustrating their users. The administrator who hasn't spent several hours in a row dealing with a printer problem has probably been on the job less than a month.

Systems administrators are often responsible for the general health and well-being of their systems. Although few wear white coats and do "rounds," most are, in one way or another, acutely aware of the emerging problems and weak spots in their networks and manage a never-ending queue of things to be fixed or investigated.

Most systems administrators also pay a good deal of attention to the well-being of their users. Problems they are having, needs that haven't been addressed, as well as their familiarity and comfort with the systems they use are important issues to the responsible systems administrator.

1.2 Emergencies

Hardware and software failures sound alarms in systems administrators' heads. The bigger the failure and the more users affected, the more quickly the system administrator will jump to the call. Some administrators are poorly equipped to determine the cause of failures. Others have advanced troubleshooting skills, sophisticated test equipment, and a lot of expertise.

Planned power outages will often involve a system administrator in an effort to properly shut down and eventually reboot hundreds of systems. Coordination with users and the timeliness of bringing the systems back up correlate highly with the administrator's level of maturity and concern for users.

Lost and corrupted files are emergencies to their owners. Although users may perceive their own problems as the most important in the world, mature systems administrators know how to balance their responsibilities to individual users with the need to look after the proper functioning of the entire network and will elect a role that is neither aloof nor harried.

1.3 Challenges

Systems administrators have their fair share of responsibilities and of headaches. From network problems to application failures, from user errors to slights from managers unable to appreciate the difficulties of their jobs unless "all hell is breaking loose," systems administrators hold out against seas of evil and help a lot of people meet a lot of deadlines.

With the challenges that large heterogeneous networks add, the caring systems administrator would likely be a dying breed were it not for the growing set of tools to help them manage these networks and automate repetitive tasks. One primary design goal of Solaris 2.x was to provide tools to do just this. You will see, as you read this book and as you learn to manage your Solaris network, the effort that is being put into system administration tools that help you do your job more effectively.

2

Product Overview and Standards

Introduction

Before embarking on the task of administering the Solaris Operating Environment, it is useful to know some of the motivation for why the product was developed in the fashion it was. In this chapter, we will introduce some of the motivating factors including a product overview and some of the standards that are merged into the Solaris 2.x product.

The Solaris product was the result of a desire to create a "standard" operating environment for the UNIX domain of computers and users. The three major developers in this market are AT&T, Santa Cruz Operation (SCO), and Sun Microsystems. Together, these three companies produce the bulk of the UNIX-based operating systems in the world. The Solaris Operating Environment is Sun Microsystems' contribution to the System V–compliant UNIX world.

The benefits and features of Solaris 2.x fall into three categories: users, software developers, and systems administrators.

- To users, the major feature is that there are few changes to the user interface. The windows-based programs will be very familiar to experienced users. Most of the basic utilities have not changed and only occasionally will some of the options have changed.

- To software developers, the major features are a common platform for building and distributing software and a host of standards which will allow development of many platforms without changes.

- The tasks of the system administrator have been made simpler. There is only one name service, NIS+, which is capable of replacing both NIS and DNS. Kernel configuration is no longer needed, and there are now some windows-based tools for doing basic administration tasks such as adding user and printers.

2.1 Product Overview

Each Solaris release consists of three parts:

- SunOS Operating System
- OpenWindows
- Deskset (calendar manager, mail tool, etc.)

The current release of the operating environment is Solaris 2.3. The three parts of Solaris 2.3 are SunOS 5.3, OpenWindows Version 3.3, and Deskset version 3.3. As a matter of interest, the Solaris 1.x product line ended with Solaris 1.3, which contained SunOS 4.1.3, OpenWindows Version 3, and Deskset Version 3.

SunOS 5.x is a version of the System V Release 4 (SVR4) operating system from AT&T. Following are some of the features included in the operating system:

- Dynamic configuration of the kernel
- Real-time scheduling class
- Fully preemptible kernel
- Full support for Sun multiprocessor architecture
- Stream network modules
- Support for threaded applications
- Tunable parameters for optimal performance

From the user perspective the intent is that there be a minimal amount of changes. The default set of commands will be the SVR4 commands and options, but there is a set of commands in the /usr/ucb directory which provide the Berkeley (BSD) commands that the user may be used to. Additionally, the Korn shell has been added as an alternative to sh and csh.

If the user does most of the routine work, such as manipulating files, editing or keeping a calendar, using the windows-based deskset, then there will be very little change from the user perspective.

The system administrator may notice the most dramatic change in the way the administrator's task is done under Solaris 2.x. The reward for migrating to Solaris 2.x and learning the administration task is a lessened workload due to use of windows-based tools and common interface for many tasks.

The System V utilities for system administration have become the default. Some of the new features the system administrator will be introduced to in this volume are:

- Automatic kernel configuration
- NIS+
- Improved security

- System V printing
- Support for 4.x diskless clients
- System V package administration

From the perspective of the software designer and developers there are many new features which will impact development activities:

- No bundled compiler
- No Sunview
- Improved documentation
- Adherence to standards
- Use of forms and menu language interpreter (FMLI)
- Korn shell

2.2 Windows and Graphics

Over the years that Sun has been shipping its operating system there have been several changes to the basic windowing mechanics. Originally, there was Sunview and NeWS (Networked Window Services) and more recently the introduction of OpenWindows, which is based on the X11 graphics standards from MIT. With Solaris 2.3, Sun has begun to support the Motif windowing methods by distributing several packages in the Software Development Kit (SDK). Since all the tasks and concepts covered in this volume can be done with no windows support, windowing is not covered here. The tools that are windows based such as `admintool` are displayed using OpenWindows and not Motif.

2.3 Standards

One of the improved features of the Solaris Operating Environment is the adherence to published standards. The use of standards is good because it allows users, administrators, and developers to learn one set of commands and programming techniques that will be used across all UNIX platforms. The following paragraphs list some of the standards organizations and the documents which have been used in the development of the Solaris Operating Environment:

2.4 AT&T

The first version of UNIX was developed by Bell Laboratories in the early 1970s and has undergone major revisions and variations to take on its present form. In 1989, AT&T announced a standard UNIX design called System V Release 4 (SVR4). The intent was to provide the best functionality from all the UNIX implementations currently running and to provide a basis for comparison for future work.

2.5   IEEE and POSIX.1

A group of users established a committee with the objective of defining a set of standards for application-level interfaces. In 1984 this group aligned with IEEE to gain worldwide acceptance of this standard. This standard has become known as *POSIX* (Portable Operating-System Interface for Computer Environments). The current revision of this standard is IEEE Standard 1003.1-1990.

2.6   ANSI

The American National Standards Institute (ANSI) develops procedures for due process of standards acceptance. It does not develop or interpret standards. ANSI verifies that all interested parties have been heard on an issue and declare that a consensus has been reached by the majority of the concerned parties. The largest contribution from ANSI to UNIX is the development of language standards for C, FORTRAN, and COBOL.

2.7   AT&T-Based Standards

The following standards are all part of the family of standards developed by AT&T to further refine the SVR4 interface.

2.7.1   ABI

The Application Binary Interface (ABI) defines a standard binary interface for compiled applications on systems running SVR4-compliant operating systems. Since it is not possible to define binary interfaces across different hardware architectures, the ABI is a family of specifications to apply as needed to different hardware types.

The ABI consists of a generic part that applies to source-level interfaces which will remain constant across hardware types. The ABI also specifies a processor-specific portion that will define the interface for a particular architecture. The generic part plus the processor-specific part will define a complete specification for a specific architecture, such as SPARC, 80x86, or 680x0.

2.7.2   SVID

The *System V Interface Description* (SVID), published by AT&T, defines an operating-system interface much the same way POSIX does. SVID defines a base system definition as well as system extensions for more robust systems. The SVID defines system call source code interfaces, user interfaces, and runtime behavior of the conforming applications.

A system may or may not conform to an SVID extension; however, all the components of an extension must be present to comply fully with the extension specification.

2.7.3   DDI/DKI

The Device Driver Interface (DDI) and the Device Kernel Interface (DKI) were developed to standardize kernel routines used in device drivers. Any device driver written to conform to these standards will be portable to any other conforming system.

2.7.4   DLPI

The Data-Link Provider Interface (DLPI) is a kernel-level support standard that specifies the format of messages that are passed to and from the data-link layer of the network model. These message formats are specified in `<dpli.h>` and are part of SunOS 5.1 as well as SVR4.

2.7.5   TPI

The Transport Provider Interface has much the same function as the DLPI. It defines the message format for a message passed to and from the transport layer of the network model. The current TLI (Transport-Level Interface) system call interface is entirely compliant with TPI.

3

Shells

Shells in UNIX act both as interactive command interpreters and as powerful programming languages. Most of the popularity and awesome power of UNIX derives from the richness of its shells as command interpreters. In fact, it almost goes without saying that proficiency in use of the shells is the most clear demonstration of competency in UNIX itself.

There is no point in trying to exhaustively cover any of the three shells available in Solaris in this chapter. Each of the three shells has been the topic of numerous books. Instead, we will provide an overview of how UNIX shells relate to the overall Solaris environment, discuss the basic functions that shells provide, introduce each of the three shells, explain the files that are used to configure each of the shells, and provide some sample scripts that will be useful for managing Solaris systems.

3.1 Basic Shell Function

The shell in UNIX systems is basically a command interpreter that takes what the user enters and transforms it into something that the UNIX kernel can understand. In this process, it parses user commands and expands arguments and metacharacters to create a complete and unambiguous command that it then submits to the kernel for execution. Incorporated into executable files, these commands can be invoked in groups, creating scripts or programs that, essentially, create new commands that the user can invoke.

3.1.1 Command interpretation

Each shell is a user-level process and has no special privilege with the kernel. At the same time, it is pervasive. From the moment that you log in, you are operating within one of the shells. Anytime you say `ls`, you're asking the shell to interpret and deliver your request to the UNIX kernel. When you say `ls -l a*`, you're asking it to do a little more work; the shell has to expand the `a*` into a string containing all filenames beginning with a lowercase "a." Once it has done this, it can pass your request to the kernel for execution.

3.1.2 Scripting

The UNIX shell also functions as a programming language with a sophisticated ability to use UNIX utilities in a manner not unlike the way in which C uses library calls. Once a series of shell commands has been stored in a file and made executable, you have essentially added a new command to the system. For systems administrators, the ability to customize and streamline their work through the use of shell scripts has long been one of the keys to managing the complexity and diversity of the typical UNIX network.

3.2 Shells Provided in Solaris 2.x

Solaris 2.x provides three shells, each offering somewhat different functionality. The first of these, the Bourne shell, has been the default shell for most UNIX systems for a long time. The C shell, developed at Berkeley, more closely resembles the C language (from which it got its name). The most recent shell to be added to SunOS, the Korn shell, is similar to the Bourne shell (it is actually a superset), but has considerably more modern features.

3.2.1 The Bourne shell

The Bourne shell was the first UNIX shell and was developed by Stephen Bourne while he was working at Bell Labs. The Bourne shell lacks some of the features of the newer shells, but is fairly universal in the UNIX world. In Solaris 2.x, there are two special-purpose shells related to the Bourne shell: the job control shell (jsh) and the restricted shell (/usr/lib/rsh).

3.2.2 The C shell

The C shell was originally developed by Bill Joy and resembles the C-programming language in syntax. With a number of enhancements (e.g., command aliasing and filename completion), the C shell has won over a large following.

3.2.3 The Korn shell

The most recent of the UNIX shells, the Korn shell is a superset of the Bourne shell; that is, all Bourne shell commands are valid in the Korn shell. With greatly improved performance and a large collection of more modern features, the Korn shell is likely to become the shell of choice. A restricted version of the Korn shell (rksh) is also available in Solaris 2.x.

3.3 Specifying the Shell

A shell can be specified in one of three ways: (1) as the default shell on logging into the system, (2) any time you wish to specifically invoke a shell, and (3) within a shell script. Each of these is explained briefly below.

3.3.1 The login shell

The shell that is defined within the passwd file for each user is their *login* shell, which is the one that they will likely use most often. The specified shell determines which configuration files are read when the user logs in and the character of interactive commands for that user.

3.3.2 Invoking a shell

Alternate shellscan be invoked at any time simply by entering their name. For example, if you are using the Bourne shell and decide you want to switch to the Korn shell, you simply enter the command ksh.

Each shell invocation is layered on top of the previous shell. Whenever you exit a shell, you will return to the one in which you were working when you invoked it. Notice in the Try This exercise how the shells are invoked and how the shell prompt changes as a result.

TRY THIS   Enter Several Shells and Exit Them

```
# echo $SHELL
sh
# ksh
# csh
nextpage# sh
# csh
nextpage# ksh
# ^D
nextpage# # nextpage# # ^D
```

If I enter ^D once more, I will exit the current shell. If this is my login shell, I will be logged out.

3.3.3 Specifying the shell within a script

You can determine which shell is used to execute a shell script by including its name on the first line of the script as shown for each of the three shells below.

`#!/bin/sh`	The Bourne shell
`#!/bin/csh`	The C shell
`#!/bin/ksh`	The Korn shell

You can also execute a script with a given shell by supplying the script name as an argument to the shell invocation using a syntax such as `/bin/sh script`. However, if you specify the wrong shell, you will generate errors even if the correct shell is specified on the first line of the script. In general, the system attempts to determine which shell is used in your script and uses it to execute the script.

3.4 Shell Comparisons

Although there is a considerable amount of overlap in the functionality of the three shells, each provides somewhat different features and enough differences in syntax that you will likely become decidedly more comfortable with one of the shells in particular. Although most UNIX users tend to have a strong preference for one particular shell, you might find that you use different shells for different purposes and will undoubtedly write or use scripts written in all three.

Shells provide a means for running commands in the background, continuing commands across more than one screen line, grouping multiple commands on a screen line, looping (e.g., through a list of filenames or hostnames), and rerunning previously entered commands (sometimes allowing you to edit them first). Therefore, your shell environment can add considerable convenience and you are likely to strongly prefer one shell over another because of its features or because of how well you know it.

The C shell, for example, has a feature which completes a filename so that you do not have to type the whole name.

TRY THIS   Try Filename Completion

```
nextpage# touch I_am_a_file_with_a_VERY_long_name_that_I_hate_to_type
nextpage# touch I_am_a_file_with_an_awfully_long_name
nextpage# set filec
nextpage# ls I*
I_am_a_file_with_a_VERY_long_name_that_I_hate_to_type
I_am_a_file_with_an_awfully_long_name
nextpage# ls I_a[ESC]
nextpage# ls I_am_a_file_with_a
```

The shell completes the filename up to the point at which it finds a conflict and then beeps at you to enter the differentiating character (i.e., _ or n in this case).

Two of the three shells support aliases that allow you to define shorthand names for commands that are too long to type every time or hard to remember. If you use the history command often so that you can reuse commands without retyping them, you might shorten it to h in the C or Korn shells:

C shell	`alias h history`
Korn shell	`alias h=history`

Shells also provide a means for evaluating arithmetic expressions and can, to a limited extent, be used as calculators.

TRY THIS   Add Numbers in the Shell of Your Choice

```
# /bin/sh
# A=`expr 6+2`
# echo $A
8
# /bin/csh
nextpage# set A=`expr 6+2`
nextpage# echo $A
8
nextpage# /bin/ksh
# A=`expr 6+2`
# echo $A
8
```

The shells also provide some degree of job control. You can move foreground tasks into the background, move them back into the foreground, and kill running processes. Job control for the Bourne shell is invoked through the job-control shell, `jsh`. This shell is an interface to the Bourne shell which provides a set of job-control commands. Another special shell associated with the Bourne shell is the restricted shell, `rsh`. The restricted shell severely limits the commands the user can execute. It is described very briefly in this chapter and in more detail in Chap. 7.

We will attempt to discuss some of the more important distinctions, but leave it to you to more fully learn the shell of your choice. To begin with, there are fairly extensive man pages on each of the shells. There are also a number of excellent books which cover shell programming, many of which explain a single shell in great depth. If you are not expert in use of the shell, we suggest that you purchase a book on the shell of your choice and offer some suggestions in the bibliography at the back of the book.

3.5   Shell Basics

Some of the basic capabilities of each of the available shells include filename expansion, command substitution, and I/O (input-output) streams. These are only briefly described in the sections below.

3.5.1   Positional parameters

The numbered arguments to shell scripts are referred to as *positional parameters.* Their names, except for the $, are only digits which represent their position in the command line. For all three shells, the 0th parameter is the name of the shell script if the command is included in a script. If, on the other hand, the commands are entered interactively, both the Bourne and Korn shells will respond with the name of the shell itself.

TRY THIS   **Write a Script That Echoes Its Name**

Create a file containing the following line, make it executable, and try it.

```
echo $0 "is my name"
```

The result should be the name of the file (i.e., the script). Try the same command while interactively using the different shells.

```
nextpage% /bin/sh
$ echo $0 "is my name"
/bin/sh is my name
```

Shells also provide a way to evaluate the number of positional parameters that have been passed and their values. The way of representing this information is different for each shell.

	Bourne	C	Korn
Number of Parameters	$#	$#argv	$#
All Parameters	$@ or $*	$argv	$@ or $*

TRY THIS   **Count Parameters**

```
#!/bin/csh
#
echo "I have been passed" $#argv "parameters"

#!/bin/ksh
#
echo "I have been passed" $# "parameters"
```

The variables that the shells provide to determine the number of parameters which have been passed are most often used in testing inside of a script to ensure that the command invoking the script has been entered correctly. The two lines displayed below show this test in the C shell and the Bourne and Korn shells.

TRY THIS   **Testing the Number of Parameters**

C shell:

```
if ($#argv !=2) then
...
else
...
endif
```

Bourne and Korn shells:

```
if test $# -ne 2
then
...
else
...
fi
```

3.5.2 Filename expansion

All three shells use metacharacters for filename expansion. The metacharacters supported by all three shells are

character	represents
?	any one character
*	any string of characters
[]	a restricted range of characters

TRY THIS   Exploit Filename Expansion in Each Shell

```
# /bin/csh
nextpage# ls fi?e.*
file.1 file.2 file.3 file.4 file.5
nextpage# ls file.[123]
file.1 file.2 file.3
```

The Bourne and Korn shells also support a negation operator which works with the range operator as shown in the example below.

```
# ls file.[!123]
file.4 file.5
```

TRY THIS   View Filename Expansion

The C Shell has an option which causes it to display expanded commands before sending them off to the kernel for execution. Let's use this shell option for looking at the expansion operation on a list of files.

```
# /bin/csh -x
nextpage# ls -1 file*
ls -1 file.1 file.2 file.3 file.4 file.5 ficult'
ls -1 file.1 file.2 file.3 file.4 file.5        ← expanded list
-rw-r--r--   1 root    other     535132 Mar 18 14:57 file.1
-rw-r--r--   1 root    other     535132 Mar 18 14:58 file.2
-rw-r--r--   1 root    other     535132 Mar 18 14:59 file.3
```

```
-rw-r--r--   1 root   other     535132 Mar 18 15:01 file.4
-rw-r--r--   1 root   other     535132 Mar 18 15:02 file.5
```

You can also view this substitution by including metacharacters within the echo command. Examine the commands in the Try This below and its response.

TRY THIS   Experiment with Metacharacters

```
$ echo *
Ch6.TOC  Ch6.TOC.bak  Chap5.ix  Chap5.ix.bak  Chap6.TOC  Chap6.TOC.bak  Chapter5
Chapter5.bak accounts capt00.fil overwrite flush disks filesys file jg ksh nis-
plus outline outline- outline.save packages quotas shells sleemail sleemail2


$ echo Can you hear me?
echo: No match
```

In the first echo command, you get a list of all of your files because the * is replaced before the echo command is executed. In the second, we get a non-match because we have no files whose names begin with the characters "me" and are followed by a single character. If we did, echo would print something like "Can you hear mex" or "Can you hear mex mey mez" depending on the number of files meeting these criteria.

3.5.3   Quoting

How quoting characters affect substitution in commands is a very important factor in preparing shell scripts. The types of quotes that you use determine whether what you type is treated literally or is evaluated (causing a substitution). It is also very important to understand how escapes and quotes can be used to neutralize metacharacters so that this substitution doesn't happen when we don't want it.

A simple example can be used to show how the different quotes cause radically different interpretation of their contents. In the Try This exercise below, we set up a variable called SUBJECT and include within different quoting characters. Notice how in the first echo command, the variable is replaced with its contents. In the second, no evaluation is done at all. In the third, the evaluation is performed but the system attempts to execute the resultant string and cannot find a command named Life.

TRY THIS   Experiment with Quoting

```
$ SUBJECT="Life"
$ echo $SUBJECT
Life
$ echo "$SUBJECT is difficult"
```

```
Life is difficult
$ echo '$SUBJECT is difficult'
$SUBJECT is difficult
$ echo `$SUBJECT is difficult`
/bin/ksh: Life:  not found
```

3.5.4   Command Substitution

Command substitution, which permits the output of shell commands to be assigned to variables and the output of one command to be used within another, takes one of two forms. The ` characters as shown in the previous section can be used to cause the commands within these quote characters to be executed. In the previous Try Me section, we got a response different than we might have expected because the contents of the quote did not resolve to an executable command. If we instead entered a valid command within our quotes, we might get a response such as

```
nextpage% Today\'s date is `date`
Today's date is Mon Dec 24 10:55:16 EDT 1993
```

The Korn shell can also use the $(command) syntax to effect command substitution. The `date` in the example above could also be expressed as $(date) in the Korn shell.

3.5.5   I/O streams

Redirection of input and output is available in all three shells. The syntax that you use for the simplest redirection is the same for each shell, but more advanced use of redirection (e.g., redirecting only errors or overriding the noclobber option) requires familiarity with the operators for the particular shell. The simplest and most common redirection operators are described as follows:

<file	standard input is redirected, input comes from file
>file	standard output is redirected to file
>>file	standard output is appended to file

To keep these operations from overwriting existing files, you can set the noclobber option. On the other hand, when noclobber is set and you want to override it, you can do so with one of the following operators.

>| or >!	standard output is redirected to file (noclobber option is ignored). The first form is used with Korn shell; the second is used with the C shell.
>>!	standard output is appended to file (noclobber option is ignored). This is used with the C shell.

The file descriptors assigned to standard I/O are the same for the Bourne and Korn shells. File descriptor 0 is standard input, file descriptor 1 is standard output, and file descriptor 2 is standard error. Under normal circumstances, all three of these are defined to be your screen.

3.5.6   Environment variables

Environment variables play a very important role in customizing the working environment for a particular user. The behavior of the shell, the commands that are recognized by the system, regardless of whether there is a default printer, and where applications look for data files may all be controlled through the set of variables that represents a particular user's environment. Environment variables differ from ordinary shell variables in one important way; they are global in nature. Once set, environment variables are available throughout your working environment. This global nature is due to the fact that UNIX passes the value of environment variables to programs executed within the shell. This is not true of shell variables which have value only within the current shell.

In the C shell, environment variables are established with the `setenv` command using the syntax `setenv VARIABLE value`. In the Bourne and Korn shells, environment variables are created and then exported; thus, they are established by using both the set and the export command using the syntax `set VARIABLE=value;export VARIABLE`. Variables that you create in this way are still available if you explicitly invoke a different shell. Similarly, environment variables set up in scripts are available even if you are using a shell different from that in which the script is written.

When a shell is invoked from within a shell, it is a "child process." It is important to understand that variables are not passed from child to parent. As an example of this, whenever you invoke a script, the variables are not available when the script has completed.

TRY THIS   Experiment with an Environment Variable

Set up an arbitrary environment variable in one shell and display its value after invoking a different shell.

```
nextpage% setenv TOP 12
nextpage% echo $TOP
12
nextpage% /bin/sh
$ echo $TOP
12
```

Some environment variables are automatically set by the shell; others have a default value, and still others have no value unless you set them. One of the most familiar environment variables is the PATH variable. It is extremely important because it tells the shell what path to follow through your file systems to find the executables that you refer to in your commands. Many environment variables are available with only one or two of the shells. You should familiarize yourself with the variables available in the shells that you support.

To display the values of your environment variables, use the env command. If you log into Solaris 2.x as root, the number of variables set when you log in is relatively small (unless you have significantly modified root's startup files). On starting up OpenWindows through use of the shell script /usr/open-win/bin/openwin, many additional variables will be defined. These are defined and exported from the script as is explained above.

3.6   The Restricted Shell rsh

The restricted shell rsh was developed for users whose access to your systems should be severely restricted for security reasons. Users of rsh cannot cd to other directories, and are, therefore, limited to their own home directories. In addition, they can only use commands that are accessible through their PATHs as established when they log in. They can only access files within the home directory and below and cannot use redirection to create new files.

3.7   Summary

Solaris 2.x provides the most popular UNIX shells along with their job-control and restricted counterparts. For further information on any of the shells, there are many excellent texts.*

You can also read the following manual pages:

```
csh(1)
jsh(1)
ksh(1)
rksh(1)
sh(1)
```

Suggested search terms for AnswerBook include *shell* and shell names. AnswerBook has some very useful information on shells and on configuring the user's environment.

---

*A couple of these that are particularly good are Gail Anderson and Paul Anderson, *The UNIX Shell Field Guide,* Prentice-Hall, 1986 and Anatole Olczak, *The Korn Shell User & Programming Manual,* Addison-Wesley, 1992.

4

The Solaris 2.x File System

To grasp the concept of a file system like that used in Solaris 2.x., you should first recognize that data when stored on disk looks little like the assemblage of files and directories that you see when you are using your account. The organization which transforms the data on disk into a series of files and directories resembling a treelike structure is an abstraction. The actual data is stored in sometimes noncontiguous chunks along with descriptive information that allows the operating system to interpret the data as a series of files and directories.

4.1 Disks

The underlying disks on which our file systems reside will vary in the overall size (storage capacity) usually ranging from a couple hundred megabytes to a couple gigabytes. They will also vary in the number of heads, sectors, and tracks that are part of their physical geometry. All these details are well hidden from the casual user.

Disks generally consist of multiple surfaces (platters) which spin rapidly together around a common spindle and devices (heads) for sensing and altering small areas on these magnetic surfaces. Most disks today have moving heads which move from track to track as required and heads on both sides of the magnetic platters providing double the storage capacity. Fixed-head disks are faster because they provide a head for each track and don't incur the time lost to switching tracks, but are considerably more expensive than their moving-head counterparts. The circular path that a head traces is called a *track*. The corresponding tracks from all surfaces are called a *cylinder*. Additionally, up to 32 cylinders can be joined into a cylinder group. The smallest addressable unit on a hard disk is called a *sector*; each sector contains a header, 512 bytes of data, and a trailer. Sectors lie end-to-end along a track. Figure 4.1 illustrates these structures.

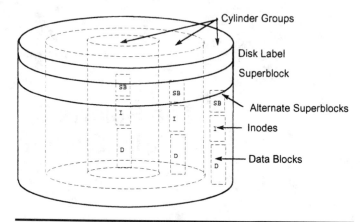

Figure 4.1 Disk file system layout.

Read-write optical disks provide functionality very similar to that of the more traditional Winchester technology just described and are increasingly used as an option for disk storage. Removable cartridges can provide tremendous offline storage for files which are not required all the time. Removable disk packs are sometimes used in environments where security constraints require that disks be locked in a secure container when not in use.

Usually, disks and the controllers which transmit instructions to them from the host CPU (central processing unit) are separate. Controllers can be supplied as circuit boards or can be integrated onto the main computer board as is the case for the SCSI (small computer system interface) controllers on SPARC-stations. Multiple disks can usually be run off a single controller resulting in some competition for bandwidth but an easy expandability since you can chain these devices together. SCSI technology permits up to seven devices to be controlled with the same controller. You will often see SCSI disks daisy-chained with other SCSI devices, like CD ROMs (compact-disk read-only memory storage devices) and SCSI tape devices. Typically, not more than four disks will be chained along with a tape device or two.

Ordinarily, all these details of disk hardware do not concern the system administrator. The commands and tools for partitioning a disk and creating file systems can be used without this knowledge. When adding a new disk to an existing system, repairing a damaged one, or trying to improve file system performance, it is useful to understand the basics of disk topology.

The `/etc/format.dat` file describes disks and provides default partition tables. The two excerpts from this file shown in Fig. 4.2 detail the 424-Mbyte disk included in a number of desktop SPARCstations. The SUN0424 is a SCSI disk with nine heads, 1151 cylinders, and 80 sectors per track. In the default configuration, partitions 0, 1, 2, and 6 are allocated space. Each value pair associated with each of these partitions indicates the starting cylinder and size (in sectors) of the partition. The swap partition (partition 1), for example, starts on cylinder

```
-------------------------------------------------------------------------
disk_type = "SUN0424" \
        : ctlr = SCSI : fmt_time = 4 \
        : trks_zone = 9 : asect = 2 \
        : ncyl = 1151 : acyl = 2 : pcyl = 2500 : nhead = 9 : nsect = 80 \
        : rpm = 4400 : bpt = 26000
...
partition = "SUN0424" \
        : disk = "SUN0424" : ctlr = SCSI \
        : 0 = 0, 33120 : 1 = 46, 65520 : 2 = 0, 828720 : 6 = 137, 730080
-------------------------------------------------------------------------
```

Figure 4.2 Excerpt from `format.dat`.

46 and is 65,520 sectors long. The overall size of this disk in sectors is 828,720. This same number can be calculated by multiplying the number of cylinders (`ncyl`), heads (`nhead`), and sectors per track (`nsect`).

If you are adding a disk which is not described in your `/etc/format.dat` file, you can use the format utility in Solaris 2.3 and higher to automatically configure and format the disk without having to get disk geometry details from your supplier, as long as the disk is SCSI-2-compliant. By using SCSI commands, the format utility is able to determine the geometry of the disk. Once it has done so, it will ask if the disk should be labeled. The format utility will use information from the `/etc/format.dat` file if the disk you are addressing is described there. If you are adding a disk which predates SCSI-2, you will have to collect `format.dat` information if it isn't provided in the existing file.

Information in the `format.dat` file describes fairly generic disk setups. The actual disk that a SUN0424 entry describes may not always be from the same manufacturer or be precisely the same size.

Also, you should note that the storage capacity of any disk on your system is likely to be as little as 75 percent of the manufacturer-reported capacity of the disk—depending on whether the manufacturer is quoting storage before or after formatting, has calculated the overhead associated with the file system, or is calculating a megabyte as 1,048,576 bytes as most computer professionals would or as 1,000,000 bytes. You should insist on knowing what figures are being quoted when you purchase a disk.

To illustrate the point, let's take a look at the SUN0424 disk attached to a local workstation. The awk script provided in Fig. 4.3 will add the size of each partition to a running total and then display the overall size. We invoke this script by piping the output of the `df -k` command which reports on disk space through the `grep` command to limit output to the disk at target 3 and then through our `awk` script to accumulate totals.

```
# df -k|grep t3|awk -f howbig
c0t3d0
318.936 MBytes (mounted)
```

As you can see, the 424-Mbyte disk is yielding about 318 Mbytes of file system storage. The swap space on this disk occupies an additional 80 Mbytes. In total, therefore, we are yielding about 400 Mbytes of our 424-Mbyte disk.

```
----------------------------------------------------------------
# howbig:  add file system sizes
#
{
if (NR == 1) {
        if ($1 != "Filesystem")
                print substr($1,10,6)
}
if ($1 != "kbytes")
        TOTSIZE = TOTSIZE + $2
}
END {
        SHOWSIZE = TOTSIZE * 1.024
        print SHOWSIZE / 1000 " MBytes (mounted)"
}
----------------------------------------------------------------
```

Figure 4.3 Calculating mounted disk storage.

We could also use the same script to report on all mounted space.

```
# df -k|awk -f howbig
2965.77 MBytes (mounted)
```

The format utility, as we shall see later, provides a partition table that details the size of each partition and gives this same kind of information.

To display basic information about local disks, use the format command. Format will display the disk address, number of cylinders, number of heads, and sectors per track. It also provides the physical device name for the device. An illustration of examining disk detail with the format command is provided in Fig. 4.4.

```
---------------------------------------------------------------------------
# format
Searching for disks...done

AVAILABLE DISK SELECTIONS:
        0. c0t1d0 <SUN0424 cyl 1151 alt 2 hd 9 sec 80>
           /sbus@1,f8000000/esp@0,800000/sd@1,0
        1. c0t3d0 <SUN0207 cyl 1254 alt 2 hd 9 sec 36>
           /sbus@1,f8000000/esp@0,800000/sd@3,0

        c0t3d0 <SUN0207 cyl 1254 alt 2 hd 9 sec 36>
          ^         ^           ^        ^    ^     ^
          |         |           |        |    |     |
          |         |           |        |    |     +-- # Sectors/Cylinder
          |         |           |        |    +-------- # Heads
          |         |           |        +------------- # Alternate Cylinders
          |         |           +--------------------- # Cylinders
          |         +------------------------------- # Disk Type
          +--------------------------------------- # Disk Address


        /sbus@1,f8000000/esp@0,800000/sd@3,0
             ^              ^           ^ ^
             |              |           | |
             |              |           | +--- SCSI logical unit #
             |              |           +----- SCSI Target #
             |              +---------------- SCSI Host Adaptor
             +---------------------------- Slot Number
---------------------------------------------------------------------------
```

Figure 4.4 Basic disk information.

In this example, you can see that the system has two disks, 424 and 207 Mbytes, on a single controller. The larger disk has fewer cylinders than the smaller one but more than twice as many sectors per track. You should also note that disk 0 is SCSI target 1 and disk 1 is SCSI target 3.

4.1.1 Partitions

Partitions represent portions of each physical disk that are treated as separate buckets for storage of files in a single file system. You can define up to seven partitions on a single disk.

Disk partitions, also called *slices,* are numbered 0 to 7. Partition 2 always represents the entire disk and when used is used exclusively. The full name of a partition is represented by an eight-character string which includes the controller number, the bus target identifier, the disk, and the partition (slice). Figure 4.5 illustrates disk partitions.

Disks with direct controllers will not include a target address and, thus, will only have six-character names. The bus target for SCSI devices is usually set through a switch on the back of the device; each SCSI device must have a unique (for your system) target. Some of these addresses are fixed. For example, a CD ROM is almost always set at SCSI target 6.

The partition associated with the address /dev/rdsk/c0t3d0s0 indicates the first partition on the first disk. Its SCSI target address is 3 and it is connected to the first controller. Figure 4.6 details this naming convention.

The format command, which allows you to format, label, repair, and analyze disks on your system can be used to display the current partitioning. See Fig. 4.7. Figure 4.8 details the fields displayed in the partition table. Format runs under Solaris with some limitations because file systems are mounted. When running within the memory-resident system environment, these limitations do not exist.

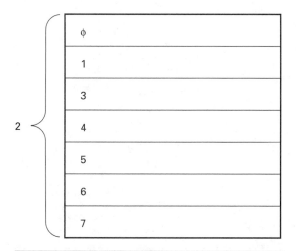

Figure 4.5 Disk partitions.

```
------------------------------------------------
/dev/rdsk/c0t3d0s0
           ^ ^ ^ ^
           | | | |
           | | | +------ slice 0
           | | +-------- disk 0
           | +---------- physical bus target 3
           +------------ controller 0
------------------------------------------------
```

Figure 4.6 Partition address.

```
------------------------------------------------------------------
# format
Searching for disks...done


AVAILABLE DISK SELECTIONS:
       0. c0t3d0 <SUN0424 cyl 1151 alt 2 hd 9 sec 80>
          /sbus@1,f8000000/esp@0,800000/sd@3,0
Specify disk (enter its number): 0
selecting c0t3d0
[disk formatted]
Warning: Current Disk has mounted partitions.


FORMAT MENU:
       disk        - select a disk
       ...
       quit
format> partition


PARTITION MENU:
       0        - change '0' partition
       ...
       print  - display the current table
       label  - write partition map and label to the disk
       quit
partition> print
Current partition table (original sd3):
Part      Tag    Flag    Cylinders        Size          Blocks
  0      root    wm       0 -   56      20.04MB       (57/0/0)
  1      swap    wu      57 -  193      48.16MB      (137/0/0)
  2    backup    wm       0 - 1150     404.65MB     (1151/0/0)
  3 unassigned   wm       0               0           (0/0/0)
  4 unassigned   wm       0               0           (0/0/0)
  5         -    wm     194 -  316      43.24MB      (123/0/0)
  6       usr    wm     317 -  852     188.44MB      (536/0/0)
  7      home    wm     853 - 1150     104.77MB      (298/0/0)

------------------------------------------------------------------
```

Figure 4.7 Using format to view partitions.

```
----------------------------------------------------------------------
7         home   wm     853 - 1150     104.77MB      (298/0/0)
^          ^      ^       ^              ^            ^   ^ ^
|          |      |       |              |            |   | |
|          |      |       + starting &   |            |   | +- # sectors
|          |      |         ending cyls  |            |   +--- # heads
|          |      +------- flags         |            +------- # cylinders
|          +-------------- tag           +-------------------- size
+------------------------- partition #

----------------------------------------------------------------------
```

Figure 4.8 Fields in partition table.

The partition tags displayed in the second column are annotations for the system administrator and are not used by the operating system. Partition 2, labeled `backup`, represents the entire disk. Partition 5 for this partition was set up as `/opt`, intended for use for third-party (non-Sun) software.

Valid tags and their numeric equivalents include the following:

0	unassigned	
1	boot	
2	root	
3	swap	
4	usr	
5	backup	
6	-	not used
7	var	
8	home	

These tags can be changed within the format utility but only to one of the values listed above. If you try to change a tag to any other value, the message `'name' not expected` is displayed. The excerpt from a dialog with format shown in Fig. 4.9 illustrates assigning a tag to partition 0.

The typical assignment of partitions is shown at the top of Fig. 4.10. Although this assignment of partitions to file systems is not strictly rigid, it is usually a good idea to follow these conventions. However, for any given disk, only some of these partitions will exist. You will rarely see a disk with all these partitions defined. Typically, a system disk will contain `root`, `swap`, and `/usr` partitions. If it is a large disk (e.g., >1 Gbyte), it might also contain `/opt` for application software or the two export partitions which support clients. A more likely setup would have these partitions spread across multiple disks as is shown at the bottom of Fig. 4.10.

This arrangement provides a more balanced I/O load across the disks and provides greater reliability since loss of a single disk doesn't affect all file systems. In this example, each of the partitions exists, but partitions are spread across several disks. Disk 1 contains partitions supporting diskless clients.

A less likely, but equally plausible, configuration of disks is illustrated in Fig. 4.11. Here we have two disks with redundant partitions. There are two root file

---

```
partition> 0
Part      Tag     Flag     Cylinders        Size         Blocks
  0 unassigned    wm        0 -   24       16.60MB      (25/0/0)

Enter partition id tag[unassigned]: ?
Expecting one of the following: (abbreviations ok):
        unassigned      boot           root         swap
        usr             backup         var          home

Enter partition id tag[unassigned]: root
```

Figure 4.9 Assigning a tag to a partition using format.

```
-------------------------------------------------------------------------
0          root
1          swap
2          entire disk
3          /export
4          /export/swap
5          /opt
6          /usr
7          /home
                                                                    /
Disk 0                       Disk 1                  Disk 2
0          root
1          swap
2          entire disk          2      entire disk      2      entire disk
                                3      /export
                                4      /export/swap
                                                         5      /opt
6          /usr
                                                         7      /home
-------------------------------------------------------------------------
```

Figure 4.10   Single- and multiple-disk layouts.

```
---------------------------------------------------
Disk 0                       Disk 1
0          root 4.1.X          0      root 5.X
1          swap
6          /usr 4.1.X          6      /usr 5.X
7          /home
---------------------------------------------------
```

Figure 4.11   Multiple OS disk layout.

systems and two /usr partitions. Most likely, a configuration like this would be set up to support multiple versions of the operating system such as might be useful in testing a software port. In the figure, root and /usr on sd0 support SunOS 4.1.X while root and /usr on sd1 support Solaris 2.x. The swap and /home partitions can be used under either OS. Depending on which root partition this workstation is booted from, the correct set of root and /usr partitions are mounted.

Another likely use of a configuration similar to that shown in Fig. 4.11 is to have a secondary and smaller disk available to allow booting the system as a dataless client in case the first disk fails. The /etc/vfstab file in the second root partition could be set up to make the dataless boot straightforward.

The Flags column in Fig. 4.8 indicates access parameters for each partition. The meaning for each flag is provided below.

w   readable and writable

r   readable only

m   mountable

u   unmountable

As you can see, only the swap partition is marked as unmountable. All partitions are both readable and writable in this example. Like partition tags, these flags are set up by the system administrator and are informational only. The mount command, for example, does not refuse to mount a partition which contains an unmountable flag.

Another way to view the partitioning of a disk is to use the prtvtoc command which displays the volume table of contents (VTOC) associated with each disk. VTOC information can be updated with the fmthard command, but this should be done only with considerable care as incorrect entries might make data in modified partitions inaccessible.

In the display shown below, the Tag and Flags fields can be interpreted with the values shown in the table following. The prtvtoc command will display information about the disk regardless of which partition you provide as an argument as long as that partition is allocated. It will always work with partition 2 since this partition, which represents the entire disk, always exists. If you specify a partition which is not allocated space, you will get a "No such device or address" message.

TRY THIS   Using prtvtoc

```
mount
...
prtvtoc /dev/rdsk/c0t3d0s2
# prtvtoc /dev/rdsk/c0t3ds2
* /dev/rdsk/c0t3d0s2 partition map
*
* Dimensions:
* 512 bytes/sector
*  80 sectors/track
*   9 tracks/cylinder
* 720 sectors/cylinder
* 2500 cylinders
* 1151 accessible cylinders
*
* Flags:
* 1: unmountable
* 10: read-only
*
```

* Partition	Tag	Flags	First Sector	Sector Count	Last Sector	Mount Directory
0	2	00	0	41040	41309	/
1	3	01	41040	98640	139679	
2	5	00	0	828720	828719	
5	6	00	139680	88560	228239	/opt
6	4	00	228240	385920	614159	/usr
7	8	00	614160	214560	828719	/export/home

```
Tags:                        Flags:
0         unassigned         00        Mountable     read & write
1         boot                         01            Not mountable
2         root                         10            Mountable read only
3         swap
4         usr
5         backup
6         -
7         var
8         home
```

4.1.2 Swap Space

Secondary storage for managing executing processes, swap space on disk, assists in the process of paging—moving portions of processes in and out of memory as required. Various rules of thumb, offered over the years to help administrators estimate how large a swap partition to allocate, are rendered obsolete by several factors. For one, dramatic drops in memory have made workstations with 16 to 64 Mbytes of main memory the norm. In addition, the swapping algorithm used in SVR4 makes conservative use of the swap partition, keeping pages in memory longer, basically until the space is needed. To fully understand how virtual swap is set up and used, refer to Chap. 17.

With Solaris 2.x, therefore, it is appropriate to have less storage allocated to the swap partition as you have main memory. Pages in memory actually become part of the virtual swap space. A new file system type, swapfs, is the pseudo–file system type used to implement virtual swap space. Available disk-based swap, plus a portion of main memory, makes up the virtual swap space. Look at the output of the swap -1 command which lists the overall swap and disk-based swap separately in units of 512-kbyte blocks.

Typical workstations should be set up with about 32 Mbytes in their swap partition regardless of the amount of memory. It could even be said that the more memory you have, the less you need swap. This was not true of earlier versions of SunOS (4.1.X and prior).

Solaris 2.x allows you to add and remove swap space without disk repartitioning. To list swap, use the swap -1 command as shown in Fig. 4.12. To add

```
------------------------------------------------------------------
swap -1
swapfile             dev  swaplo blocks   free
swapfs                -        0 122048 112808  <-- overall swap
/dev/dsk/c0t1d0s1    32,9      8  66232  66232  <-- disk-based swap
                      ^  ^
                      |  |
                      |  +------------------------- minor device number
                      +---------------------------- major device number

------------------------------------------------------------------
```

Figure 4.12 Looking at swap usage.

```
-------------------------------------------------
mkfile 1m /export/home/swap

swap -a /export/home/swap

swap -l
swapfile                  dev  swaplo blocks    free
swapfs                     -        0 124088 114840
/dev/dsk/c0t1d0s1        32,9        8  66232  66232
/export/home/swap          -         8   2040   2040
-------------------------------------------------
```

Figure 4.13 Adding swap space.

swap, you first create a file that is the same size as the amount of swap that you want to add. Then you issue the `swap -a` command to add this to the virtual swap space. This process is illustrated in Fig. 4.13. To remove swap, you do the reverse. First, you issue the `swap -d` command to release the swap space. Next, you remove the swap file with `rm`. The swap file that you create does not need to be on the local disk, but can be NFS mounted (as is always the case with diskless clients).

Notice the last line in Fig. 4.13. This is the swap space that you just added. To add this file to virtual swap each time your system is booted, you only need to add it to your `/etc/vfstab` file with a line like that shown below.

```
/export/home/swap1 - - swap - no -
```

You should also notice how little swap is being used in this example. Monitoring swap space in your environment with applications that are commonly used, will help you determine how much swap space you really need.

4.1.3 The boot block

The boot block is an extremely important disk block and is stored in the first 8 kbytes of the first cylinder group. It stores information that is used to boot the system. On file systems not used for booting, the boot block is empty. The boot block is normally stored with the root partition, but can be stored in other partitions as well.

4.2 File Systems

Once a disk has been partitioned, it is ready to hold file systems. For the most part, each partition that is allocated space will be set up as a file system. The structures for keeping track of files and free space will be built when the file system is being created. Most of the file systems that you deal with for Solaris systems will be `ufs` file systems. This file system type, which stands for UNIX file system, is the standard for SVR4. This file system type is also known as the "Berkeley Fat Fast File System." You are also likely to work with file systems which are accessed through NFS and RFS (network file system and remote file sharing). Support and management of distributed file systems is covered in Chap. 10.

A ufs file system can be as large as 1 tbyte and may contain files as large as 2 Gbytes. You will seldom encounter file systems or files anywhere near these limits.

4.2.1 The superblock

Details about the beginning and the end, the size and the status of a file system, and free space in the partition are kept in an important structure known as the *superblock*. The superblock is also used to keep track of such things as the date and time when the file system was last accessed and where it was last mounted and its state. The file system state (clean, stable, active, or bad) is used by fsck and during booting to determine whether the file system needs to be checked. *Clean,* for example, means that the file system was unmounted properly and is therefore consistent; the file system check is skipped. During the boot process, you may notice the messages that are displayed when this determination is made. They will display messages like these:

```
checking filesystems
/dev/rdsk/c0t3d0s5: is clean
/dev/rdsk/c0t3d0s7: is clean
/dev/dsk/c0t3d0s5 mounted
/dev/dsk/c0t3d0s7 mounted
```

Clean—has been properly unmounted and is undamaged

Stable—is mounted, but has not been modified

Active—has been updated since mounting

Bad—is inconsistent, needs repair

In the ufs system, there are numerous copies of the superblock. The duplicate copies are used in system recovery if the initial superblock has been damaged. When you first create a file system with the newfs command or during installation, the addresses associated with the superblocks will be shown on the screen. Any of the duplicate superblocks can be used with the fsck command. For example, with the file system being created in Fig. 4.14, the command fsck -F ufs -o b=69632 would check the integrity of the file system using the superblock stored at address 69632.

The backup superblocks are replicated in each cylinder group within the file system. The number of backup superblocks is more than adequate for recovery from almost any disk disaster. In fact, if you find that you cannot retrieve a good superblock from the many choices provided, chances are your disk controller is causing your problems.

It is not necessary to copy these sector addresses when you create a file system. The newfs command can be run at any time with the -N option. This op-

```
--------------------------------------------------------------------------
#newfs /dev/rdsk/c0t1d0s7
/dev/rdsk/c0t1d0s7:     409680 sectors in 569 cylinders of 9 tracks, 80 sectors
        209.8MB in 36 cyl groups (16 c/g, 5.90MB/g, 2688 i/g)
super-block backups (for fsck -F ufs -o b=#) at:
 32, 11632, 23232, 34832, 46432, 58032, 69632, 81232, 92832,
 104432, 116032, 127632, 139232, 150832, 162432, 174032, 184352, 195952,
 207552, 219152, 230752, 242352, 253952, 265552, 277152, 288752, 300352,
 311952, 323552, 335152, 346752, 358352, 368672, 380272, 391872, 403472,
#
--------------------------------------------------------------------------
```

Figure 4.14 Backup superblocks.

tion causes newfs to print out the partition and superblock information without actually creating the file system.

TRY THIS   Retrieve Backup Superblock Addresses

```
boson# newfs -N /dev/rdsk/c0t3d0s0

/dev/rdsk/c0t3d0s0: 34992 sectors in 108 cylinders of 9 tracks, 36 sectors

   17.9MB in 7 cyl groups (16 c/g, 2.65MB/g, 1216 i/g)

super-block backups (for fsck -F ufs -o b=#) at:

32, 5264, 10496, 15728, 20960, 26192, 31424,

boson# newfs -N /dev/rdsk/c0t1d0s0

/dev/rdsk/c0t1d0s0: 41040 sectors in 57 cylinders of 9 tracks, 80 sectors

   21.0MB in 4 cyl groups (16 c/g, 5.90MB/g, 2688 i/g)

super-block backups (for fsck -F ufs -o b=#) at:

32, 11632, 23232, 34832,
```

The sync command, often issued before halting a system and as part of the shutdown process, updates the superblock from data stored within memory to ensure the integrity of the data on your disk. Sync works only with local disks, however.

System administrators never manipulate the superblock. Instead, it is used by numerous system commands and utilities like fsck, which uses the information in the superblock to check the validity and integrity of file systems and is updated whenever the file system is changed (e.g., when you edit a file). The superblocks of mounted file systems are usually stored in memory for faster access, since these structures are updated frequently as files are used and updated.

Another important function of the superblock is to keep track of the free list, the structure containing pointers to all unused disk space. Changes in files and in the free list can be lost if a system is shut down improperly.

There is one condition under which the sync command should not be used. When fsck has been used to repair file system damage, the corrections are made directly to the disk itself. If the system administrator then issues the sync command, the corrected superblock will be overwritten with the in-memory superblock and the inconsistencies will reappear.

4.2.2 File system components

As was pointed out at the beginning of this chapter, the file system organization that is presented to you when you are using a UNIX shell or viewing your files through File Manager is an abstraction. The structures that create this view and maintain the content of your files as well as their description are explained in this section.

4.2.2.1 Inodes.

The *inode*, short for index node, is a structure which contains information about a file. Much of the information contained in this structure is familiar to the casual user who has seen it displayed in long listings while issuing the `ls -1` command—the filename and owner, group, access permissions, file length, the type of file, number of links, and the date last modified. The inode also stores the date and time of the file's creation and its last access. End users who do all of their work through the deskset, viewing their files as icons within File Manager, may view this information in the File Properties window of File Manager where most of this information is displayed along with additional data concerning *binding*—how the file is associated with applications and print methods.

The filename is the piece of information that is actually not contained in the inode itself. Although this may seem odd at first, it is quite in keeping with the UNIX tradition. Like `userids` and `groupids`, files are known to the system by numeric values and presented to the user by "friendly" names. The name of each file is stored in another file—the directory file—representing the directory in which the file is located. This is an important concept. Directories are actually files containing filenames and inode numbers and are used to link the two.

In Fig. 4.15, the short octal dump of a directory file, you can see four of the files: the . and .. entries which connect the directory into the file system tree, and two user files, `table1.rs` and `table2.rs`. The structure for directories is defined in a header file, `/usr/include/sys/dirent.h`. Figure 4.16 displays this structure.

Each record in the directory structure has four fields as described in the excerpt from the header file used to define the structure. The inode number uniquely identifies a file. Preceding each filename is a filename length; commands such as `ls` use this length field in reading and printing out the file in-

```
--------------------------------------------------------------------------------
# od -bc Figs | head 8
0000000 000 000 052 017 000 014 000 001 056 000 000 000 000 000 025 000
         \0  \0   *  017  \0  \f  \0 001   .   \0  \0  \0  \0  \0 025  \0
0000020 000 014 000 002 056 056 000 000 000 000 052 020 000 024 000 011
         \0  \f  \0 002   .    .  \0  \0  \0  \0   * 020  \0 024  \0  \t
0000040 164 141 142 154 145 061 056 162 163 000 000 000 000 000 000 052 021
          t   a   b   l   e   1   .   r   s  \0  \0  \0  \0  \0   * 021
0000060 000 024 000 011 164 141 142 154 145 062 056 162 163 000 000 000
         \0 024  \0  \t   t   a   b   l   e   2   .   r   s  \0  \0  \0
                     ==================================
--------------------------------------------------------------------------------
```

Figure 4.15 Inside a directory file.

```
----------------------------------------------------------------------
/*
 * File-system independent directory entry.
 */
struct dirent {
        ino_t           d_ino;          /* "inode number" of entry */
        off_t           d_off;          /* offset of disk directory entry */
        unsigned short  d_reclen;       /* length of this record */
        char            d_name[1];      /* name of file */
};
----------------------------------------------------------------------
```

Figure 4.16 The directory structure.

formation. The filename lengths in the displayed portion of the directory are 1, 2, 9, and 9.

4.2.2.2 File types. Every file in the file system has a type associated with it, stored in the file's inode. These file types are recognized by the operating system to some extent. That is, certain commands will balk if you try to run them against the wrong file type. Others will not, sometimes with fairly bizarre results. For example, the cd command will not allow you to change directory to a file that is not a directory. On the other hand, you can attempt to edit a directory with vi (even though it refuses to overwrite the file), and you can display "garbage" on your screen by using the cat command against an executable.

TRY THIS   Display an Executable File

```
%cat /usr/sbin/fsck
```

A more fine-grained differentiation of files by type is available at the user level through the mechanism of file binding that File Manager, other desktop tools, and the file command use.

4.2.3 Regular files

The most common type of file is a regular (also called "ordinary") file. Regular files encompass a wide variety of what you and I think of as file types, such as your text files, source code and compiled programs, operating-system commands, and system configuration files. Ordinary files are identified by a hyphen in the first column of a long listing (e.g., ls -l).

Other file types are directory files, block and character special files, FIFOs (named pipes; first in–first out), and symbolic links.

4.2.4 Block and character special files

Block and character special files are usually associated with devices and provide two mechanisms for reading and writing to disk. The primary difference is in whether the transfer is accomplished using a block buffer or directly to memory as in a "raw" or character interface. Another difference is the amount of data that is transferred; block interfaces transfer data in 512-byte chunks.

TRY THIS   Block and Character Devices

Use the `ls` command to look at the contents of the `/dev/dsk` and `/dev/rdsk` directories associated with your disks. You will see both a block and a character device associated with each of your partitions.

```
$ ls /dev/dsk
c0t3d0s0  c0t3d0s2  c0t3d0s4  c0t3d0s6  c0t6d0s0  c0t6d0s2  c0t6d0s4  c0t6d0s6
c0t3d0s1  c0t3d0s3  c0t3d0s5  c0t3d0s7  c0t6d0s1  c0t6d0s3  c0t6d0s5  c0t6d0s7
$ ls /dev/rdsk
c0t3d0s0  c0t3d0s2  c0t3d0s4  c0t3d0s6  c0t6d0s0  c0t6d0s2  c0t6d0s4  c0t6d0s6
c0t3d0s1  c0t3d0s3  c0t3d0s5  c0t3d0s7  c0t6d0s1  c0t6d0s3  c0t6d0s5  c0t6d0s7
```

The devices you should see in each of these directories represent the block and character (raw) devices for disk partitions on your system. The Try This exercise in Sec. 3.4 illustrates these devices. Whether or not these devices will actually correspond to the devices on your system depends on whether you have added or removed devices since the last time you booted with a kernel reconfiguration request.

The particular system queried for the output shown above has a single disk (SCSI target 3) and a CD ROM (SCSI target 6). There are eight device files for each of the two devices in each of the directories. Do the devices that you see in these directories correspond to the devices that you expect to see on your system? Notice that partitions are listed regardless of whether they are allocated space on your disks. These files are built automatically when you install your system or add a device and boot with a `/reconfigure` file in place. This is part of the process of autoconfiguration which Solaris 2.x provides to simplify systems administration.

4.2.5   Directories

As we have seen, *directories* are really files that contain inode numbers and filenames along with some information which helps to locate the actual files. This simple yet elegant structure provides an easy mechanism for nesting directories within directories and the abstraction of the flexible treelike structure that is one of the claims to fame of early UNIX. (Since then many other operating systems have adopted this construct.)

Like inodes, directories are changed only through the use of commands like `mv` which updates the directory structure. When a file is moved with `mv` within a single directory, the command simply changes the filename in the directory file. If the file is moved across subdirectories or file systems, more than one directory structure must be updated to accommodate the change. Between directories, the file must actually be moved on the disk to assume a position in the cylinder groups associated with another file system.

4.2.6 FIFOs (named pipes)

A *pipe* is a mechanism that is used to effect one-way transfers of data between running processes. You can view the named pipe as a mechanism for a stream of bytes to be communicated between processes, one writing and the other reading.

Normally, pipes are set up within programs and are not represented within the file system. Pipes have a temporary (while processes are running) existence and require that the communicating processes share a common ancestry so that knowledge and use of the pipe can be coordinated.

FIFOs, or named pipes, are different. A named pipe is represented by a file. The first character in a long listing of a named pipe is p. Like block and character special files, named pipes are created with the mknod command.

TRY THIS   Set Up a Named Pipe

```
$ mknod mypipe p
$ ls -l mypipe
prw-r-r- 1 root  other    0 Jan 1 12:04 mypipe
$ rm mypipe
```

Named pipes are more flexible than pipes because by existing in a directory, they can be opened by any process with access to them. Programmers don't have to worry about the sequence with which pipes are created and shared between parent and child processes because they are always available.

Most likely, applications that use named pipes will create the required files during the installation process.

4.2.7 Links

The simple filename-inode relationship provides an additional flexibility that is expressed through the mechanism of links. A single file may have more than one name associated with it. In fact, this is very common. Links can be used to provide shortcuts to files. That is, by creating a link in the current directory to a file with a long full pathname, such as linking /opt/apps/trans1/data2 to data2, it is possible to treat the file as if it were located in the current directory without having to duplicate it.

Links can be hard or symbolic. Hard links are indistinguishable from the original files themselves, but may not cross file systems or refer to directories. When you create a hard link, an entry is added to the directory, but the same inode is used and operations on the file are the same regardless of which filename is used. The file looks and acts as though it is a copy of the original, but it occupies no additional space unless the directory file must be enlarged to accommodate the new filename.

Symbolic links are quite different, but also provide the benefit of adding little space to the file system. Symbolic links simply point to the original file. The link file contains the fully qualified pathname of the file to which the link refers. Notice how the length of the file is the same as the length of the filename. Symbolic links can cross file system boundaries as well as refer to directories.

Because symbolic links point to other files, most commands (e.g., cat, od) operate on the file that the links point to; you will not, therefore, see the content of the link file. We can determine, however, that the link file's length is the same as the full pathname of the file that it points to by using the command below where we echo the name and use awk to calculate the length; it exceeds the length provided in the long listing by one; this is because echo adds a carriage return.

```
lrwxrwxrwx 1 root other 25 Dec 22 11:34 link ->/usr/include/sys/dirent.h
# echo /usr/include/sys/dirent.h|awk ' {print length($0)}'
26
```

The ln command is used to create hard and symbolic links. With the -s option, it creates symbolic links. Solaris 2.x also includes the more obvious link and unlink commands to create and remove hard links.

TRY THIS   Create Links

```
$ echo "Be excellent to each other" > file0
$ ln file0 file1
$ ln -s file0 file2
$ ls -l fil*
-rw-r--r-- 2 slee sysadmin 27 Jan 1 12:21 file0
-rw-r--r-- 2 slee sysadmin 27 Jan 1 12:21 file1
lrwxrwxrwx 1 slee sysadmin 5 Jan 1 12:22 file2 -> file0
$ rm file0
$ ls -l fil*
-rw-r--r-- 1 slee sysadmin 27 Jan 1 12:21 file1
lrwxrwxrwx 1 slee sysadmin 5 Jan 1 12:22 file2 -> file0
$ cat file1
Be excellent to each other
$ cat file2
cat: cannot open file2
```

Notice how file0 and file1 appear to be identical while file2 points to file0. When we remove the original file (file0), the hard link (file1) is still valid. After all, it continues to rely on the original inode. On the other hand, file2 now points to a file which no longer exists. It is a "broken link." Although it may appear healthy in the long listing, operations which attempt to use the link will fail with a `cannot open` message.

The use of links can impact backup and restore operations. You should make sure that you know, for example, whether the original file or a link is stored and recovered when you use backup and restore software. The tar command, for example, stores a symbolic link rather than the file that it points to. In some cases, this may be what you want. In others, it may not be.

4.3 File System Types

Solaris 2.x supports a large number of file systems other than the `ufs` file system that we have been discussing. By supporting foreign file systems, Solaris 2.x acquires a large degree of file interoperability. Once mounted, a foreign file system can be used just as if it were a `ufs` file system, with few exceptions (CD ROM writability and DOS naming conventions).

```
---local
```

ufs   The BSD Fat Fast File System from the Tahoe Release. This is the standard file system for Solaris and the one that you will deal with almost exclusively.

hsfs   ISO 9660 file system for CD ROM. Based on the High Sierra format, Sun's implementation of this ISO standard includes the Rock Ridge extensions which provide all `ufs` functionality except for writability.

pcfs   PC (personal computer) file system provides read-write access to DOS-created floppies (floppy disks). MS-DOS file naming conventions are enforced; translations between upper- and lowercase and truncations of names to eight or fewer characters for the filename and three or fewer in the file extension.

```
---remote
```

NFS   Network file system. Supports mounting of file systems over the network. NFS is covered in considerable depth in Chap. 17.

rfs   Remote file sharing. Similar to NFS, rfs supports mounting of file systems over the network, but only support `ufs` file systems; however, it also permits mounting of remote devices. Like NFS, rfs is described in more detail in Chap. 17.

```
---pseudo
```

tmpfs   Uses local memory for reading and writing, providing very fast access, guaranteed files and directories will not be preserved between reboots or unmounts, so should be used only for temporary files. Performance enhancement is achieved by caching writes to files and can be quite noticeable if you are using a large number of short-lived files. Does compete with other commands being executed because can compete for memory if there are a large number of tmpfs files.

lofs   The loopback virtual file system provides a means to duplicate or overlay an existing file system.

`proc`	Provides access to the image of each running process in the system. Names of files in `/proc` represent the process IDs of the corresponding processes. The `ps` command and debugging tools use this to process images accessible through standard system calls.
`fifos`	Provides access to named pipes used in interprocess communications.
`fdfs`	Provides access to filenames using file descriptors.
`namefs`	Provides dynamic mounting of file systems through Streams.
`specfs`	Provides access to special character and block devices.
`---`	

4.4 Creating File Systems

The `newfs` command is a front end to `mkfs` and simplifies creating a `ufs` file system; `newfs` calculates approximate parameters, which it then passes to `mkfs`. These parameters describe how the file system will be set up and effectively establish tradeoffs that determine how efficiently space will be allocated and how well it will perform. Some of these parameters can be overridden with options to the `newfs` command. The default parameters selected by `newfs` are optimized for performance of what Sun considers a conservative estimate of the typical file system. In general, optimizing for performance is the choice to make unless you are very concerned about disk space or expect to use more than 90 percent of the actual space available.

With keen insights into how your file system is to be used and whether you care more about maximizing the used disk space or improving disk performance, you can tune your file system using these parameters. If you are going to have only very large files, for example, you will not need as many inodes for a given partition size, so you will increase the bytes per inode parameter that details how much disk space is allocated for each inode.

If, on the other hand, you expect to have a great many small files and symbolic links, you will need a greater number of inodes, or less disk space for each inode. In our opinion, the typical `ufs` file system has far too many inodes for a given amount of space. The default assumes an average file size of 2 kbytes (2048 bytes).

In the example shown in Fig. 4.17, the 2048 bytes per inode parameter (the default) indicates that the average file is expected to be about 2 kbytes long. If the `newfs` command included the `-i` option and specified a value of 4096, (e.g., `newfs -N -v -i 4096 /dev/rdsk/c0t3d0s7`), the space allocated for each inode would be doubled; the number of inodes would be halved. Keep in mind that we are using the `-N` option with the `newfs` command so that you can execute these commands without actually changing anything about your file systems. You will need to omit the `-N` parameter to create a new file system.

A few of the parameters associated with a file system can be changed on the fly with the `tunefs` command. These parameters are dynamic and affect the way individual files are read and written, but not the overall structure of the file system on the disk. By entering the `tunefs` command without parameters, you

```
--------------------------------------------------------------------------
# newfs -N -v /dev/rdsk/c0t3d0s7
mkfs -F ufs -o N /dev/rdsk/c0t3d0s7 214560 80 9 8192 1024 16 10 73 2048 t 0 -1 8
```

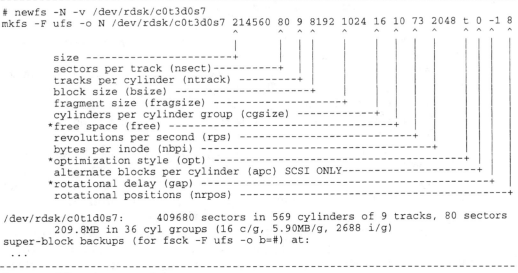

```
/dev/rdsk/c0t1d0s7:    409680 sectors in 569 cylinders of 9 tracks, 80 sectors
         209.8MB in 36 cyl groups (16 c/g, 5.90MB/g, 2688 i/g)
super-block backups (for fsck -F ufs -o b=#) at:
 ...
--------------------------------------------------------------------------
```

Figure 4.17   File system parameters.

can conveniently list the options which can be changed without recreating the
file system.

Unmount a file system before changing any of its parameters with tunefs.

TRY THIS   List Tunable File System Parameters

```
# tunefs /dev/dsk/c0t1d0s7
ufs usage: tunefs tuneup-options special-device
```

where tuneup-options are

-a   maximum contiguous blocks

-d   rotational delay between contiguous blocks

-e   maximum blocks per file in a cylinder group

-m   minimum percentage of free space

-o   optimization preference (space or time)

When using tunefs, note that although the syntax is easy, the decisions are
tough, and the parameter values you specify can have considerable impact on
the performance of your file systems. You are encouraged to explore the implications of changes before straying from the defaults established through years
of experience with typical file systems. Familiarity both with your device driver and applications will aid in making these decisions.

The -a option allows you to reset the maximum number of disk blocks that
will be written contiguously before forcing a rotational delay. The default is

one, appropriate for most disks since they require an interrupt for each disk transfer and, thus, cannot write more than one block at a time.

The -d option allows you to specify the rotational spacing between consecutive blocks of a single file.

The -e option specifies the largest number of blocks that a single file can occupy in a single cylinder group. This limit prevents large files from consuming too much space in a cylinder group and slowing down accesses for subsequently allocated files. If, however, you know that your file system will mostly contain large files, a large value here is appropriate.

The -m parameter represents the amount of disk space in a file system that is held back from users. Typically, 10 percent of the space in any given file system appears "missing" to the average user. When you examine the kbytes and used columns of the df -k command, and calculate the percentage, you will note that it is considerably different from what is reported; the avail column also appears in error. This 10 percent is held back from the users to prevent the file system from getting so full that it performs badly. In a pinch, you could modify this file system parameter to make additional space available. However, you would first unmount the file system. In addition, by resetting this value to less than 10 percent of the space available, the file system switches from time to space optimization. Throughput to your disk can be dramatically reduced, as much as a factor of 3. For both these reasons, the decision to reset the minimum free space should not be made lightly. On the other hand, the space set aside when you reserve 10 percent of very large disks can be considerable. Calculate 10 percent of a 2-Gbyte disk; we are talking about hundreds of megabytes. You would have to give serious thought before sacrificing this amount of space.

You can use the newfs command with a -N option to print out a listing of the parameters that newfs would use without actually creating the file system.

You can also retrieve the command line that was used to generate a particular file system by entering the mkfs command with the -m option.

```
# mkfs -m /dev/rdsk/c0t3d0s7
mkfs -F ufs -o nsect=80,ntrack=9,bsize=8192,fragsize=1024,cgsize=16,free=10,
rps=73,nbpi=2048,opt=t,apc=0,gap=0,nrpos=8,maxcontig=7 /dev/rdsk/c0t3d0s7
214560
```

Whenever you create a new file system, it will contain a lost+found subdirectory. This is used in fsck's recovery process to hold files that need to be reattached to the file system; it is generally empty.

4.5 Making File System Available (Locally)

In order to mount a new file system, you will need to create a mount point which is usually an empty directory, although it doesn't need to be empty. Previous contents are hidden while the file system is mounted. One nice way to distinguish mount points from other directories is to create an empty file within them that proclaims the directory as a mount point:

```
boson# mkdir myfilesys
boson# touch myfilesys/"File system is not mounted"
boson# mount /dev/dsk/c0t1d0s7 myfilesys
```

When the file system is not mounted, `ls` will display the "File system is not mounted" message. This will prevent user panic when the file system is not mounted and the files would otherwise appear to have been erased.

Mount points for local file systems are usually created at the base of the root file system (in /). However, this is not necessary; a mount point can exist at any level in the directory structure. Often, file systems or directories which are mounted from remote systems are mounted at a higher level in the file system structure.

4.5.1 Mounting and unmounting file systems

Mounting file systems makes them accessible to processes and users. Most local file systems are mounted as part of the boot process. The mount and unmount commands, which can be executed only by root, attach file systems to points in the directory tree structure known as *mount points* (Fig. 4.18).

The mount command can be used for both local and remote file systems. NFS, for example, allows you to mount specific directories within file systems

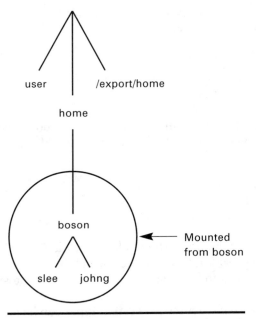

Figure 4.18 File system mount points.

rather than the entire file systems, depending on what the file server is sharing and what you want. This will be more thoroughly covered in Chap. 9.

Assuming that we have a CD ROM mounted through an entry in /etc/vfstab, we are going to substitute it with another. Notice the messages that refer to the file system type. The first CD ROM (which we reinsert at the end of this dialog) contains a ufs file system, while the other is an ISO 9660 file system. Note the use of mount options.

TRY THIS   Mount a File System

```
# umount /cdrom
# mkdir /home/slee/clipart
# touch /home/slee/clipart/"CD is not mounted"
# mount /dev/dsk/c0t6d0s2 /home/slee/clipart
mount: /dev/dsk/c0t6d0s2 write-protected            <- oops
#mount: -r /dev/dsk/c0t6d0s2 /home/slee/clipart     <- specify
                                                    read only

mount: /dev/dsk/c0t6d0s2 is not this fstype.        <- oops, again
#mount -F hsfs -r /dev/dsk/c0t6d0s2 /home/slee/clipart  <- specify
                                                    ISO 9660

# ls /home/slee/clipart                             <- success
animals    comm       food      holidays   maps      office    tools
arch       computer   foreign   icon       medical   safety    traffic
bkgrnds    dingbat    framers   illustrat  military  space     trans
borders    electric   games     industry   money     sports    usa
business   flags      hands     landmark   music     stars
# umount /home/slee/clipart
# mount -F hsfs -r /dev/dsk/c0t6d0s2 /cdrom
hsfs mount: /dev/dsk/c0t6d0s2 is not an hsfs file system.
# mount -r /dev/dsk/c0t6d0s2 /cdrom
```

Use verify option to display the command executed when you specify mount /export/home. Notice the additional information that is obtained from the /etc/vfstab file.

```
# mount -V /export/home
mount -F ufs /dev/dsk/c0t1d0s7 /export/home
```

Other mount options include the file system type (-F option) which we have seen in many of the examples so far, the -m option which mounts without updating the /etc/mnttab file, and -r, which specifies that a file system be mounted read-only.

Additional options specific to particular file system types can be used following a -o in a mount command. The ufs -specific options include

f	"Fakes" an entry in the /etc/mnttab file without mounting anything. Remove faked entry with editor.
n	Option, like the generic -m option above, mounts without updating the /etc/mnttab. The umount command will warn you that file system is not in mnttab, but will unmount it just the same.
rw	Specifies read-write mount.
ro	Specifies read-only mount.
nosuid	Disallows setuid execution for better system security.
remount	Changes read-only mount to read-write mount.

TRY THIS   ufs -Specific Mount Options

```
# mount -o ro /export/home
# mount|grep home
/export/home on /dev/dsk/c0t3d0s7 read only on Fri Jan 1 15:02:32 1993
# mount -o remount /export/home
# mount|grep home
/export/home on /dev/dsk/c0t3d0s7 remount on Fri Jan 1 15:03:51 1993
```

4.5.2 The vfstab file

The file, /etc/vfstab (virtual file system table), describes regularly mounted file systems. Included are local file systems as well as those which are mounted over the network. The fields are separated with spaces or tabs and include the device name, device name for use with fsck (which runs against the raw partitions of a disk), the mount point, the file system type, the sequence in which the file system will be checked with fsck, whether the file system should be mounted when the system is booted, and special mount options (e.g., ro which indicates read-only mount).

File systems which are not mounted when the system boots can be subsequently mounted without including all the detail in the boot command. For example, the last line in the listing below specifies that the CD ROM is not to be mounted at bootup. With this line in the /etc/vfstab file, the device can be mounted by issuing the command mount /cdrom rather than the more verbose command mount -r /dev/dsk/c0t6d0s2 /cdrom. The rest of the line specifies that the device will not be checked with fsck, is to be mounted on /cdrom, holds a ufs file system, and is not mounted at boot time.

#device	device	mount	FS	fsck	mount	mount
#to mount	to fsck	point	type	pass	at boot	options
#						
#/dev/dsk/c1d0s2	/dev/rdsk/c1d0s2	/usr	ufs	1	yes	-

```
/proc              -                /proc        proc   -   no    -
fd                 -                /dev/fd      fd     -   no    -
swap               -                /tmp         tmpfs  -   no    -
/dev/dsk/c0t3d0s0  /dev/rdsk/c0t3d0s0  /         ufs    1   no    -
/dev/dsk/c0t3d0s6  /dev/rdsk/c0t3d0s6  /usr      ufs    2   no    -
/dev/dsk/c0t1d0s7  /dev/rdsk/c0t1d0s7  /export/home ufs 3   yes   -
/dev/dsk/c0t3d0s5  /dev/rdsk/c0t3d0s5  /opt      ufs    4   yes   -
/dev/dsk/c0t1d0s0  /dev/rdsk/c0t1d0s0  /root41   ufs    5   yes   -
/dev/dsk/c0t1d0s1  -                -            swap   -   no    -
/dev/dsk/c0t1d0s6  /dev/rdsk/c0t1d0s6  /usr41    ufs    7   yes   -
/dev/dsk/c0t6d0s2  -                /cdrom ufs   ufs        no    ro
```

You are likely to receive CD ROMs in one of two formats: ufs or ISO 9660. Each requires a different mount command or /etc/vfstab entry. The entry shown in the vfstab file below only works for ufs. If you followed the Try This exercise in Sec. 3.8, you should have noted the two file system types we specified in our attempts to mount CD ROMs. Since you are unlikely to want to modify your /etc/vfstab for each of the files, I suggest that you create a second entry for the ISO 9660 CDs. Since you cannot differentiate the second entry by the first field of the /etc/vfstab file (you would be using the same CD drive), you need to differentiate the second entry by the mount point; this way, the mount command knows which entry to use. The only other entry that needs to be different is, obviously, the file system type; hsfs is the file system type for ISO 9660.

By adding the line below to the /etc/vfstab file just displayed, you can mount ISO 9660 CD ROMs with the mount /hsfs command and ufs CD ROMs with the mount /cdrom command. You should create /hsfs; it can be a traditional mount point (i.e., a directory) or can be symbolically linked to /cdrom depending on where you want to use the mounted file system.

```
/dev/dsk/c0t6d0s2 - /hsfs hsfs - no ro
```

4.5.3 The mnttab file

The /etc/mnttab file contains information about currently mounted file systems. Unlike the vfstab file, this file is not modified by the system administrator. The mount and unmount commands maintain the file. The tab-separated fields include the device, the mount point, the file system type, mount options (e.g., ro, rw, and ignore), and the time at which the file system was mounted.

```
/dev/dsk/c0t3d0s0 /         ufs   rw,suid   725118103
/dev/dsk/c0t3d0s6 /usr      ufs   rw,suid   725118103
/proc /proc              proc   rw,suid   725118103
fd /dev/fd               fd     rw,suit   725118103
/dev/dsk/c0t1d0s7 /export/home ufs suid,rw,dev=80000f 725118107
/dev/dsk/c0t3d0s5 /opt     ufs   suid,rw,dev=80001d 725118108
/dev/dsk/c0t1d0s0 /root41  ufs   suid,rw,dev=800008 725118109
```

```
/dev/dsk/c0t1d0s6    /usr41   ufs    suid,rw,dev=80000e   725118111
boson:(pid135)       /net     nfs    ro,ignore,map=-hosts,indirect,dev=21c0000
   725118146
boson:(pid135)       /home    nfs    ro,ignore,map=auto_home,indirect,dev=21c0001
   725118146
```

4.5.4 The `mountall` and `umountall` commands

The `mountall` and `umountall` commands allow you to easily mount or un-mount groups of file systems by file system type, regardless of whether they are local or remote, or because they are included in a file which is formatted like the `vfstab` file. If there are several file systems that should be mounted only once in a while, you could include their mounting information in a separate file and use it with the commands shown below.

```
mountall /etc/vfstab.special
umountall /etc/vfstab.special
```

To mount file systems by type, use the `-F` option as shown here:

```
mountall -F nfs
```

To mount only local or only remote file systems, use one of these commands:

```
mountall -l
mountall -r
```

Combining these options is allowable as long as the options are consistent. The first command below is fine; the second contradicts itself since `nfs` file systems are always remote. This command will cause `mountall` to complain that the options are incompatible.

```
mountall -l /etc/vfstab.special
mountall -l -F nfs
```

4.6 Beyond Manual Mounts

All versions of the mount command require root privilege. This is reasonable with system disks which should not be mounted and unmounted by the casual user who may not understand the implications of file integrity and shared disks. On the other hand, when we are dealing with CD ROMs or file systems on floppy disks, it would often be more convenient if anyone could issue the mount and unmount requests. In addition, it would be nice if file systems could be mounted and unmounted as needed. Two tools exist in Solaris 2.x to overcome this problem: Volume Management and Automounter. Volume Management is discussed in Sec. 4.8. Automounter is covered in Chap. 9.

4.7 Options for Disk Storage

Some options for disk storage go beyond what is provided in Solaris 2.x, but may provide added value in situations where reliability and availability are critical. One technique for significantly improving reliability is called *disk mirroring*. With disk mirroring, all data are written to a second disk which is a duplicate of the first and can be used in its place in the case of disk failure. Obviously, some overhead is incurred with mirroring since each disk write requires two or three write operations.

Almost the opposite concept, dual porting allows a disk to be connected to more than one host so that failure of any component on the host does not prevent access to the data on the disk. When a disk is dual-ported, one controller must be the master and the other a slave at any point in time.

Another advance in disk technology is disk striping in which groups of disks can be treated as though they were a single larger disk, enabling creation of larger file systems and a larger logical partition (slice). With disk striping, the data written to disk are interleaved. This also improves read and write performance for serial applications. Disk concatenation, on the other hand, appends disks end-to-end to create a single large logical disk.

Many of these options for storage are available through use of Online: DiskSuite, a product which can be used with Solaris to provide enhanced file system performance and reliability.

Other options to consider when designing your file system strategies include hierarchical storage systems which automatically move infrequently used files to slower and cheaper media improving access times to files which are frequently used and maintaining adequate free space in file systems that they perform well. *Rewritable optical* media is often an excellent choice for price and reliability when considering this technology.

4.8 Volume Management

New in version 2.2, Volume Management makes it possible for users to mount floppies and CD ROMs without having to have root privilege. It provides automatic mounting for CD ROMs and diskettes. If a CD or diskette is in the drive when the system is booted, it is automatically mounted. If a user inserts a diskette, they will have to notify the Volume Management tool using the `volcheck` command.

CD ROMs are automatically mounted on `/cdrom/` if the CD has a name and `/cdrom/unnamed_cdrom` if it does not. If the CD ROM does not contain a file system, it is mounted on `/vol/dev/aliases/cdrom0`. Figure 4.19 illustrates the contents of `/cdrom` when a Sun User Group CD ROM (`sug94_1`) is mounted.

Diskettes are automatically mounted on `/floppy/` if the CD has a name and `/floppy/nonunique` if it does not. If the CD ROM does not contain a file system, it is mounted on `/vol/dev/aliases/floppy0`.

Users can eject CD ROMs which are mounted by Volume Management by using `eject cd`, `eject cdrom`, or `eject floppy`. This accomplishes the unmount and ejects the device.

```
----------------------------------------------------------------
# cd /cdrom
# ls -l
total 14
lrwxrwxrwx   1 root      nobody         9 Dec 28 09:03 cdrom0 -> ./sug94_1
dr-xr-xr-x   2 nobody    nobody       512 Dec 20 08:50 solaris_2_3_ab
dr-xr-xr-x   2 root      sys         4096 Nov 16 12:19 sug94_1
dr-xr-xr-x   2 nobody    nobody       512 Dec 22 09:35 unnamed_cdrom
----------------------------------------------------------------
```

Figure 4.19 Contents of cdrom with SUG CD ROM mounted.

You can check if Volume Management is running by looking for its deamon in the processes. This ps command will check for the running process:

```
# ps -ef|grep vold
root 175 1229 09:03:28 ? 0:08 /usr/sbin/vold
root 1004 876 7 02:59:48 pts/2 0:00 grep vold
```

4.8.1 Compatibility with older mount commands

If you try mount commands from releases preceding Solaris 2.2, you are likely to see an error message when you try to mount a CD ROM or floppy saying that the device is already mounted, that the mount point is busy, or that the allowable number of mount points has been exceeded.

4.8.2 Configuration of Volume Management

Volume Management has a configuration file, /etc/vold.conf (see Fig. 4.20), which you can edit to modify its default behavior. You would also modify this file to add a second CD ROM or diskette.

The use lines in this file correspond to individual devices. See Fig. 4.21.

4.8.3 Sharing with Volume Management

You can also configure Volume Management so that mounted CD ROM and diskettes are automatically made available across the network. If you add share cdrom* to the /etc/rmmount.conf file (see Fig. 4.22), all CD ROMs will be available for sharing once they are mounted. You can also share a specific CD by name by using its name as shown here.

```
share sug94_1
```

4.9 Summary

Managing Solaris 2.x file systems involves creating and tuning them as well as making them available to the users who need them. Understanding and maintaining file systems requires knowledge about disk partitioning, file systems types (disk-based, network-based, and pseudo-network-based), and the share and mount commands which will be covered in Chap. 9.

```
----------------------------------------------------------------
# @(#)vold.conf 1.16      93/05/17 SMI
#
# Volume Daemon Configuration file
#

# Database to use (must be first)
db db_mem.so

# Labels supported
label dos label_dos.so floppy
label cdrom label_cdrom.so cdrom
label sun label_sun.so floppy

# Devices to use
use cdrom drive /dev/dsk/c0t6 dev_cdrom.so cdrom0
use floppy drive /dev/diskette dev_floppy.so floppy0

# Actions
insert /vol*/dev/diskette[0-9]/* user=root /usr/sbin/rmmount
insert /vol*/dev/dsk/* user=root /usr/sbin/rmmount
eject /vol*/dev/diskette[0-9]/* user=root /usr/sbin/rmmount
eject /vol*/dev/dsk/* user=root /usr/sbin/rmmount
notify /vol*/rdsk/* group=tty /usr/lib/vold/volmissing -c

# List of file system types unsafe to eject
unsafe ufs hsfs pcfs
----------------------------------------------------------------
```

Figure 4.20 Default /etc/vold.conf.

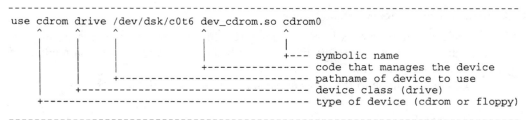

Figure 4.21 Fields in use command in /etc/vold.conf.

```
-------------------------------------------------
# @(#)rmmount.conf 1.2      92/09/23 SMI
#
# Removable Media Mounter configuration file.
#

# File system identification
ident hsfs ident_hsfs.so cdrom
ident ufs ident_ufs.so cdrom floppy
ident pcfs ident_pcfs.so floppy

# Actions
action cdrom action_filemgr.so
action floppy action_filemgr.so

-------------------------------------------------
```

Figure 4.22 Default rmmount.conf file.

The manual pages for the following commands are useful:

```
devinfo(1M)
df
format
fmthard(1M)
fsck(1M)
newfs(1M)
prtvtoc(1M)
rmmount
swap(1M)
volcancel
volcheck
vold
volfs
volmissing
```

In Answerbook, look for the sections on adding and maintaining peripherals, Volume Management, and administering file systems.

Installation

5

Preinstallation Issues

Before you begin to install any Solaris system, you should have a clear idea what role the system will play in your network. Some systems are clearly single-user workstations, while others are shared or function as file servers or boot servers. Some systems are installed as standalones, while others receive most of the software they use from other systems on the network.

You also need to evaluate your readiness for the Solaris 2.x installation. Make sure that the system you are about to install has the proper disk and memory configuration. Specific requirements for any Solaris 2.x system will be included in the installation documentation provided with the release. We will only touch on them briefly and in a general sense here.

5.1   Requirements for Installing Solaris 2.x

Each release of SunOS 5.x will have its own space and memory requirements for running the operating system locally. SunOS 5.2, for example, requires that you have 150 Mbytes of disk space and 16 Mbytes of memory to install a standalone system. Since these requirements change between releases, it is a good idea to make your slices larger than required. This may avoid the need to repartition your disk before the next upgrade. For a standalone system, you should have a 424-Mbyte disk or larger in order to install everything you will need to function effectively.

Since SunOS is only distributed on CD ROM, you will need to have a CD ROM drive somewhere on your network accessible to you. This drive does not have to be attached to the system you are installing, however. You can use a drive attached to another host on your network provided it will respond to requests from the host you are installing. This requires that the host with the drive have the name and address of the host you are installing either in its local files or in its NIS maps.

If you are installing Solaris 2.x on a system which has been running SunOS 4.x, you should be aware of several possible compatibility problems. Certain peripherals (mostly disk drives or SBus cards) may not yet be ported to Solaris 2.x. In addition, some applications may not run while others may run only using binary compatibility mode. If this is the case, you will want to be sure to install this option. It is included in all clusters except the core configuration.

5.2   Roles Systems Play

Common terms used to define the roles that hosts play in a given network include *client* and *server,* with a number of more specific descriptors. The terms that you should be familiar with are described below.

5.2.1   File server

A *file server* is a system which provides file storage and retrieval for users. This term is used primarily for systems which house home directories, but data files can be served as well.

5.2.2   Application server

An *application server* is a system which is used to house a particular application or set of applications. Often, application servers are file servers as well.

5.2.3   Boot server

A *boot server* is a system which provides operating system support for clients. Boot servers may support dataless or diskless clients or both. Boot servers can be homogenous or heterogenous depending on whether their clients are of the same or different kernel architectures.

5.2.4   Install server

An *install server* is a system which is used to support installations of new hosts over the network. Install servers are configured similarly to servers which support diskless clients. Primarily, they provide access to a CD ROM for hosts which do not have a drive. For install servers which will be used to install a large number of clients, it can be considerably more efficient to copy the contents of the CD ROM onto the install server's hard disk.

If you are installing many hosts using the same configuration, you can preconfigure the installation and greatly streamline the installation process by configuring your install server with autoinstall capabilities. Instructions for configuring a server to allow automatic installation are included in the installation guide for your specific release of Solaris 2.x.

5.2.5   Mail and calendar servers

Mail and calendar servers provide a centralized place to store and administer mail files or calendar files for users. Centralizing these functions is often a good idea since it simplifies the maintenance of mail aliases and makes managing the mail system at a large site considerably easier. A single server will often provide both mail and calendar files.

5.2.6 Client systems

Clients are systems that use the services of other hosts on the network. Usually, clients depend on servers for users' files, operating system, or application support. Systems which depend on a server for naming services are also called clients.

5.2.7 Standalones or "diskful" systems

A *standalone* is a system which is self-sufficient even though it may be connected to a network. These systems rely on software resident on their own disks to boot and run. They often get home directories and applications from other systems. There is some disagreement as to which term—*standalone* or *diskful*—better describes this configuration. Neither term is completely appropriate. Diskful systems can, in fact, not be self-sufficient just as clearly as most self-sufficient systems are ordinarily not standing along, but are network-connected. Sometimes, the term *networked standalone* is used to convey the concept of a self-sufficient yet networked system.

If you are installing a system which is not connected to a network, then, clearly, it can only be a standalone. Standalone systems can run even if the network is down, but with certain reservations. If the systems depend on other systems for naming information (this is usually the case) or applications (this is often the case), they will function properly only if you stop them from trying to bind to their name server or hard mounting partitions from other systems.

5.2.8 Dataless clients

A *dataless client* is one that "has no data." It has a local root directory and local swap space. It gets operating system support as well as applications and home directories from other hosts on the network. Dataless clients mount /usr, /usr/kvm, and their root file system from a boot server. One primary advantage of dataless systems is that volatile files are not stored on them, but are stored on shared servers. This facilitates the work of installing and upgrading these systems since there are relatively few files to back up and you only need to create a new root file system. In spite of this advantage, dataless clients do not require dedicated space on the file server; this makes this configuration option even more attractive. Diskless clients, in comparison, require root and swap space amounting to at least 40 Mbytes.

5.2.9 Diskless clients

A *diskless client* is one that has no disk and gets the operating system as well as applications and home directories from the network. Obviously, any system without a disk can only run as a diskless client. On the other hand, diskful systems can be set up to run in *diskless mode*; that is, they can get all their operating support—/, /usr, and their swap space—from another host.

5.3 Standard Client Configurations

Setting up individual systems is seldom done without reference to your entire network. Your choice of how completely to install any particular host will depend on many factors, including performance on your network and the number of hosts from which you can obtain applications and packages that you do not load locally.

Some of the factors that you need to evaluate when deciding how to configure clients involve NFS and client performance, disk space, and the ease with which file systems are administered. Clearly, clients will perform best when files and applications are local. Under these same conditions, the NFS load on your network will also be minimized. On the other hand, you will have many copies of files and applications to administer and file systems on many clients which need to be backed up. The dataless client represents a good balance of centralized administration and good performance.

Most sites with a large number of workstations will define a small number of client configurations that they will support. This is a good practice, since it greatly simplifies both the installation and the maintenance of these systems. Using the standard SVR4 disk partitioning and a naming convention for additional disks that is consistent for your site will also facilitate system management and make later setup of tools like Automounter and setup of scripts or software for automated backup software that much easier.

5.4 Configuration Clusters

Four standard software configurations are embodied in the configuration clusters that are provided with SunOS. Each configuration cluster includes an increasingly complete set of all the software packages that make up SunOS. As will be further described in Chap. 7, you can select only the bare minimum of the files required to run the operating system, or you can select the complete set of packages.

The four configuration clusters include core, end user, developer, and the entire distribution. The core system contains only the bare essentials. This cluster will allow your workstation to boot and execute UNIX commands. The end-user cluster also contains OpenWindows. This includes the OpenWindows deskset as well as fonts and menus. The developer's cluster adds the files necessary to develop applications. Although compilers and debuggers are no longer included in Solaris, the developer's cluster contains header files, archive libraries, manual pages, and other compilation tools. The entire distribution cluster, naturally, includes all software packages that are included on the distribution CD ROM.

The four configuration clusters define a simple, but coarse set of choices that provides a reasonable amount of functionality for four different types of users.

These choices, however, are merely an installation convenience. Starting with any of the configuration clusters, you can add and omit any of the packages that comprise Solaris. Selecting and omitting packages during installation is covered in the next chapter. Chapter 11 explains how to add packages at a later time.

5.5   Gathering Information for the Installation

Depending on how your network is managed, you will need to collect various pieces of information before you begin your installation. You will need a host-name, and IP (Internet Protocol) number. You will need to determine whether the system will be a client of a naming service like NIS+ and, if so, what do-main it belongs in. If the system is to be a client of another, for home directo-ries, mail or calendar files, applications or for its operating system, you will need to have the name and IP address of the systems providing this support available during installation.

If you are upgrading a system from a previous SunOS, most of this informa-tion has already been established for this host. It will be easier if you copy it before you shut the system down or fetch it from NIS or /etc files on another host. However, it is possible to retrieve it from the host you are installing any-time before you start the actual installation. While you are running `sunin-stall` and selecting your configuration options, you can still open a command tool, and mount the old root partition to retrieve this data.

You will, of course, need to know the root password before the installation and, most likely, will assign the same password during the installation. This, however, depends on how system security is handled at your site.

You should also have the names and IP numbers of all servers which will pro-vide support to this system. This will allow you to set up these and test these mounts while you are configuring the new host.

If this is a new system, you should make sure that you have all the cables and that you have checked for available power outlets and network connections. It is a good idea to have spare cables, terminators, and test equipment on hand in case you run into problems attaching the host to your network.

An easy way to make sure you have all the information you will need is to have a form ready with answers to the installation questions you will be asked. You should also provide space on this form to note information that you en-counter during the installation or to note any problems that you had so that you can avoid them on the next system. Keep any product sheets that came with the system and make sure you have serial numbers and hostIDS for main-tenance purposes and later software licensing.

5.5.1   Hostnames

A hostname can include up to 64 characters and, in Solaris 2.x, can include up-percase characters, numbers, and hyphens (but should not begin or end in a hyphen).

Most sites will allow users to name their own hosts, although some sites have rigid naming schemes or conventions which limit these choices. A chemistry department, for example, might name hosts after the elements in the periodic chart of elements, while a federal agency might name hosts after countries. Whatever your naming scheme, take this issue seriously. The personalization of hosts on your network is something your users are likely to care about more than you might imagine.

5.5.2 IP numbers

IP addresses are always rigidly defined since they must be unique and must be members of the network address assigned to your site. If your organization is small and not connected to the Internet, you can get away with using almost any addresses, but you should be aware of how IP addresses are constructed and used and understand that you will need to obtain a site-specific network address should you decide to connect your network to the Internet.

Make sure before you install a system that you know what its IP address is or should be. If you use multiple network addresses and routers, make sure the IP address that you are using will allow proper routing to this host.

5.5.3 Subnet masks

If your site implements subnet addressing, you need to determine the correct subnet mask to use. The most common use of subnet masks is to divide the address space of a class B network (e.g., 128.220.0.0) into a number of class C-sized subnets. This type of addressing clearly differentiates divisions within the overall organizational structure and, to some extent, isolates traffic within these divisions.

The simplest way to think about subnet masks is to imagine a dividing line between the bits that are set and those that are not. The set part represents the network address, while the unset part is left to number each host on the network. Thus, a mask of 255.255.255.0, is the default for a class C network where the first 3 bytes represent the network and the last byte, the host. Used with a class B network, on the other hand, it specifies that the third byte is to be used as part of the network address even though this byte, by TCP/IP (Transmission Control Protocol/IP) definitions, is part of the host address.

```
255.255.255.0
  ^           ^

network     host
```

Although subnet masks are almost always specified at byte boundaries, this is not a strict requirement. A mask of 255.255.255.192 is valid; it uses 2 bits of the last byte to break the address space of a class C network into four subnets (or a class B into more than a thousand subnets).

5.5.4 Network Information

Solaris 2.x systems can be NIS or NIS+ clients, or they can refer to files in `/etc` for information about themselves and other hosts on the network. Have the domain name and server name ready if this host will be an NIS or NIS+ client.

5.5.5 Servers

Since any particular host may go to a number of servers for various types of support, have a list with the names and addresses of servers along with details on the file systems which they provide for this particular client. You might use a form like that shown below to collect this information. Include the path for applications and nonstandard locations. Also mark those directories which you plan to set up to Automount; this will help you remember to ensure that they are included in the Automount maps and not to establish the mount during installation. Most of this information will not be unique to this particular host, but will be the same for a number of hosts which are configured using the same guidelines. Figure 5.1 shows a sample form.

5.5.6 Host configurations

On the same or a different form, collect the information which is unique to this host. This data sheet will help you to manage your client configurations over the long haul and will be valuable to anyone who might need to take over management of some or all of these systems. Figure 5.2 shows a sample form.

Installation is also a good time to collect information that you will need later in managing your network, including the system serial number, Ethernet address, architecture, peripherals, location, and user's name. Having a form on hand to collect this information and keeping track of host information provided with the system is an extremely good idea. Even if the host you are installing

```
--------------------------------------------------------------------------
                                                              auto-
Support Provided       Server Name           Server IP Address   mounted
=================      ==================    ==================  ========
operating system       _____    _____
root and swap          _____    _____
home directories       _____    _____  _____
mail files             _____    _____  _____
calendar files         _____    _____  _____
applications and data  _____    _____  _____
_____      _____    _____  _____
_____      _____    _____  _____
_____      _____    _____  _____

printers               _____    _____  _____
_____      _____    _____  _____
_____      _____    _____  _____
_____      _____    _____  _____
--------------------------------------------------------------------------
```

Figure 5.1 Client mount specifications form.

```
-----------------------------------------------------------------
hostname:               _____
client type:            o stand   o dataless   o diskless
IP address:
subnet mask:            _____
naming service:         o NIS+     o NIS        o FILES
role:                   o master   o replica    o client
domain:                 _____
type of install:        o quick    o custom
# diskless clients:     _____
# architectures:        _____
software configuration: o all      o developer     o user      o core
additional packages
        required:       _____   _____
                        _____   _____
                        _____   _____

packages to
        omit:           _____   _____
                        _____   _____
                        _____   _____
-----------------------------------------------------------------
```

Figure 5.2 Client configuration form.

```
------------------------------------------
hostname:               _____
system serial number:   _____
hostid:                 _____
ethernet address:       _____
architecture:           _____
peripherals:            _____
                        _____
                        _____
                        _____
printers used:          _____
                        _____
                        _____
                        _____
location:               _____
user's name:            _____
OS version:             _____
date installed:         _____
------------------------------------------
```

Figure 5.3 Host information form.

has been in use at your site for years, you may not have a reliable record of all this information. Figure 5.3 shows a sample form.

5.6 Planning Partitions

When planning how to partition your disks, consider the role that the particular system will play before deciding how much room each partition will require. The following table lists the normal partition assignments. Except for servers with diskless clients, slices 5 and 6 are seldom used.

Even if you have more than one disk and choose to spread your partitions across them, it is best to follow these conventions in assigning slices to file systems since they will make sense to other UNIX administrators.

```
/dev/sd0a      /dev/dsk/c0t0d0s0      /

/dev/sd0b      /dev/dsk/c0t0d0s1      swap

/dev/sd0d      /dev/dsk/c0t0d0s3      /export

/dev/sd0e      /dev/dsk/c0t0d0s4      /export/swap

/dev/sd0f      /dev/dsk/c0t0d0s5      /var or /opt

/dev/sd0g      /dev/dsk/c0t0d0s6      /usr

/dev/sd0h      /dev/dsk/c0t0d0s7      /export/home
```

On your worksheets, include both the old and new devices naming conventions, as was done here, to make it easier to get accustomed to the new device naming scheme.

For boot servers, you must set aside enough space to support the diskless and dataless clients that will boot off this server. The /export partition will contain both the /export/root and /export/exec directories. It should be large enough to accommodate 20 Mbytes for each diskless client's root partition, 10 Mbytes for the template files, and 15 Mbytes for each architecture (e.g., sun4c) that is supported. Dataless clients will require additional space only if their architecture is different from that of the server and other clients. In this case, you will have to load the architecture-specific kvm files for these clients.

```
Template Files                         10

Number of Diskless Clients    ___ * 20 =    ___

Number of Architectures       ___ * 15 =    ___

Total Space for /export                    ___
```

If the system will provide OS support both for Solaris clients and clients still running 4.x, you will need to provide considerable space for the 4.x SunOS partitions.

Application servers will need a larger /opt or /usr/local partition, depending on where you decide to keep application software.

Print servers will need additional space for spool directories and log files.

If you do not have a separate partition for /var, make sure that the root slice is large enough to accommodate this file activity. The same holds true for mail and calendar servers. Mail files, in particular, can become very large; if at all possible, /var on a mail server should be a separate partition.

The suninstall routine runs completely in physical memory so that you will be free to modify the sizes of any of your partitions (slices) during the installation if you need to. You will not need to be concerned about the location of your root and swap partitions while you do this.

5.7 Making Backups

If you are installing a system which has been in use on your network, back it up before the installation and keep a printout of the old partition table so that you can easily determine which partitions you need to preserve (e.g., /export/home) and which you should overwrite. You can repartition the disk at this time, but usually not without having to reinstall the partitions that you want to preserve.

A printout of your /etc/fstab file (or /etc/vfstab file, if this is an earlier release of Solaris 2) along with the output of a df (or df -k) command will contain enough information to give you confidence that you are preserving the right partitions. If the host has more than one disk, make sure that you do not confuse them when installing Solaris. What was sd2 might be c0t0d0. The easiest way to get a listing of your existing partitions is to use the format utility. As superuser, use format, then select the disk whose partition you wish to list. You will then enter partition and when the next menu appears, say print. This sequence of commands will provide a listing of the existing partitions. If you are running in OpenWindows, you can easily cut and paste this listing into a file and print it. Figure 5.4 illustrates this use of the format utility. This listing provides information about the partitions which are defined and their sizes, but not the names of the file system which are built on each. You can match this information against your listing of the /etc/fstab file. In this example, partitions e and h, corresponding to slices 4 and 7, have no space allocated to them.

Backing up existing partitions is important, even if you will be preserving them. The new device naming conventions make the likelihood of an inadvertent overwrite of file systems more likely. Even were this not the case, however, a complete backup before installing a new operating system is always a good idea in case anything goes wrong.

You will also want to separately preserve a number of host configuration files so that you will not have to recreate them or rediscover the knowledge of your system that they contain. Some of these files will not be compatible with their Solaris 2.x counterparts. Still, the information that they contain can be very helpful in rebuilding your system after the installation. A simple example of this is the definitions of printers including in the /etc/printcap file. If this file is available after you've installed Solaris 2.x, you can easily recreate the list of printers that the use of this particular workstation expects to access.

Here's a list of files which you should preserve even though they will not be used directly in Solaris 2.x:

The /etc directory contains so many configuration files—including fstab, printcap, hosts, services—that it should probably be preserved in its entirety for later reference.

The /etc/fstab will help you update the /etc/vfstab file or add file systems to your Automount maps.

The /.rhosts file should be saved so that you can re-create the trust matrices that existed before the installation.

The /etc/hosts file should be saved. It will contain the host names and IP numbers of hosts from which this host may have booted in the past. If the host was not an NIS client, but used /etc files for network information, there may be many addresses in this file that are important to the workstation's user.

```
----------------------------------------------------------
        format      - format and analyze the disk
        repair      - repair a defective sector
        show        - translate a disk address
        label       - write label to the disk
        analyze     - surface analysis
        defect      - defect list management
        backup      - search for backup labels
        quit
format> quit
boson#


boson# format
Searching for disks...done

AVAILABLE DISK SELECTIONS:
        0. xy0 at xyc0 slave 0
           xy0: <Fujitsu-M2361 Eagle cyl 840 alt 2 hd 20 sec 67>
        1. sd0 at sm0 slave 0
           sd0: <CDC Wren VII 94601-12G cyl 1923 alt 4 hd 15 sec 68>
        2. sd2 at sm0 slave 8
           sd2: <FALCON 2.0GB-ST42000N cyl 2633 alt 2 hd 16 sec 83>
Specify disk (enter its number): 2
selecting sd2: <FALCON 2.0GB-ST42000N>
[disk formatted, defect list found]
Warning: Current Disk has mounted partitions.


FORMAT MENU:
        disk        - select a disk
        type        - select (define) a disk type
        partition   - select (define) a partition table
        current     - describe the current disk
        format      - format and analyze the disk
        repair      - repair a defective sector
        show        - translate a disk address
        label       - write label to the disk
        analyze     - surface analysis
        defect      - defect list management
        backup      - search for backup labels
        quit
format> partition


PARTITION MENU:
        a        - change 'a' partition
        b        - change 'b' partition
        c        - change 'c' partition
        d        - change 'd' partition
        e        - change 'e' partition
        f        - change 'f' partition
        g        - change 'g' partition
        h        - change 'h' partition
        select   - select a predefined table
        name     - name the current table
        print    - display the current table
        label    - write partition map and label to the disk
        quit
partition> print
Current partition table (original sd2):
        partition a - starting cyl      0, # blocks     79680 (60/0/0)
        partition b - starting cyl     60, # blocks    159360 (120/0/0)
        partition c - starting cyl      0, # blocks   3496624 (2633/0/0)
        partition d - starting cyl    180, # blocks    531200 (400/0/0)
        partition e - starting cyl      0, # blocks         0 (0/0/0)
        partition f - starting cyl    580, # blocks     79680 (60/0/0)
        partition g - starting cyl    640, # blocks   2646704 (1993/0/0)
        partition h - starting cyl      0, # blocks         0 (0/0/0)

partition> quit


FORMAT MENU:
        disk        - select a disk
        type        - select (define) a disk type
        partition   - select (define) a partition table
        current     - describe the current disk
----------------------------------------------------------
```

Figure 5.4 Using the format command to list disk partitions.

Many of the files in /var should be saved since they represent ongoing work. The /var/spool/mail files should be saved and installed in /var/mail. The /var/spool/calendar files should also be preserved and reinstated following the installation. The crontab files in /var/spool/cron/crontabs should be saved, although it is probably a good idea to examine them to make sure the commands in these files are consistent with Solaris 2. If you use uucp you should also preserve the /var/spool/uucp directory; its new location is /var/uucp. If the system was previously an NIS+ server, you should preserve /var/nis.

It is also a good idea to save root's configuration files: /.cshrc, /.login,/.logout, and /.profile.

5.8   Introducing New Hosts

If the host you are installing is completely new to your network, you will have to add its name and IP address to the /etc/hosts file or the NIS hosts map on servers it will access. Both the new system and servers which will support it will need to know how to communicate with each other before the client will be able to operate on the network. If the new host is diskless or dataless, it will not be able to boot until this information has been provided. Further, if /usr/partitions are shared with a restrictive host list, this host will need to be added to the list or to the netgroup that it refers to.

New hosts can be added to the NIS master, or to the /etc files the specific server(s) if you are not using NIS or NIS+. If you are using NIS+, you can use Host Manager to add the new client's hostname and IP address.

If you will not be using a local CD ROM drive, you will have to establish an install server from which the new client can boot from a CD ROM or CD ROM image which has been placed on the disk.

5.8.1   Using Host Manager

Using the Host Manager Tool from Admintool, it is possible to prepare the network for a client that is yet to be installed. Standalone, dataless, and diskless clients can be subsequently installed with little trouble since all the information relating to their network identities will be already established. When the client machine is initially booted, it will probe the network for information about itself and installation screens which normally collect this information from the person installing the system will simply not appear. This technique also centralizes the introduction of new hosts to your network.

To use Host Manager, you must have set up the admin group (group 14) set up in NIS+ or NIS. Select Host Manager from the Admintool as shown in Fig. 5.5. Select your naming service as depicted in Fig. 5.6. Existing host names will appear in your window (see Fig. 5.7). Use the Add Host… option under the Edit menu to bring up a form in which you can enter all the information about the new host. Figures 5.8 through 5.10 illustrate how this information is entered.

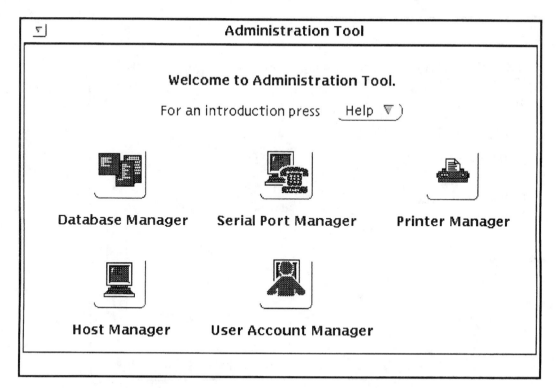

Figure 5.5 Administration Tool.

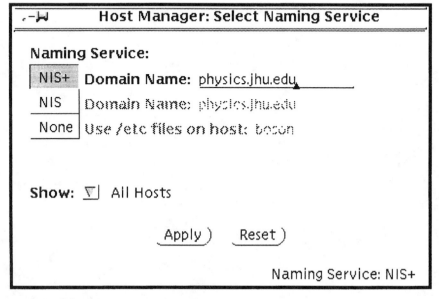

Figure 5.6 Selecting a name service.

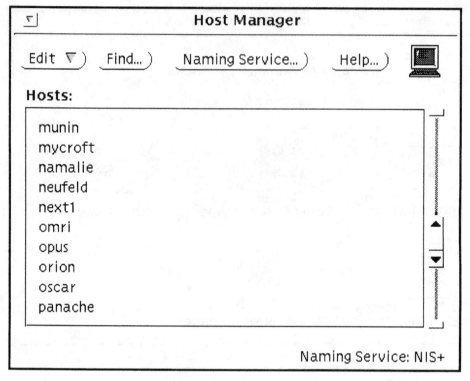

Figure 5.7   Listing hosts with Host Manager.

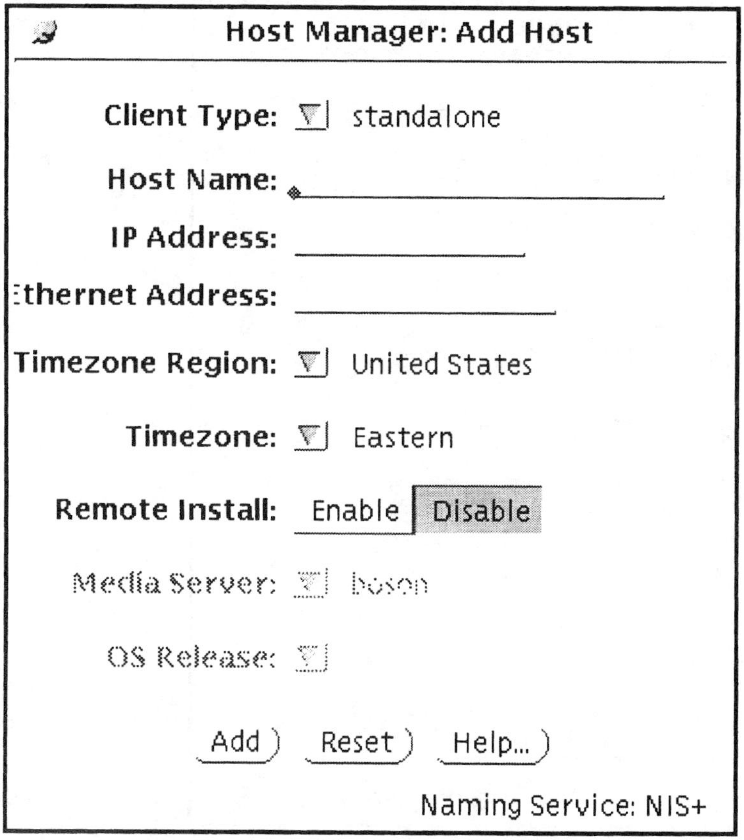

```
┌─────────────────────────────────────────────────┐
│  🖎        Host Manager: Add Host               │
│  ─────────────────────────────────────────────  │
│                                                  │
│        Client Type:  ▽│ standalone              │
│                                                  │
│         Host Name: ◆_____     │
│                                                  │
│         IP Address:   _____               │
│                                                  │
│   Ethernet Address:   _____               │
│                                                  │
│   Timezone Region:  ▽│ United States            │
│                                                  │
│          Timezone:  ▽│ Eastern                  │
│                                                  │
│    Remote Install:  Enable │ Disable            │
│                                                  │
│       Media Server: ▽│ boson                    │
│                                                  │
│        OS Release:  ▽│                          │
│                                                  │
│         ( Add )   ( Reset )   ( Help... )       │
│                                                  │
│                        Naming Service: NIS+     │
└─────────────────────────────────────────────────┘
```

Figure 5.8 Adding a host with Host Manager.

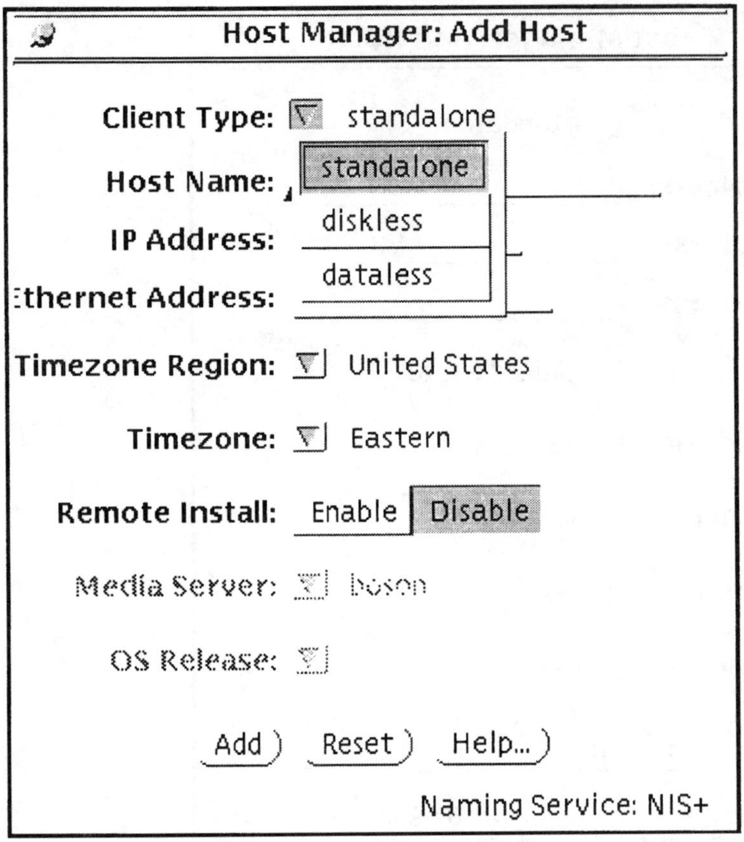

Host Manager: Add Host

Client Type: ▽ standalone

Host Name: | standalone

diskless

IP Address: dataless

Ethernet Address:

Timezone Region: ▽ United States

Timezone: ▽ Eastern

Remote Install: Enable | Disable

Media Server: ▽ boson

OS Release: ▽

Add) Reset) Help...)

Naming Service: NIS+

Figure 5.9 Selecting host type.

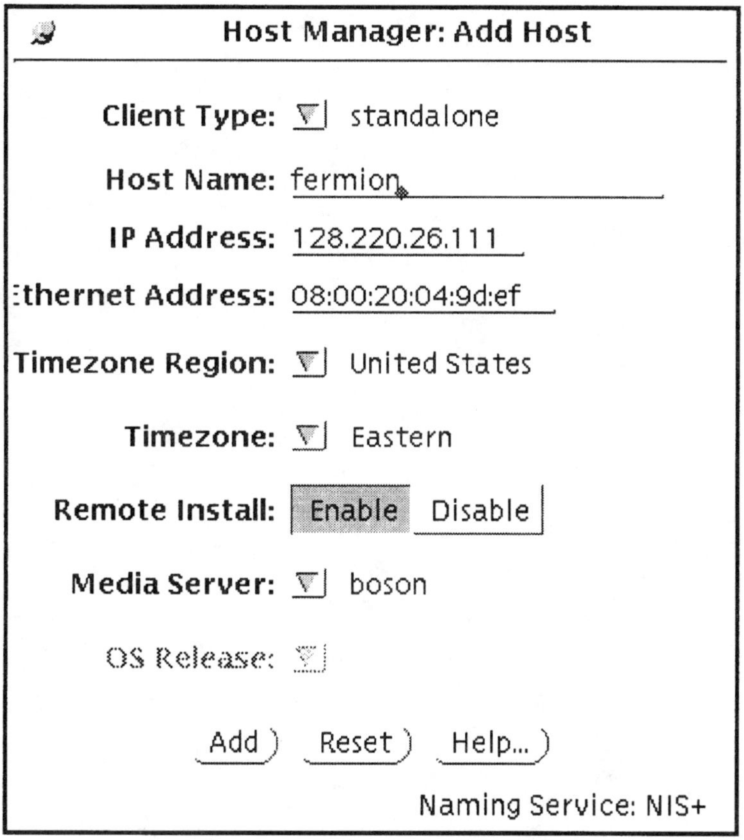

Host Manager: Add Host

Client Type: ▽| standalone

Host Name: fermion

IP Address: 128.220.26.111

Ethernet Address: 08:00:20:04:9d:ef

Timezone Region: ▽| United States

Timezone: ▽| Eastern

Remote Install: | Enable Disable |

Media Server: ▽| boson

OS Release: ▽|

Add)   Reset)   Help...)

Naming Service: NIS+

Figure 5.10 Entering host addresses and zone information.

5.9 Summary

Preparing to install Solaris 2.x systems involves making sure that you have all the information that you need and have a clear picture of the role that host will play in your network. Host Manager can simplify installation by allowing you to preconfigure clients before they are actually attached to the network.

6

Installing Solaris 2.x

Before you begin to load Solaris 2.x onto the disk of the system you are installing, you will have to boot off the Solaris 2.x CD and configure the system by specifying the configuration that you want. This configuration process involves describing this host and the environment in which it operates. You will be providing its name and address, specifying where it gets name services and file systems from, and entering information about the regional area and the current date. Following this process, you will select the software to be loaded onto this host.

The exact menus and choices for installation of Solaris 2.x will undoubtedly change somewhat between each subsequent release of the software. The steps in this chapter, therefore, may only approximate the choices you will make during installation. Refer to the installation guide for the particular subrelease for more specific instructions.

6.1 The Solaris 2.x Installation CD ROM

The SunOS CD will contain the software for multiple architectures. Depending on the type of system you are installing, you may have to construct a boot command that selects the correct software. In general, newer systems will require only that you enter `boot cdrom` to the `ok` prompt if the CD ROM is local. The exact command depends on the type of system and its boot prom. Some of the older systems, like the 4/110 and the SPARCstation 1 or 1+, will require the address of the software on the CD ROM. For example, to boot a SPARCstation 1 or 1+ from a local CD ROM, use the command `boot sd(0,6,2)`.

If you find yourself with only the > prompt, enter n (for new mode) and the `ok` prompt should appear.

If the CD ROM is located elsewhere on the network, you will have to boot the host using an install server so that you can use the CD ROM or software from the CD ROM which has been preloaded onto its hard disk. Booting from an install server will require a boot command that accesses the network. This, again, will require a command which corresponds to the particular type of host you are installing. Newer systems will boot with a `boot net` command, while older systems will require a boot command that specifies the Ethernet controller, such as `boot le()`. You will need to configure your boot server before you can install a client using this technique.

Since a Solaris 2.x installation doesn't use a miniroot like older (4.x) versions of SunOS, there is no requirement that you have a dedicated swap partition for the installation. Instead, `suninstall` runs completely in memory, allowing you greater flexibility in moving and resizing your partitions.

The character-based installation procedure allows you to install the system with a Sun monitor or an ASCII terminal. Most installation selections will not require you to enter a carriage return at the completion of the selection but will execute on selection.

Depending on the particular release, you may have to do a full install, recreating the root and `/usr` partitions. Often, an upgrade option is available when you are upgrading between subreleases of the operating system (e.g., between Solaris 2.2 and 2.3). Upgrades will modify only those files which have changed between releases rather than re-creating the root and `/usr` file systems. If an upgrade is possible, the choice will appear on the initial screen of the `suninstall` program.

Once Solaris 2.x is booted, you will use the `suninstall` utility to load your system.

6.2 Using `suninstall`

The `suninstall` utility may be available in a number of different languages. If so, you will be presented with a menu with commands in different languages from which you select the one that you want. That language will then be used in all subsequent menus.

Navigating around the installation menus may seem a little frustrating until you have become accustomed to the keys which move you between fields and choices. The tab character is used to move from field to field, the return key applies a choice, and the arrows move between choices for a field with a menu of choices.

The first piece of information that you will need to enter about the host you are installing is the hostname. Then `suninstall` will ask for the IP address and whether the system is connected to a network. It will also ask about the region in which you are located and the current date and time. It will ask about naming services. It will also ask about the disks in your system. If you have more than one disk, you can decide to preserve one in its entirety and leave it unconfigured as far as the install is concerned. Alternatively, you can preserve individual partitions or slices provided you do not need to change the partitioning of the disk and affect these slices in the process.

If the install process tells you that a partition is too small for the software that you've selected, you can change its size or reduce the files that you are trying to load either by selecting a smaller installation cluster or selectively omitting packages within a cluster that you don't need. The list indicates the space required by each package. This might help guide you in deciding which packages you might want to mount from servers rather than loading on each individual system.

Keep in mind that you can mount specific packages from your servers if everything will not fit on the local disk. You can also add packages later that you omit at installation time. Chapter 11 describes this process in detail.

During the installation process, you can select which file systems or directories to mount and from where and you can test the mounts as well; mounts set up in this way are hard mounts. The lines inserted into your /etc/vfstab file will cause these file systems to be mounted at boot time. If you prefer to have these file systems mountable on demand, either do not include them in this step or modify the /etc/vfstab files, later changing the column that specifies a boot time mount to no.

It is a good idea to Automount file systems and directories which are not continuously needed; this improves overall NFS performance and helps keep your systems from hanging when network resources are not available.

The install process will list shared file systems, making it very easy for you to select the proper source directories.

The forms displayed in Figs. 6.1 through 6.8 illustrate this step in the installation process during which you select file systems for mounting. The remote file systems form says none until you add mounts. For each file system you want to mount, select the file system and then tab to the accept button and hit return. Once the file systems appear in the list, you know that your mount table (/etc/vfstab) has recorded the mount information. The Can Mount? column records the status of any mount testing that you've done.

6.3 Summary

The suninstall utility in Solaris 2.x will take you through a series of forms and menus as you install your system. Once you've mastered the keyboard strokes for making selections from these forms, the process is easy and will allow you to monitor space usage and test mounts during the installation.

```
┌─────────────────────────────── Solaris Install ────────────────────────────────┐
│ ┌──────────────────────[ Custom Install Configuration ]──────────────────────┐ │
│ │                                                                            │ │
│ │ ( System Type... )         Standalone                                      │ │
│ │                                                                            │ │
│ │ ( Software Selection... )  Solaris 2.3, Entire Distribution                │ │
│ │                                                                            │ │
│ │ ▓▓Disks/File Systems...▓▓  c0t3d0: /, swap, /opt, /usr                      │ │
│ │                                                                            │ │
│ │                                                                            │ │
│ │                                                                            │ │
│ │                                                                            │ │
│ │ ( Remote File Systems... )                                                 │ │
│ │                                                                            │ │
│ │                                                                            │ │
│ │                                                                            │ │
│ │                                                                            │ │
│ │                                                                            │ │
│ │                                                                            │ │
│ ├────────────────────────────────────────────────────────────────────────────┤
│ │   ( Begin Install )      ( Props... )      ( Cancel... )   ( Help... )      │
│ ├────────────────────────────────────────────────────────────────────────────┤
│ │ <Return> Select; <Tab> Next Field; <F1> Help                               │
└─────────────────────────────────────────────────────────────────────────────────┘
```

Figure 6.1 Solaris installation.

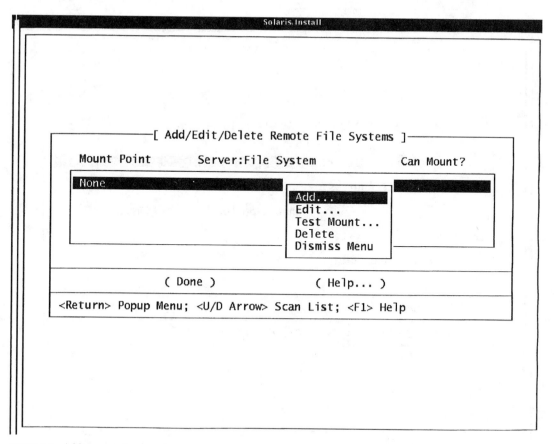

Figure 6.2   Adding remote mounts.

```
┌──────────────────────────── Solaris Install ────────────────────────────┐
│                                                                          │
│                                                                          │
│                                                                          │
│           ┌─────────[ Add A New Remote File System ]──────────┐          │
│           │                                                    │          │
│           │        Server: ████████████████████████           │          │
│           │                                                    │          │
│           │    IP Address:                                     │          │
│           │                                                    │          │
│           │                    ( Show Exported File Systems... )│         │
│           │                                                    │          │
│           │ Enter Remote File System:                          │          │
│           │                                                    │          │
│           │    Local Mount Point:                              │          │
│           │                                                    │          │
│           ├────────────────────────────────────────────────────┤         │
│           │  ( Test Mount )    ( Apply )    ( Dismiss )    ( Help... )│    │
│           ├────────────────────────────────────────────────────┤         │
│           │ <Return> Commit; <Tab> Next Field; <F1> Help       │          │
│           └────────────────────────────────────────────────────┘         │
│                                                                          │
│                                                                          │
│                                                                          │
└──────────────────────────────────────────────────────────────────────────┘
```

Figure 6.3   Form for remote file systems.

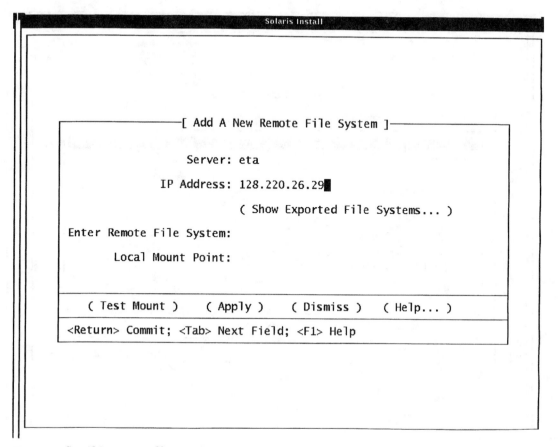

Figure 6.4 Specifying remote file systems.

```
┌──────────────────────── Solaris Install ────────────────────────┐
│                                                                  │
│  ┌─────────[ File Systems Exported By: eta ]──────────┐          │
│  │                                                    │          │
│  │  Select An Exported File System To Mount:          │          │
│  │  ┌──────────────────────────────────────────────┐  │          │
│  │  │ /usr                                         │  │          │
│  │  │ /cdrom                                       │  │          │
│  │  │ /usr/local                                   │  │          │
│  │  │ /usr/X11R5                                    │  │          │
│  │  │ /export/home                                 │  │          │
│  │  │ /export/home                                 │  │          │
│  │  │ /export/data1                                │  │          │
│  │  │ /var/spool/mail                              │  │          │
│  │  │ /var/spool/calendar                          │  │          │
│  │  │ /export/exec/kvm/sun4c.sunos.4.1.3           │  │          │
│  │  │ /export/exec/kvm/sun4m.sunos.4.1.3           │  │          │
│  │  │ /usr                                         │  │          │
│  │  └──────────────────────────────────────────────┘  │          │
│  │                                                    │          │
│  │     ( Apply )        ( Dismiss )      ( Help... )  │          │
│  │  ──────────────────────────────────────────────   │          │
│  │  <Return> Select; <U/D Arrow>: Scan List; <F1> Help│          │
│  └────────────────────────────────────────────────────┘          │
│                                                                  │
│                                                                  │
└──────────────────────────────────────────────────────────────────┘
```

Figure 6.5   Listing exported file systems.

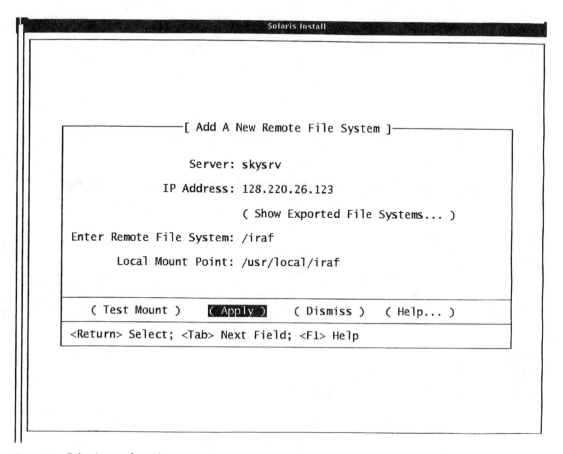

Figure 6.6   Selecting apply option.

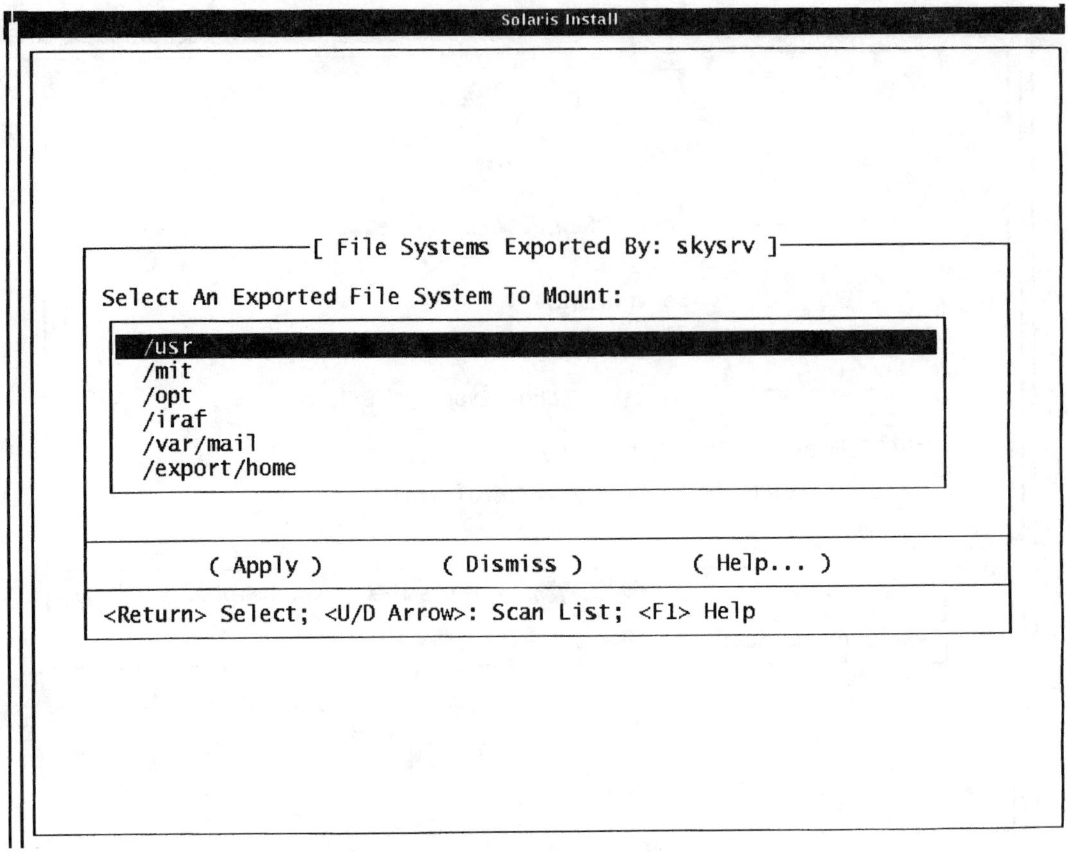

```
                              Solaris Install

            ┌──────[ File Systems Exported By: skysrv ]──────┐
            │  Select An Exported File System To Mount:        │
            │  ┌──────────────────────────────────────────┐   │
            │  │ /usr                                      │   │
            │  │ /mit                                      │   │
            │  │ /opt                                      │   │
            │  │ /iraf                                     │   │
            │  │ /var/mail                                 │   │
            │  │ /export/home                              │   │
            │  └──────────────────────────────────────────┘   │
            │                                                   │
            │      ( Apply )      ( Dismiss )     ( Help... )  │
            │  <Return> Select; <U/D Arrow>: Scan List; <F1> Help │
            └───────────────────────────────────────────────────┘
```

Figure 6.7   Solaris host-exported file systems.

```
┌──────────────────────────── Solaris Install ────────────────────────────┐



     ┌─────────[ Add/Edit/Delete Remote File Systems ]─────────┐
     │  Mount Point        Server:File System        Can Mount? │
     │ ┌──────────────────────────────────────────────────────┐ │
     │ │/usr/local/iraf    skysrv:/iraf                  ?     │ │
     │ │/usr/local         eta:/usr/local               Yes    │ │
     │ │                                                       │ │
     │ └──────────────────────────────────────────────────────┘ │
     │                                                          │
     │         ( Done )                ( Help... )              │
     │ <Return> Popup Menu; <U/D Arrow> Scan List; <F1> Help    │
     └──────────────────────────────────────────────────────────┘



└──────────────────────────────────────────────────────────────────────────┘
```

Figure 6.8 Testing file system mounts.

Basic Administration

7

Maintaining User Accounts

The process of setting up and maintaining user accounts is one of the primary responsibilities of systems administration. This is no surprise. Supporting users of the network is what systems administration is all about.

When you set up a user account, you are not only making it possible for someone to log into a host on your network but also creating, at least initially, the environment in which that individual will work. Fortunately for administrators of large networks, the tools for adding and configuring user accounts are maturing and are allowing greater degrees of automation, sometimes across disparate UNIX platforms.

Solaris provides a number of tools for setting up and configuring user accounts, managing account security, and providing users with networkwide access to their files and applications. In this chapter, we will discuss account configuration and maintenance, consider organizational policies that influence systems administration, provide details on account configuration files, and explain how to use Solaris tools to best automate account management.

7.1 Knowing Your Site

How you set up accounts at your site will depend on several important factors. Foremost among these, account management practice depends heavily on organizational policies that influence system administration activities: the importance of security and privacy and the ownership of resources that you are allocating and providing access to. Large financial organizations and military agencies are likely to view their computer systems as vulnerable assets. They are likely to have guidelines regarding ownership and use of computer assets, the rules for securing accounts, and procedures for systems administration firmly established. University laboratories, on the other hand, may be more flexible as long as you keep your systems available for use and safe from attack.

Another key factor in how you manage your accounts is the character of your user base. Programmers are likely to need more control over their accounts and workstations than end users who use only application software. In addition, the degree to which control over your systems is centralized or spread across different administrative groups will influence how you manage local resources.

Whether you are supporting only Sun systems, only Solaris, only UNIX-based operating systems, or a range of platforms running a variety of operating systems will determine how much benefit you will get out of software meant to simplify or standardize your work. How large a group you are responsible for will influence how much you are able to do "manually" along with the variety of systems that you need to support. Maintaining several hundred identical systems can be much easier than supporting half a dozen systems from different vendors. Each system requiring you to maintain expertise in its idiosyncrasies adds considerable complexity to your job.

The systems administration tools built into Solaris will help maintain all your Solaris systems. By writing customized scripts, you should be able to extend control to other UNIX platforms as well.

7.2   Establishing and Implementing Policies

Many of the decisions you make as systems administrator will be influenced by organizational policy as well as guidelines that you create to facilitate administration of your network. It is very important that you let your users know what the rules are for security and legitimate use of their accounts. You should also be sure that how much control and responsibility each of you is assuming in the configuration and maintenance of a user's account is understood; this will avoid a lot of unnecessary frustration and misunderstanding later on. A reference card or memo that summarizes your site's policies is probably the most you should expect your users to read.

In order to properly develop and enforce policies, regardless of whether your organization has established guidelines, you will need the support and coordination of your management. If you do not have this, you are likely to encounter considerable frustration.

Some issues likely to require policy on are

- Naming conventions
- Process for assigning and changing passwords
- Account configuration and maintenance
- Disk quotas
- File and resource ownership

7.2.1   Naming conventions

A simple example of policy is the naming conventions that you use in setting up your user accounts. Some sites can afford to let all users select their own individual user login names. For other sites, this is not practical. The ease with which users can send mail to each other or browse each others' calendars will depend, in part, on the predictability of user login names.

In addition to user login names, you might also set policies on users' mail addresses. The mail system permits you to assign aliases for email (electronic mail) which can more approximately match the user's real name. The ease with which we can send mail to individuals at Sun is due to the fact that user email addresses are usually based on the individuals' names. If John Doe worked for Sun, his email address would more than likely be `John.Doe@Sun.COM`. Similarly, many organizations use first initial–middle name combinations for user login names, and John Doe would probably be `jdoe` in most organizations. At the same time, no naming convention is perfect. When John Doe's new boss, Jane Doe, shows up for work, you have a conflict.

7.2.2 Assigning and changing passwords

Sites will vary on the rules for setting up and changing passwords. Some sites create passwords for users and may or may not allow the users to change them. In the past, security-conscious organizations rarely could allow users to select their own passwords because they would choose passwords that were easy for others to guess. Solaris 2.x has implemented password restrictions which prevent this from happening. New passwords are screened against a number of security criteria. For one, a password cannot be identical to the user's login name and cannot be a shifted or reversed variation of the user login name. In addition, it must be at least six characters long, and contain at least two characters and at least one digit or special character. These restrictions are not placed on passwords that the superuser assigns, but you, as system administrator, should be careful to use good judgment in assigning passwords, especially for the root account.

Solaris also supports password aging with several parameters. Passwords can expire at a given date, or you can set minimum and maximum times with the following three parameters:

Minimum change	Least time must pass before a user is able to change password
Maximum change	Longest a user can go without changing password
Expiration date	Last date user will be able to log in

The minimum age is primarily intended to keep users from changing their passwords according to policy and then changing them right back again. Using both minimum age and maximum age provides a means to force users to change their passwords every so often and retain them long enough to have the desired effect.

You should use password aging parameters with some consideration to your users. Your aim is not to frustrate them, cause them to need to write their passwords down, or to get them into situations where good security would dictate that their passwords be changed (e.g., someone else has learned their password), but they are prevented from changing their passwords because the minimum has not been reached.

7.2.3   Account configuration and maintenance

How much you configure accounts for your users and how much they are permitted to modify their setups depends on policy as well as the sophistication of your users. If your users are programmers, you will not likely have to worry about changes that they make to their environments. If your users are more computer-naive, you will likely provide the environment that they require and will want some degree of control over it so that you can keep track of your configuration and modify it without a lot of individual attention to each account.

7.2.4   Disk quotas

Another decision that you will make in setting up user accounts is how space is controlled. Disk space is usually one of the more expensive and contentious of computer resources. Maintaining file systems and managing backup and restoration of user files can be time-consuming and frustrating. If you are able to establish and enforce quotas and monitor disk space, you will be much happier than if you have users constantly filling up disk space and looking for more. A balance of sensitivity to users' requirements and a need to maintain and ensure the reliability of systems and data is best.

Whenever possible, you should be proactive in monitoring space. If you let your users know when space is getting tight and when they are approaching or exceeding 90 percent of their quotas of disk or file space, they are likely to view your monitoring space as concern and do what they can to keep things under control.

7.2.5   File and resource ownership

File ownership is another issue which can be subject to organizational policy. Most organizations will feel that they, and not the individual users, own the files in a user's account. After all, these files often represent the organization's business. The extent to which individual users are allowed to share their files or use them for their personal gain depends on the organization's policies and the nature of the files themselves. Security-conscious organizations are likely to have strict rules about file ownership.

Removing user accounts is also an activity that can call this policy into play. Whether the files of a user who is leaving the organization should be erased, archived, or bequeathed to another should not be an ad hoc decision.

Ownership of resources in a more general sense is also an issue that will heavily influence how you do your job. In some organizations, the computer staff, as a service provider, is assumed to be the owner of computer resources and has a significant degree of control over how they are controlled and allocated. Other sites take the opposite approach, and computer resources are considered the property of the departments which use them. Either scenario can work; the most difficult position for system administrators is to have a position of responsibility with little jurisdiction to leverage their judgment.

7.3   Making Choices

There are a number of choices that you make on a sitewide basis rather than for each individual user account. Chief among these, you select to use a naming service or to use the /etc files for user and system information. By the time you are ready to set up user accounts, you have probably already made this decision since it also impacts how host and other system information is maintained. You also must decide how and where to set up your user accounts. This latter decision will influence how easily your systems will be to back up and maintain and the mechanisms that you will use to maintain availability.

7.3.1   Name services

Solaris 2.x provides several choices for naming services. These are described in more detail in Chap. 13, which provides considerable detail in setting up and using NIS+. Other naming services that you may use include NIS, the much less versatile and powerful predecessor of NIS+, and Domain Name Service (DNS), the naming service used across the Internet (not included in Solaris). You can also elect to use the traditional UNIX /etc files, but this is practical only for very small networks.

The choice of naming service should be made for the largest possible domain that you control. If your network is heterogeneous, you might elect to use more than one naming service to accommodate different platforms or to use software which provides you a uniform and single-point access to managing accounts across dissimilar platforms.

If you are primarily a Sun site, the services provided by NIS+ and the account management tools described in this chapter will provide you considerable flexibility and control over your network.

7.3.2   Location of home directories

Individual home directories can be located on the disks of individual client workstations or on file servers. Consolidating user homes on file server generally provides larger amounts of disk storage and much easier maintenance and backup strategies.

Automounter, described in detail in Chap. 10, provides a way for you to make users' home directories available on any system on the network in an easy-to-manage, transparent way. If your users might not always work on the same workstation, automounting their homes is an efficient way to make their homes available to them without requiring superuser intervention each time they stray from their normal workstation.

7.3.3   Mail and calendar servers

Deciding where to establish mail and calendar files for your users should depend on whether your users do all their work at a particular workstation and what facility you have provided for looking up mail addresses and calendar locations. Since both addressing mail and browsing calendars can require a user@host address, it is important that users are able to determine what hostname to use.

Localized mail services for users who basically stay put do not require any special setup. If you manage a large network, it may be difficult for your users to know how to address mail to each other without having to keep track of their hostnames.

Mail aliases can solve this problem for mail. If the mail alias, /etc/mail/aliases or the aliases table in NIS+, includes a line equating Nicole to nicole@ducksoup, users can address mail simply to Nicole. Calendar Manager, however, does not have a way to look up users or refer to an alias's file.

Centralized mail and calendar services facilitate addressing. If users can address a message they want to send to Nicole to nicole@mailhost and browse Nicole's calendar as nicole@calhost, they do not need to concern themselves with where Nicole is logging in on the network.

7.4 Skeleton Account Setup

Common with System V versions of UNIX, skeleton account configuration directories are supported in Solaris 2.x. By preconfiguring these skeleton directories for users of different UNIX shells or different application software, you are making user account configuration and management much simpler.

7.4.1 Shell Configuration Files

The most common use of skeleton directories is to provide the different shell configuration files that each of the shells uses. For users of the C shell, for example, you might provide a .cshrc, .login, and .logout file with paths and environment variables set up as a convenience to your users.

Bourne and Korn shell users will require a different set of configuration files. Individual directories for each of these shells allow you to select the proper setup for each user by simply specifying a single directory.

Solaris 2.x provides prototypes for these files. If you copy the appropriate prototype files into separate skel directories for each of the shells, and rename them appropriately as shown below, you will be able to specify the specific skel directory when you are installing a new account and have these files automatically copied. In the example, we have called the shell-specific skel directories B (for the Bourne Shell), C (for the C shell), and K (for the Korn shell).

```
# mkdir /etc/skel/B /etc/skel/C /etc/skel/K
# cp /etc/skel/local.profile /etc/skel/B/.profile
# cp /etc/skel/local.profile /etc/skel/K/.profile
# cp /etc/skel/local.cshrc /etc/skel/C/.cshrc
# cp /etc/skel/local.login /etc/skel/C/.login
```

If shell configuration files are not included in your accounts when you set them up, system default files will be used to initialize the shell environment for your users.

For Bourne and Korn shells user, the local `.profile` is used after the global file, `/etc/profile`, is executed. It is, therefore, a good idea to put your systemwide settings in `/etc/profile` and commands and setups for individual users in their local `.profile` files.

7.4.2 Deskset configuration files

Additional files that you might want to include in your skeleton directories include the configuration files for deskset tools. Calendar Manager, File Manager, the Clock, and several other tools are configurable through startup files. Though these files are usually created as a result of user selection and setup of tool properties, you can modify the initial configuration by installing configuration files into each user account, sometimes simplifying or standardizing the configuration of tools is beneficial to your users.

7.4.3 Directories and links

Symbolic links and directories set up in skeleton directories are not re-created in home directories as you might expect.

If you create a symbolic link in a skeleton directory, new accounts will receive a copy of the original file, not a symbolic link. If you create a directory in a skeleton directory, new accounts will receive a useless file with data from the directory file, but this file will not be recognized by the system as a directory. Symbolic links and directories should, therefore, be set up outside the skeleton configuration utility provided by the administration tools.

7.5 Account Configuration

At the very least, when you set up an account, you must create a user login name, numeric userid, primary group, and default shell for the new user. Ordinarily, you will do much more than this. You are likely to set parameters for password aging, build account configuration files, establish secondary group memberships, configure shell variables and search paths for application software, configure the deskset tools, and start file and disk quota accounting.

There is another set of things that you do if you are configuring a workstation for this user as well. We are treating these activities separately and cover the setup of workstations elsewhere.

7.5.1 Login names, userids, and groups

Creating a login name for your user is simply a matter of selecting a unique string of from two to eight characters. Each character can be a letter or a digit, except the first. It must be a letter. The numeric userid, on the other hand, is a unique number which is used internally for file ownership. When you list files in the long format (ls -l), both user login names and group names are extracted from system files (the /etc/passwd and /etc/group files) or are retrieved from the name service. For example, when someone asks for a long file listing with the ls -l command, the userid is replaced in the listing with the user login names as long as this information can be located. At some point or another, you've probably seen a listing with a numeric identifier in place of the userid you might have expected to see. This is often the case when you've just loaded files from another system and the owner's userid does not correspond to the userid of any user on your network.

Groups are defined in a very similar manner. Groups have both names and numeric identifiers. When you set up a user, the primary group, expressed in the passwd file or table, is included as a numeric identifier. If this value is associated with a group that is defined in the /etc/group file (or the group table), long listings will display the group name rather than the numeric value.

As an example, the systems administration group, group 14, which has special privilege in Solaris 2.x, is not defined in the /etc/group file when you install a system. When you list files created by anyone whose primary group is 14, the resultant display will show 14 rather than a string value like sysadmin. Compare the two lines below, which show a long listing of a file before and after including the line sysadmin::14: to the /etc/group file.

```
drwxr-xr-x 2 slee 14 512 Mar 12 11:24 C
drwxr-xr-x 2 slee sysadmin 512 Mar 12 11:24 C
```

You can request a long listing without invoking the userid to username conversion by using a -n option in place of the -l. This will display the userid and groupid.

TRY THIS   List Files with and without Name Conversions

```
# ls -l /etc | head -5
total 362
-r--r--r--    1 root     sys      144 Feb 2 16:37 TIMEZONE
drwxrwxr-x    2 adm      adm      512 Nov 3 14:15 acct
lrwxrwxrwx    1 root     root     14 Feb 2 16:44 aliases -> ./mail/aliases
-r-xr-xr-x    1 root     bin      82 Feb 16 12:35 auto_home

# ls -n /etc | head -5
total 362
-r--r--r--    1 0        3        144 Feb 2 16:37 TIMEZONE
drwxrwxr-x    2 4        4        512 Nov 3 14:15 acct
lrwxrwxrwx    1 0        0        14 Feb 2 16:44 aliases -> ./mail/aliases
-r-xr-xr-x    1 0        2        82 Feb 16 12:35 auto_home
```

The user and group names that appear in the first list command are derived from your /etc files (or NIS+ tables) while the numeric identifiers are stored in the inode that stores descriptive information about each of these files. If you look at your /etc/passwd file, you should see a line like that shown below. In this example, we use the grep command to display information on a single user (in this case, the pseudo-user adm). In looking at the Try This exercise that we just displayed, you can see how the user adm was derived from this file by matching on the userid field.

```
# grep adm /etc/passwd
adm:x:4:4:0000-Admin(0000):/var/adm:
```

What the system actually does is better represented by the awk command shown below. Here, we are passing the /etc/passwd file through an awk command that selects records whose third field exactly equals 4. When it finds such a match, it prints the first field. You can see from this command that it has accurately matched on the entry for adm and printed its username.

```
# cat /etc/passwd | awk -F: '$3 ~ /^4$/ {print $1}'
adm
```

In Solaris 2.x, userids should be assigned within the range 100 to 60,000 (don't enter the comma). Userids below 100 are generally reserved for system usage (e.g., root and pseudo-users like cron and uucp) and userids 60,001 and 60,002 are associated with the nobody and noaccess users.

Even if you are responsible for only a portion of the user base in a networked environment, your userids should be unique across the entire network or group of interconnected networks.

7.5.2 Passwords and password security

Often, you will set an initial password to secure a new account. However, it is usually the responsibility of the user to reset this password at first login. The -f option of the passwd command allows you to force the user to enter a password on the next login.

In Solaris 2.x, a password cannot be identical to the user's login name and cannot be a shifted or reversed variation of the user login name. In addition, it must be at least six characters long, and contain at least two characters and at least one digit or special character. These restrictions are not placed on passwords the superuser assigns, but you should follow them just the same.

When you establish a password with the passwd command or when you set up a user account with one of the tools described below, you can also set the aging parameters to ensure that the password will be changed at some interval. All aging parameters are kept in the /etc/shadow file. (If you are using NIS+, aging parameters are stored in the passwd table.) The date when the password was last changed and the number of days of inactivity permitted for the account are also stored in this file. Dates in the /etc/shadow file are stored in "absolute" date format—the number of days since January 1, 1970.

TRY THIS   Set an Account Expiration Date

Set up an account with an expiration date and grep on the user's login identifier in the /etc/shadow file to see how the value is stored.

Here is an example: Say we have set up a user's account to expire at the end of September 1994. Expressed in days since January 1, 1970, the value stored in the shadow file is 9038 and the entry will look something like this:

```
# grep slee /etc/shadow
slee:0cGh5rviJRCvU:8443:::::9038:
```

Dates are stored in the absolute date because this is efficient. It is not, however, necessarily convenient for you when you want to determine whose passwords are about to expire. You can use the Modify User Form of the User Account Manager tool to retrieve this information for any particular user, but this may be far too time-consuming if you have a lot of users. An alternative to fetching this information is the awk script shown in Fig. 7.1a. You would invoke this script by retrieving fields from the shadow file as shown in Fig. 7.1b.

The script can also be used to translate a single number by calling it with a command that looks like this:

```
# echo 9038 | awk -f showdate
Sep 30, 1994
```

All the other fields in the shadow file are explained in the manual page and labeled in Fig. 7.2; enter man shadow for a complete explanation of each field.

7.5.3   Group membership

Every user has a primary group as defined in the passwd file. This group determines the group associated with every file or directory the user creates, unless explicitly changed. An individual can be a member of any number of other groups as well and thus able to share files with a given subset of the user population as defined by the group permissions on the target files.

It may be a matter of policy at your site whether users share files outside their primary groups. If monitoring file systems for proper group and world (everybody) permissions is important, you might prepare scripts to do this monitoring for you.

7.5.4   Shell configuration

You also select the individual's default shell. If the user will be using the shell, rather than working solely with the Deskset and applications, the choice of

```
# interpret absolute date as calendar date
BEGIN {
          days[0]=0
          days[1]=31; days[2]=28; days[3]=31; days[4]=30
          days[5]=31; days[6]=30; days[7]=31; days[8]=31
          days[9]=30; days[10]=31; days[11]=30; days[12]=31
          MO[1]="Jan"; MO[2]="Feb"; MO[3]="Mar"; MO[4]="Apr";
          MO[5]="May"; MO[6]="Jun"; MO[7]="Jul"; MO[8]="Aug";
          MO[9]="Sep"; MO[10]="Oct"; MO[11]="Nov"; MO[12]="Dec";
}
{
# decipher what info we are passed
if ($NF 1)
                         NAME=$1
          else
                         NAME=""
}
else {
# rightmost argument is string (user login name)
          NAME=$NF"\t"
          DAYIX="None"
}
len=length(NAME)
if (len>0)
          if (len 1461) {
                         ++LEAPS
                         YR=YR+4
                         DAYIX=DAYIX-1461
          }
          if (DAYIX (cumdays[i])) {
                         ++i
                         }
          DAYIX=DAYIX - cumdays[i-1]
          print NAME MO[i], DAYIX", " YR
}
else print NAME "None"
}
```

(a)

Figure 7.1 (*a*) An awk script for interpreting absolute dates

```
# cat /etc/shadow | awk -F: '{print $1, $8}' | awk -f showdate
root       None
daemon     None
bin        None
sys        None
adm        None
lp         None
smtp       None
uucp       None
nuucp      None
listen     None
nobody     None
noaccess   None
slee       Sep 30, 1994
fred       None
vail       Feb 16, 1994
```

(b)

Figure 7.1   *(Continued)* *(b)* invoking the script.

```
slee:0cGh5rviJRCvU:8443:::::9038:
^        ^              ^   ^^^^^     ^
|        |              |   |||||     |
|        |              |   |||||     +--   flag (not used)
|        |              |   ||||+-------    expire
|        |              |   |||+--------    inactive
|        |              |   ||+---------    warn
|        |              |   |+----------    max
|        |              |   +-----------    min
|        |              +----------------   lastchg
|        +-----------------------------     password
+-------------------------------------      username
```

Figure 7.2   Shadow file fields.

shell can be very important. The user may be very fluent in one of the three available shells. There are also a lot of features which will be available in one shell and not the others. Refer to Chap. 3 for some of these differences.

More importantly, you will set up variables which determine the applications and files that are visible to the user during login and may be necessary for accessing certain applications and utilities. The configuration files that are installed into a new account customize the working environment. For example, the MANPATH variable lists a path of directories which are searched when the user enters man command. Since you are likely to have man pages which are not part of the standard OS distribution (included with application software or some that you define yourself), this variable needs to include the new directories before the user can see these man pages. Similarly, LPDEST and LD_LIBRARY_PATH, along with a large group of variables detailed in Chap. 4, provide important support to some of your users. The LPDEST variable, for example, allows you to set a default printer by user rather than by the host on which the user is working. The LD_LIBRARY_PATH is important for applications which refer to software libraries not included in the standard locations (e.g., /usr/openwin/lib). Lines such as those shown below are included in the configuration files to establish these options for your users. The local and global files that are used with each of the shells are

```
                local                       global
                =====                       ======
Bourne          .profile                    /etc/profile
CShell          .cshrc .login .logout       /etc/.login
Korn            .profile                    /etc/profile
```

If you do not install the configuration files for the appropriate shell in the user's home directory, only the default script from /etc will be used. If you elect to install the skeleton files in the user's home, both files will be used; the /etc file will be read before the user's file so that the user's settings will have precedence.

```
C Shell:            setenv MANPATH /apps/lang/man:/usr/man
Bourne/Korn Shells:MANPATH=/apps/lang/man:/usr/man;export MANPATH
```

If you are using the C or the Korn shell, you can also take advantage of the alias command to create shortcuts to common commands or to group several commands together. For example, to create a short name for the history command, it is common to equate it with the single letter h.

```
C Shell:    alias h history
Korn Shell: alias h=history
```

Another important variable for sites where security is important is the umask variable, which determines default permissions for files and directories that the user creates. A umask text 022 file creation mode mask can be set up in the .cshrc or .profile file.

The umask variable determines permissions by performing what is called an *exclusive OR* operation; that is, it masks whatever bits are normally set. With a umask of 022, files will be created with the permissions set to 644 (rw-r-r-), which gives read and write access to the owner and read to everyone else. Directories would be given the permissions 755 (rwxr-xr-x). The easiest way to calculate the umask to use is to subtract the permissions you want from 777 for directories and from 666 for files. If you want your user's files to be created with the permissions set to 644, use the mask 022. The two calculations correspond to the reasonable assumption that files should not, by default, be executable while directories require this permission if they are to be searched.

7.5.5   Deskset configuration

By setting up configuration files, you determine not only whether your users go directly into OpenWindows on login but also the contents of their root menu, the layout of their screen, and the configuration of their desktop tools when they do.

For example, if your site makes heavy use of groups to allow users to share files within projects, you might want to add all the members of a user's group to that user's browse list for Calendar Manager. In this way, your users will not have to collect this information and create the list for themselves. A cm.rc file containing the line shown below would add the three users listed into the owner's browse menu.

A .cm.rc file containing the line shown below would add the three users listed into the owner's browse menu.

```
Calendar.CalendarList: ccg@wizard slee@nextpage jerry@mh
File                   Holds Configuration Options for
====                   ================================
.Xdefaults             OpenWindows X Properties
.cm.rc                 Calendar Manager
.desksetdefaults       Calctool, Clock, File Manager
.mailrc                Mailtool
```

It might also be very advantageous to set up the site-specific bindings for File Manager that determine how files are represented and what happens when a user double-clicks on an icon or drags it into the PrintTool. Setting up deskset defaults for your users is completely optional. In using the tools, your users have access to menus and forms that allow them to configure their own defaults. On the other hand, if you want to take advantage of a chance to make economy of scale changes or to configure account options that you think will be most useful for your users, the simplest way is by creating deskset configuration files within your skeleton directories so that they will populate your user accounts whenever you create them.

You can do things like set everybody's calculator to default to binary by adding the following line to their .desksetdefaults file.

```
deskset.calctool.base: BIN
```

or to set the mode of the calculator for financial analysis

```
deskset.calctool.mode: FINANCIAL
```

or the clock to a 12-h digital display:

```
deskset.clock.digital12Hour: true
```

You can set up vi as the default editor to call when someone double-clicks on a file in file manager with the line:

```
.desksetdefaults:deskset.filemgr.otherEditor:  shelltool  sh  -c  "sleep  3;vi
$FILE"
```

If you establish your account configuration by including your configuration files for shells and desktop tools in the /etc/skel directories, each account that is subsequently created will get the new setup almost automatically; you still have to use the option to include the skeleton files when you create an account. Existing accounts, on the other hand, will not receive the new files unless you explicitly copy them. The script contained in Fig. 7.3 will update new

```csh
#!/bin/csh
#
#     update_accts
#
set HOMEDIR="/export/home"
foreach dir ('ls $HOMEDIR')
    if (-d $dir) then
        set LN='grep ^$dir":" /etc/passwd | awk -F: '{print $1, $4, $7}''
    if ("$LN" !="") then
        set WHO='echo $LN | awk '{print $1}''
        set GPR='echo $LN | awk '{print $2}''
        set SHELL='echo $LN | awk '{print $3}''
        set SKEL='echo $SHELL | awk -f getshell | tr "sck" "BCK"'
        echo "Updating $dir from /etc/skel/$SKEL"
        foreach cf ('ls -a /etc/skel/$SKEL')
          if (! -d $cf) then
            if (-f $HOMEDIR/$WHO/$cf) then
              mv $HOMEDIR/$WHO/$cf $HOMEDIR/$WHO/$cf.$$
              echo "Old $cf backed up to $cf.$$" | mail $WHO
            endif
            cp /etc/skel/$SKEL/$cf $HOMEDIR/$WHO/$cf
            chown $WHO $HOMEDIR/$WHO/$cf
            chgrp $GRP $HOMEDIR/$WHO/$cf
            echo " Using /etc/skel/SKEL/$configfile"
          endif
        end
      endif
    endif
end
```

Figure 7.3 Script for updating accounts from /etc/skel directories.

accounts from the skeleton directories and back up existing copies so that any changes your users may have made will not be lost.

This script will update all home directories in /export/home. It first checks that each directory corresponds to a username in the /etc/passwd file. For all directories that correspond, the script determines which shell is the user's default and uses this information to select the correct skel subdirectory. The script backs up preexisting copies of the file to files which have the same names but have a dot followed by the process identifier attached to create a unique filename. Notice how we send mail to the user indicating that that user's old configuration file is backed up under this name.

If you configure your users' desktop, you should realize that there will always be users who resent your efforts to standardize account setup and others who won't even realize that you've done something to make their tools nicer to use. Always try to find a compromise between what makes your job more manageable and keeps your users happy.

7.5.6 Application configuration

When you install applications for your users, you may have to update their accounts for these applications to work properly. Updating users' search paths and adding shell variables used by the application software is a common aspect of account management. For some application software, you might create subdirectories or symbolic links to configure the application efficiently for their use. Some applications require the use of shell variables so that they know where their files are located on your system. An example (for the C shell) is setenv IPHOME /usr/local/info-power, which, entered as a separate line, sets up a C-shell environment variable that enables the Info-Power distributed network information application to find its files.

7.5.7 Establishing and monitoring quotas

Quotas are first established by the file system and then by the individual user. When quotas are turned on for a file system, Solaris will monitor space and file usage within that file system. Individual limits for the amount of disk space and the number of files that a user is allowed to maintain are set up by the system administrator and stored in a file at the base of each file system being monitored.

When you establish quotas, you can set them up for disk space or the number of files or both. You also set both hard and soft limits; the users can exceed their soft limits and will be warned by the system that they have exceeded their quotas. Once they have exceeded their hard limits, they cannot create new files and may even lose files if they attempt to edit them and are prevented from writing them back to disk. Quota monitoring has a slight impact on performance.

Generally, you will not want to divide the available space into equal chunks and establish this amount as your quota. If you do, you are sure to make a good amount of your disk resources unavailable for use. Some individuals will never even come close to using their fair share of disk space, while others will fill space as long as it is available. To reserve space for those who will not use it is foolish. At the same time, if your quotas are excessively generous, you might as well not enforce them at all. In general, giving each user between 1.5 and 2 times the space which represents a fair share will provide the desired account-ability without artificially limiting your users.

If you are willing to establish equal quotas for users, you can use one indi-vidual as a model and establish quotas for everyone else without having to edit the parameters individually.

7.5.7.1 Turning on quotas.   There are several steps involved in setting up quotas. You need to identify the file systems for which you want quotas established, make sure that quota monitoring starts up when the system is booted, and es-tablish quotas for your users. Quotas can only be set for ufs file systems.

The steps you must take to establish quota for a file system are

- Create the quotas file.
- Add quota checks and enabling to the bootup files.
- Add quota option to the /etc/vfstab file.
- Establish quotas for individual users.

The first thing you want to do is establish the file system that you want to mon-itor and create an empty quotas file at its base.

```
# cd /export/home
# touch quotas
# chmod 600 quotas
```

To start quotas when a system is booted, add these lines to the /etc/rc2.d/S01MOUNTFSYS file. These lines will check quotas and start quota monitoring.

```
# Check and enable quotas
echo -n "setting up quotas:">/dev/console
/usr/bin/quotacheck -a>/dev/console 2>&1
echo "done.">/dev/console
/usr/sbin/quotaon -a
```

Edit /etc/vfstab to specify quotas with an rq indicator in the mount options. At this point, you still have specified the use of quotas for a certain ufs file sys-tem, but haven't yet established quotas for any individuals.

The edquota command gives you a line for each file system which has quo-tas enforced. You specify quotas in 1-kbyte chunks. For example, 30000 means 30 Mbytes. The edquota command interprets data from the quotas file, lets you edit it, and then writes it back in the proper form.

```
# edquota slee
fs /export/home blocks (soft=0, hard=0) inodes (soft=0, hard=0)
```

Users are generally given a week to remove files once they have exceeded their quotas. After this, they will be unable to create new files and will likely have problems editing old ones as well. This limit can be changed globally with the `edquota -t` command. If you have users who travel a lot, it might be more manageable to extend the limits so that they won't return from a trip and find themselves unable to work. Proper limits depend very much on your users and how much disk space you have to spare.

You can also change the quotas for an individual user at any time or turn quotas off for an individual by replacing that person's limits with 0s. You can turn quotas off for the file system at any time by using the `quotaoff` command. Use the `quotaon` command to start quotas (or reboot the system): `# quotaon -a`.

7.5.7.2 Reporting on Quotas. If you are going to enforce quotas, you should also be careful to monitor quotas and be proactive in managing your space. The Solaris 2.x quota system includes commands which prepare reports on quota usage. If you have a large user population, you can easily prepare customized scripts to examine these reports and provide warnings about individuals who are approaching or exceeding their limits. (See Fig. 7.4.)

7.6 Account Management Tools

The User Account Manager in Solaris 2.x facilitates some but not all of what you need to do to set up and maintain user accounts. User Account Manager provides an OpenLook application that can be used to add and remove users from your system and modify some of the account parameters (such as the default shell). It can also be used to configure many of the site-specific or application-specific variables that your users will need if the parameters or files are set up in skeleton directories ahead of time. User Account Manager is invoked through the Administration Tool (admintool) (Fig. 7.5). Once you select User Account Manager from admintool's palette, you will need to identify where you are keeping your account information. If you are using NIS or NIS+, account information will be added to the appropriate database; otherwise, the `/etc` files are updated on the selected host. Figure 7.6 illustrates the selection of name service. User Account Manager is shown in Fig. 7.7.

7.6.1 User Account Manager

When you are adding a user, User Account Manager performs the following tasks for you:

- Checks user login name and userid against existing users
- Checks to ensure that secondary groups exist
- Updates `passwd` and shadow files (or NIS, NIS+ equivalents)
- Adds user to selected secondary groups
- Sets parameters for password aging (optional) or expiration date

```
# repquota /export/home
                        Block limits                File limits
User             used    soft    hard   timeleft  used  soft    hard  timeleft
slee     --     13477   40000   60000             307   0       0
vail     --      8014   40000   60000             123   0       0
filehog  --     38499   40000   60000             912   0       0
danielle --     13162   40000   60000             672   700     800
fred     +-     58499   40000   60000   4 days    904   900     1000  4 days
nicole   --         1   40000   60000               1   700     800
----------------------------------------
#    over90 — report on quotas exceeding 90%
#    Usage: repquota /export/home | awk -f over90
#
BEGIN {
     print "Users Approaching or Exceeding Quotas"
     print "===================================="
}
if ($3 < "A") {
     SPACE = substr ($2,1,1)
     Files = substr ($2,2,1)
     if (length($1) < 8)
          WHO = $1 "t"
     else
          WHO = $1
     MSG = ""
     TIMELEFT = ""
# disk space used
     if ($4 > 0
          PCT = $3/$4 * 100)
     else
          PCT = 0
     IX = index(PCT,".")
     if (IX == 0)
          IX = length(PCT) + 1
     if (SPACE == "+") {
          MSG = "<== Over Disk Quota "
          TIMELEFT = "\t Time Left: " substr($0,38,12)
          print WHO "\t" substr(PCT,1,IX-1) "%" MSG, TIMELEFT
          }
     else if (PCT > 90) {
          MSG = "<== Over 90% Disk Quota "
          print WHO "\t" substr(PCT,1,IX-1) "%" MSG
          }
# files used
     if (SPACE == "+")
          if ($9 > 0)
               PCT = $8/$9 * 100)
          else
               PCT = 0
     else
          if ($7 > 0)
               PCT = $6/$7 *100)
          else
               PCT = 0
     IX = index)PCT,".")
     if (IX == 0)
          IX = length(PCT) + 1
     if (SPACE == "+") {
```

Figure 7.4   Monitoring quotas.

```
          MSG = "<== Over Files Quota "
          TIMELEFT = "\t Time Left: " substr($0,38,12)
          print WHO "\t" substr(PCT,1,IX-1) "%" MSG, TIMELEFT
          }
      else if (PCT > 90) {
          MSG = "<== Over 90% Files Quota "
          print WHO "\t" substr(PCT,1,IX-1) "%" MSG
          }
}
}
-----------------------------------------------------------------------------
# repquota /export/home | awk -f over90
Users Approaching or Exceeding Quotas
=====================================
filehog    96%<== Over 90% Disk Quota
danielle   96%<==  Over 90% Files Quota
fred       146%<== Over Disk Quota          Time Left: 4.2 days
fred       100%<== Over Files Quota         Time Left: 4.2 days
```

Figure 7.4   (*Continued*)

- Creates home directory (optional)
- Copies configuration files from skeleton directory (optional)
- Configures automount for home directory (optional)
- Adds user to mail aliases if mail service is specified (optional)
- If NIS+ is used, User Account Manager can select user's credentials

If you are deleting a user, User Account Manager does the following:

- Removes the user entry from the passwd and shadow files
- Removes user from the groups he or she is associated with
- Removes the home directory and its contents (optional)
- Removes the mailbox (optional)

You can also use the tool to change some of the fields, for example:

- Changes default shell
- Adds user to additional groups, removes from others

Some of the fields' values must be within ranges. For example, the userid should be between 100 and 60,000. The tool will check if the requested userid is already assigned, but will not provide the next number in sequence if you assign userids in this way (Fig. 7.5).

User Account Manager (Fig. 7.6) will not create subdirectories or symbolic links in your users' home directories. Basically, any files that exist in the skeleton directory will be copied into the new home directory when you specify the skeleton directory. If you include a symbolic link, the original file will be copied.

```
┌──────────────────────────────────────────────────────┐
│  ⌐        User Account Manager: Add User              │
│  USER IDENTITY                                         │
│              User Name: ▪_____                      │
│                User ID: _____                     │
│          Primary Group: nobody____                     │
│      Secondary Groups: _____          │
│              Comment: _____           │
│            Login Shell: ▽│ Bourne  /bin/sh             │
│  ACCOUNT SECURITY                                      │
│              Password: ▽│ Cleared until first login    │
│            Min Change: 0____ days                      │
│            Max Change: _____ days                      │
│           Max Inactive: _____ days                     │
│       Expiration Date▽│ None ▽│ None ▽│ None           │
│               Warning: _____ days                      │
│                                                        │
│  HOME DIRECTORY                                        │
│       Create Home Dir: _│ Yes if checked               │
│                  Path: _____          │
│                Server: _____          │
│          Skeleton Path: ......................         │
│                                                        │
│       AutoHome Setup: _│ Yes if checked                │
│          Permissions ReadWrite Execute                 │
│              Owner: ✔  ✔  ✔                            │
│              Group: ✔  │  ✔                            │
│              World: ✔  │  ✔                            │
│  MISCELLANEOUS                                         │
│            Mail Server: _____         │
│                                                        │
│      Cred. Table Setup: ✔ Yes if checked               │
│                                                        │
│            Add )  Reset )  Help... )                   │
│                                                        │
└──────────────────────────────────────────────────────┘
```

Figure 7.5 User Account Manager: add user.

If you want symbolic links and subdirectories, you must create these outside of the scope of AdminTool. (Fig. 7.7).

The chart below makes some comparisons between what the User Account Manager supports in setting up user accounts and what the `useradd` command supports. One of the more important distinguishing features is the ability that the User Account Manager (UAM) has to set up accounts remotely. The other is the point made earlier that useradd can be invoked from a script. The third issue of considerable weight is whether the tool can update NIS+ tables. Although `useradd` does not update NIS+ maps, including the `useradd` command

```
┌────────────────────────────────────────────────┐
│ ⊽|         User Account Manager                 │
│                                                 │
│   Edit ⊽ )   Find... )   Naming Service... )  Help...│
│                                                 │
│    User Name    User ID    Comment              │
│   ┌─────────────────────────────────────────┐  │
│   │ sil          347      Stan Lippman       │  │
│   │ simon        374      David Simon x524   │  │
│   │ singh        353      Avinash Singh x5   │  │
│   │ sjc          211      Steve Conard       │  │
│   │ skb          502      Sharon Busching    │  │
│   │ skd          322      Susan Domokos x7   │  │
│   │ skipper      538      Bill Skipper       │  │
│   │ skumar       151      Suman Kumar        │  │
│   │ sl           175      Steve Lawrence     │  │
│   │ slee         253      S. Lee Henry, x7   │  │
│   │ slee2        111      S. Lee Henry, x7   │  │
│   └─────────────────────────────────────────┘  │
│                                                 │
│    Naming Service: NIS+, Domain: physics.jhu.edu│
└────────────────────────────────────────────────┘
```

Figure 7.6   User Account Manager.

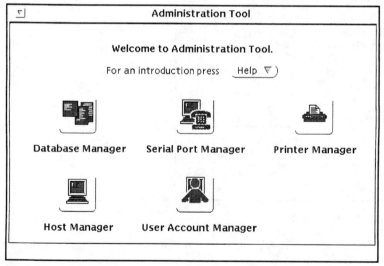

Figure 7.7   AdminTool.

in a script would provide an opportunity to use NIX+ commands to update its tables in the same context.

	adds acct	updates	can use skel files?	can specify expiration date?	can specify aging?
	---------	-------	-----------	---------	------
UAm	remote/local	files/NIS	yes	yes	yes
useraddlocal		files	yes	yes	no

The copy option saves you time by filling in fields for you from an existing entry. You don't have to reenter the group associations and select the default shell and Automount options if they are the same.

Automount, by the way, will mount home directories /export/home, /export/home2 as /home so that users only need to think of their homes as /home/username.

In versions of Solaris 2.x prior to Solaris 2.3, UAM may have sometimes run into trouble. If you, for example, give it inconsistent or incorrect information, it may have set up accounts incompletely. For example, if you added a user, but asked for that user to be added to groups which did not yet exist, it may have added the user to the /etc files or database but failed to create the account or update the groups. Error message like the one shown below might have popped up.

```
The operation failed
with this status:
Error code is 175, failure mode is DIRTY.
Error 142 setting up system database entries:
Error 44 adding group entries:
_user_groups_nis: User 'slee' could not be added to the following groups
because they do not exist: 876 543
```

DIRTY failures refer to conditions in which some, but not all, of the requested operation has been performed; you cannot, therefore, simply fix the problem and try again. You have to clean up first.

In Solaris 2.3 and later, you are not likely to see dirty failures since AdminTool checks more thoroughly before adding new accounts.

CLEAN failures, on the other hand, refer to error conditions in which no action was taken due to the error. In this case, the problem can be repaired and the action reinitiated. An example of this is trying to add a user with an invalid login name or userid.

```
The operation failed
with this status:
Error code is 113, failure mode is CLEAN.
Invalid username: S.Lee
```

If you use the tool to change the default shell, configuration files for the new shell will or will not be copied, and those for the old shell will or will not disappear.

7.6.2 `useradd, usermod, userdel`

An alternative to using the UAM tool are the `useradd`, `usermod`, and `userdel` utilities that are included in Solaris largely because of its System V heritage. In `/usr/sbin`, the `useradd, usermod, userdel` utilities are command oriented tool that permit you to set up, modify, and remove accounts with much of the same functionality as the UAM.

The `useradd` utility is a tool for creating accounts and has much of the same functionality as the UAM. Like the UAM, `useradd` adds the user entries from the `/etc/passwd` and `/etc/shadow` files. It also creates the supplemental group memberships if you use the `-G` option and creates the home directory if you use the `-m` option. Also like the UAM, this tool will optionally copy skeleton files; you provide the path for the skeleton directory following a `-k`. You can specify an expiration date with the `-e` option, but there is no option for password aging; password aging can be set up with the `passwd` command options `-n`, and `-x` (for the minimum and maximum day limits).

The `useradd` utility will reject requests which are in error; for example, it will not add entries to the passwd and `/etc/shadow` files if specified secondary groups do not exist.

The biggest disadvantage of `useradd` is that it only adds users to the local system. It cannot pass newer user information to a naming service like NIS+, though it can refer to the name service to ensure that user login names and userids are unique.

The biggest advantage of useradd is that it can be called from within a script that you create to both set up an account and customize it to the particular requirements of your site.

7.7 Extending the Tools

As mentioned several times earlier, you can create scripts to help configure your accounts. Preparing scripts of your own allows you to take advantage of existing tools while facilitating customization that meets your peculiar needs.

In configuring accounts, custom-made scripts can facilitate setting up links and directories that applications may require, and add commands to customize the deskset and working environment to best meet your users' needs. The script contained in Fig. 7.8 uses a model directory and duplicates directories, files, and links in the target directory. In the script, we use `/etc/skel/setup` as the model directory. You can specify another location by changing the `SRC=` line of the script. Notice how the script tests the type of each file and does not copy directories or links, but re-creates them with the appropriate command. This script is written in the Korn shell.

```ksh
#!/bin/ksh
#
# dup_dir          copy files, directories, and links from sample directory
#                  to home directory of user (passed as argument)
#
SRC=/etc/skel/setup
HOMEDIR=/export/home
DEST=$1
[[ $# =lt 1 ]] && {
          print "Usage: $0<username>"
          exit
}
for file in `ls $ SRC`
do
          print "Duplicating $file"
          [[ -d $SRC/$file ]] && {
                mkdir $HOMEDIR/$DEST/$file
                chown $1 $HOMEDIR/$DEST/$file
                }
          [[ -L $SRC/$file ]] && {
                target=`ls -l $SRC/$file | awk ' {print $11}'`
                ln -s $target $HOMEDIR/$DEST/$file
                }
          [[ -z $SRC/$file ]] && {
                touch $HOMEDIR/$DEST/$file
                chown $1 $HOMEDIR/$DEST/$file
                }
          [[ -f $SRC/$file && ! -L $SRC/$file ]] && {
                cp $SRC/$file $HOMEDIR/$DEST/$file
                chown $1 $HOMEDIR/$DEST/$file
}
done
```

Figure 7.8 Script for duplicating configuration directory.

Simple updates to user's configurations can be an enormous amount of work if you have hundreds or thousands of users. By creating a handful of "generic" scripts, you can make this job extremely easy; however, you should always proceed with caution and test your scripts before applying them to your users' accounts, since it is easy to make a mistake.

The script contained in Fig. 7.9 copies a file to every account included in the local /etc/passwd file. It does not copy the file for system users such as root

```
#!/bin/ksh
#
#
#         cp2homes copy file to all home directories in local /etc/passwd
#
[[ $# -lt 1 ]] && {
          print "Usage: $0<filename>"
          exit
}
FILE=$1
for LN in `cat /etc/passwd | awk -F: '{print $1":"$3":"$6}'`
do
          WHO=`echo $LN | awk -F: '{print $1}'`
          UID=`echo $LN | awk -F: '{print $2}'`
          HOMEDIR=`echo $LN | awk -F: '{print $3}'`
          if [[ $UID -ge 100 && $UID -le 60000 ]]
          then
                    print "Copying $FILE for $WHO"
                    cp $FILE $HOMEDIR
                    chown $WHO $HOMEDIR/$FILE
          fi
done
```

Figure 7.9 Script for copying file to all local homes.

and uucp (i.e., it checks the numeric userid and selects userids larger or equal to 100 and smaller than 60,000).

Updating shell variables is an ideal candidate for this technique. Usually, you will not want to overwrite your users' configuration files. You can, however, use a command such as sed to make the updates you want and leave the rest of the file intact.

For example, the following lines could be used in a script to add a new directory of manual (man) pages to a user's MANPATH variable. The sed part of these lines is adding the pathname, /opt/map/bin, to the beginning of the MANPATH variable. We subsequently write the output to a temporary file and then copy it back into place. This is a C-shell example (note the use of .cshrc).

```
cat ~$WHO/.cshrc | sed "s,MANPATH=,MANPATH=/opt/map/bin:,">
/tmp/.cshrc
mv /tmp/.cshrc ~$WHO/.cshrc
chown $WHO ~$WHO/.cshrc
```

The script in Figure 7.10 uses grep to remove and echo to include mail variables for Korn shell users.

```ksh
#!/bin/ksh
#
#          mk_mailpath add MAILPATH for user, remove incompatible MIL
#                           variable if it exists
#
[[ $# -lt 1 ]] && {
     print "Usage: $0<username>"
     exit
}
WHO=$1
HOMEDIR=/export/home
EXISTS=`grep MAILPATH $HOMEDIR/$WHO/.profile`
if [[ -z $EXISTS ]] #MAILPATH does not exist
then
     print "Adding MAILPATH for $WHO"
     EXISTS=`grep MAIL $HOMEDIR/$WHO/.profile`
     if [[ -z $EXISTS ]] # MAIL does not exist
     then
          echo "MAILPATH=~$WHO/mbox:/news/mbox"[ggt]
$HOMEDIR/$WHO/.profile
     else
          cat $HOMEDIR/$WHO/.profile |\
               grep -v MAIL > /tmp/.profile
          mv /tmp/.profile $HOMEDIR/$WHO/.profile
          echo "MAILPATH=~$WHO/mbox:/news/mbox">>
$HOMEDIR/$WHO/.profile
          chown $WHO $HOMEDIR/$WHO/.profile
     fi
fi
```

Figure 7.10 Script for setting up MAILPATH variable.

7.8 Account Security

Secure passwords are not all there is to creating and managing secure accounts. File and directory permissions determine what access other valid system users will have to another user's files.

The most important task of account security is communicating to your users what is expected of them and why the organization would want files to be shared only according to planned groups and projects.

You can develop scripts to monitor file and directory permissions and screen for possible permission problems in your home accounts. The find command, for example, can be used to display all directories with world write permission as shown below.

If you are interested in locating files with wide-open permissions (everyone having read, write, and execute access), a simple find command would flush this information from your system.

TRY THIS   Find Wide-Open Files

You can start this find command from any directory, and it will look through that directory and recursively through all directories contained within that directory. It will not follow symbolic links to the files or directories to which they point, though it will report on the permissions of the links themselves.

```
# cd /export/home
# find . -perm 0777 -print
```

TRY THIS   Find Files with World Write Permission

To locate files that anyone can write to, you can modify the find command to match only on permission bits set in the command. In the following command, any file which has the world write bit set will be listed (starting in the current directory). The -ls command provides a long listing where -print only prints the file name.

```
# find . -perm -0002 -ls
```

7.9 Summary

Maintaining User Accounts involves determining your users' needs and preferences, monitoring disk usage and security, and managing applications. AdminTool and scripts that you create to meet the specific needs of your site can make this task manageable.

8

Administering Printing Services

Administering printing services in Solaris 2.x involves configuring printers, defining and managing forms and printwheels, optionally maintaining access lists for printer usage, and tracking down causes of print problems. This chapter describes the print model, the commands for setting up and maintaining the print service, and includes scripts to help you monitor printer usage and analyze printer problems.

8.1 The SVR4 Print Subsystem (Overview)

The LP Print Service is a set of utilities that manage shared-background printing on a networkwide basis through the use of network listen utilities, spooling services, and a powerful and versatile scheduling process. The service itself comprises a set of user commands that create or cancel print jobs (or requests) and track their status, a scheduler that sends print jobs to a particular printer, a set of commands for managing the print queue, and the directories and files which describe and control the print jobs in progress.

The Solaris 2.x Print Service provides interoperability between SVR4 and BSD systems so that print services can be shared within mixed UNIX networks. PostScript filters are bundled into the operating system so that PostScript printers can be used without additional software.

Based on the SVR4 Print Service, the print subsystem also supports the use of printed forms and replaceable printwheels by monitoring what is mounted and what is requested, intercepting print jobs when a form or printwheel must be mounted, and sending an alert to the systems administrator or designee.

Extensive capabilities are also included to set up and manage printer access lists and to group printers into classes to facilitate routing print jobs to available printers. For example, if a particular printer is out of service or otherwise not accepting requests, the job can be automatically printed elsewhere.

Print Service does the following:

- Administers and schedules print requests
- Filters files to match print request with printer type (when needed)
- Starts the program that initializes the printer
- Tracks the print job and manages the print queue
- Monitors printed forms and printwheels
- Requests a change of form or printwheel when a print job requires it
- Alerts the administrator when there are print problems

Generally started at boot time through the `/etc/init.d/lp` script, the print service can also be started and shut down on demand by calling the script with one of the commands as shown below.

```
/bin/sh /etc/init.d/lp start
/bin/sh /etc/init.d/lp stop
```

Notice that `start` and `stop` are parameters to the script which evaluate your request and properly start up or shut down the service.

Print Service requires the following software packages:

SUNWlpr (this is the root portion of Print Service)

SUNWlpu (this is the usr portion of Print Service)

If these are not loaded on your system, you can install them with the following commands (replace `Solaris 2.3` with a later release if appropriate). Refer to Chap. 11 for a more complete description of package administration.

```
# mount -F hsfs -o ro /dev/dsk/c0t6d0s2/cdrom
# pkgadd -d /cdrom/Solaris_2.3 SUNWlpr SUNWlpu
```

8.2 The Print Model

The SVR4 print model schedules the requests of multiple users for multiple printer resources. It keeps track of special requirements of print jobs (e.g., special forms or printwheels), and alerts the systems administrator when there are problems or the printer needs attention.

The print model also extends beyond the local system to support print requests from other hosts on the network and to send local requests to remote print servers. Network printing involves the use of processes which listen for remote requests from other SVR4 as well as BSD (e.g., SunOS 4.1) hosts.

8.2.1 The Service Access Facility

The Service Access Facility (SAF) controls terminal and modem access as well as network services such as remote printing. It manages local and network services through the use of well-defined interfaces.

The Service Access Controller (sac) is started by the init process and monitors both serial ports and network ports. When the system goes into multiuser mode, sac starts up in response to an entry in /etc/inittab. It forks a child process for each port monitor: ttymon for serial ports and listen for network services, such as printing.

Listen processes do just that; they "listen" for requests that arrive at specific network connections. Connection-oriented in nature, they invoke servers in response to requests that arrive from other hosts.

Each instance of listen is configured through the sacadm command. Information specific to the particular listen process is configured with the port monitor administration command pmadm, which associates Print Service with a port monitor and uses nlsadmin for information about the service process and the FIFO used for listen services.

You can list the listen services which are servicing System V and BSD requests as shown below. Notice that the service tag field SVCTAG, displays the process being monitored: lp on the SVR4 systems and lpd on the BSD systems.

```
# pmadm -l
PMTAG PMTYPE SVCTAG FLGS ID
tcp listen lp - root - - p - /var/spool/lp
/fifos/listenS5 #
tcp listen lpd - root \x00020203867b0e01000
0000000000000 - p - /var/spool/lp/fifos/listenBSD #
```

If you use the manual procedures for setting up printers, you will issue commands to sacadm and pmadm to configure the listen service for the printer. If you use Print Manager, this will be done for you. Service Access Controller is illustrated in Fig. 8.1.

8.2.2 The print scheduler

Central to the entire Print Service, the print scheduler lpsched maintains Print Service files, sets up print requests from user input, schedules jobs for printing, and is notified each time the lp command is issued by a local user. It monitors the processing of print jobs and starts an interface script to initialize the printer prior to sending a new print job. Optionally, the interface program can do things like set up the banner page using arguments that are passed along to it from the lp command. It also interprets other parameters of the print request, such as the requested number of copies, and conveys this information to the printer; this is the remote print model.

```
+-----+      +---------+      +-------------------+      +---------+
| lp  |----->| lpsched |----->| interface program |----->| printer |
+-----+      +---------+      +-------------------+      +---------+
                |   |   |
           +-----+  |   +-----> executes filters (if needed)
           |        |
           V        V
    sets up spool  selects printer
    directory files
```

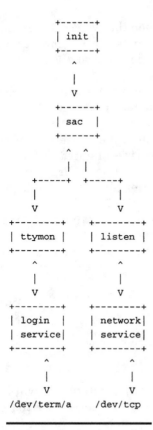

Figure 8.1 Service Access Controller (sac).

The scheduler also manages requests that arrive from remote systems through the registered network listen services. These services both listen for print requests from print clients and confirmations from print servers. The lp-Net daemon then handles the request.

Remote requests from other Solaris 2.x systems come through lpNet on the requesting host. Remote requests from BSD clients come through the BSD print daemon, lpd on the remote host.

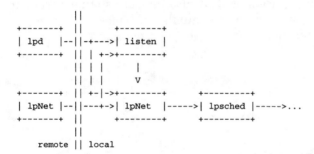

In scheduling a job, lpsched evaluates the information provided by the requester and sets up the print job in the spool directory, /var/spool/lp/requests, in a subdirectory by the same name as the requesting host. Requests from nextpage for example, are stored in /var/spool/lp/requests/nextpage. Additional files are created in /var/spool/lp/tmp/nextpage that further describe the print request and store the output of print filters.

TRY THIS   Check if Scheduler is Running

```
# lpstat -r
scheduler is running
```

When the system boots, there should be one and only one lpsched running. This lpsched process forks a child process when it is managing a particular print job on a particular printer. This child process, in turn, forks another process which immediately execs the interface script. This happens so quickly that you will rarely see this third lpsched. The process of forking and executing other processes keeps the original (parent) lpsched free to handle incoming requests and manage the print queue.

In order to understand this process, you should have a clear handle on the difference between a process fork and a process exec. Briefly, a fork creates a child process identical to the parent process; this process inherits critical attributes from the parent process (e.g., userids, file descriptors, shared-memory segments). An exec, on the other hand, overlays the calling process with an altogether independent executable. A forked process returns control to its parent, while an exec simply exits when it is done.

Thus, the job of the third lpsched is simply to start the interface script via the exec call. The child (second) lpsched monitors the print job and stays around until the print job has completed.

While a print job is active, you can see the child lpsched which is handling it in your processes:

TRY THIS   Check If Scheduler Is Running

```
# ps -ef | grep lpsched
root 160 1 80 12:35:48 ? 0:01 /usr/lib/lpsched
root 184 160 8 12:35:55 term/a 0:00 /usr/lib/lpsched
root 315 291 9 12:53:31 pts/3 0:00 grep lpsched
```

Once the print job has completed, the second lpsched will disappear, soon to be replaced by a new child process managing yet another item in the print queue if there are additional requests.

8.2.3 Spool directories

Print requests are stored in subdirectories which correspond to the name of the requesting host as shown in Fig. 8.2. Parameters of each print request are stored in files in the /var/spool/lp/requests directory. Data files, including filtered output (when filtering was needed to match the content type with the particular printer), are stored in /var/spool/lp/tmp.

Examining the contents of the spool directories will help you in understanding the print process.

8.3   Describing Printers

There are a number of ways of describing a printer, such as the manufacturer, the type of input expected, the speed, and the size of paper that can be used. Some of this information must be provided during printer installation. Some needs to be considered only if you are installing an uncommon printer that is not already defined in the terminfo database.

Describing printers to your users is as important as describing them to your system. For users, the most important descriptors involve color, resolution, and quality (versus draft quality) as well as information about where the printer is located. The lpadmin command provides an option to allow you to attach a description to each printer so that your users will have an easier time determining where to send their print jobs and pick them up later. The command shown below will attach the description "Draft printer outside computer room" to the printer scribe.

```
lpadmin -p scribe -D "Draft printer outside computer room"
```

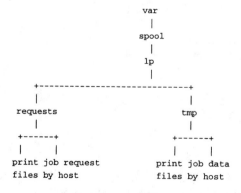

Directories and Files

```
                          var
                           |
                         spool
                           |
                          lp
                           |
        +-----------------------------+
        |                             |
     requests                        tmp
        |                             |
     +------+                      +------+
     |      |                      |      |
   print job request           print job data
   files by host               files by host
```

Figure 8.2 Spool directories.

Users will see this description when they issue the `lpstat` command as shown below:

```
% lpstat -p scribe -l
printer scribe now printing scribe-57. enabled since Wed Apr 21 12:44:13 EDT
199
3. available.
  Form mounted:
  Content types: PS
  Printer types: PS
  Description: Draft printer outside computer room
  ...
```

Describing printers to your system involves describing the printer's capabilities. For Print Service, you need to provide the type of printer and the content type(s) it can handle. You also need to know how the printer is attached and the Print Service (host) that is supporting it.

8.3.1 Printer types

Usually derived from the manufacturer's name, but often generic (e.g., postscript), printer types are used by Print Service to extract extensive parameters about a printer's capabilities and characteristics from the `terminfo` database. Information such as character sequences which effect certain printer functions (e.g., a page eject) and margin descriptors are included in `terminfo`.

The printer type is, therefore, the name of a `terminfo` entry. Information from the `terminfo` database is used to initialize the printer before each print job. The default is "unknown," but even this corresponds to a set of parameters detailed in the `terminfo` database.

Printer Manager allows you to select a printer type from a list of known printer types. Printers can be assigned to more than one type if they can emulate other printers. It is not unusual for sophisticated printers to emulate simple ones. Figure 8.7 near the middle of this chapter illustrates this.

The `lpadmin -p -T` command allows you to assign a particular type or list of types to a printer as illustrated in the example below:

```
# lpadmin -P scribe -T spinwriter,ep40
```

If you don't have an entry in `terminfo` that will work for your printer, you can build a description and add it with the `terminfo` compiler `tic`, but this is a time-consuming task requiring that you know considerable detail about your printer.

Most printers will either be described in the `terminfo` database or can be used with a preexisting description. The organization of the `terminfo` database is unusual, but easy to decipher. Each directory within `/usr/share/lib/terminfo` contains printer and terminal descriptions of devices starting with the same letter.

TRY THIS   List Some Printer Descriptions

```
nextpage# ls /usr/share/lib/terminfo
1 3 5 7 9 B H P a c e g i k m o q s u w y
2 4 6 8 A G M S b d f h j l n p r t v x z
nextpage# ls /usr/share/lib/terminfo/P
PC6300PLUS PS PS-br PSR
PC7300 PS-b PS-r
```

8.3.2 Printer classes

An added flexibility provided by Print Service is its capability to group printers into classes. This allows Print Service to use some discretion in where to send print jobs according to whether a print filter is required, a required preprinted form is mounted, or the printer is available. If a class of printers receives a print request directly from a user, the print scheduler can send the job to any printer in the class and, thereby, avoid using a printer which may be backed up at the time. Unfortunately, this ability of the scheduler to balance the print load across printers works only for printers which are attached to the local host. The scheduler, after all, doesn't have access to information about what printers on remote hosts are doing.

Whenever a print job is sent to a class of printers which are all attached to remote hosts, the scheduler sends the job to the first printer defined in the class.

Unlike printer types which are strictly defined by terminfo, a printer class can be a fairly arbitrary grouping, such as all draft printers. The keyword "any" can be thought of as a class that includes all printers.

A printer class is created anytime a printer is added to it with the command lpadmin -p -c command (unless, of course, it already exists). An example of this command used to add the printer scribe to the printer class sysprinters is shown below.

```
# lpadmin -p scribe -c sysprinters
```

Similarly, a printer class, but not the printers belonging to it, "disappears" when the last member of a class is removed from the class.

To remove a printer from a class, use the lpadmin command as shown below.

```
# lpadmin -p scribe -r sysprinters
```

Use the command shown below to remove a class. This command will not remove the printers belonging to the class. If print jobs are queued for the class you are about to remove, wait first for them to finish or reroute them to another printer with lpmove.

```
# lpadmin -x sysprinters
```

When a class is created, you must use the `accept` command before print jobs can be queued for it. Similarly, you should reject further jobs with the `reject` command before removing a printer class.

```
# accept sysprinters
```

To list printer classes, use the following `lpstat` command.

```
# lpstat -c all
members of class sysprinters:
  scribe
  magic
```

8.3.3   Content types

Content types represent the format of files that a printer is asked to print. Both print jobs and printers have a content type associated with them. The content type of a print job corresponds to the format of the file (or input) that is to be printed. The content type of a printer corresponds to the type of file (or input) that it is expected to print (e.g., a PostScript printer is expected to print files formatted with the PostScript language.)

The most common type of file is `ascii` text. Other common content types include PostScript, `tex`, `troff`, and `raster`. Printers can usually print plain `ascii` (i.e., simple) files as well as files in their intended format. Whenever the content type of the printer matches the content type of a file, printing is simple and straightforward. When these types do not match, a filter is often required to turn the file into the format expected by the printer.

On configuring a printer, if you specify the content type as "none," all files will be filtered. The word "none" signifies that the content type of the printer does not match any known content type. On the other hand, if you specify "any," no files are filtered. The word "any" signifies that the content type of the printer matches anything. In reality, you will seldom use none or any with your printers.

The `-I` option of the `lpadmin` command associates a particular content type with a printer. More than one content type can be associated with a single printer when this is appropriate.

```
# lpadmin -p scribe -I PS
```

8.3.4   Print filters

Print filters, as mentioned in the previous section, are utilities that convert one content type to another in order to provide a printer with something it can print. A common example is a filter which creates a PostScript version of a plain text file.

TRY THIS   Examine Function of Print Filter

```
$ cd /usr/lib/lp/postscript
$ echo hello | postdaisy | tail      <—send text to filter
1 pagesetup
(hello)1                             <—the text we entered (surrounded by
cleartomark                             PostScript commands)
showpage
restore
%%EndPage: 1 1
%%Trailer
done
%%DocumentFonts: Courier
%%Pages: 1
```

You will see a lot of PostScript language commands ending with lines that look like what is displayed here. Notice how the single word *hello* has been inserted into one of the lines just before the "showpage" command that causes the composed page to be displayed. Clearly, the effect of the filtering is to turn the single word into a large file of PostScript commands which lay out the page, select a font and size, and print the word *hello*.

Print filters must be registered with the Print Service with the `lpfilter` command before they can be used. Similarly, to take a print filter out of service, you must unregister it (or delete it) so that the Print Service will no longer use it. Each of these commands is shown below.

```
lpfilter -f <filtername> -f <pathname>
lp filter -g <filtername> -x

# lpfilter -f postdaisy -F postdaisy.fd
# lpfilter -f postdaisy -x
```

Since filters are simply programs that reformat data, it is possible to build your own and register them with the Print Service. You need to know a lot about a particular printer or a printer language (e.g., PostScript) to build a filter that correctly transforms your data. More than likely, applications that you use will produce output in a format that your printers can use or that can be transformed using existing filters.

Information about filters is stored in the file `filter.table` in `/etc/lp`. Below, a single line from this file clearly contains information that details when the filter should be used (i.e., when converting "daisy" input to PostScript output).

```
:any:any:daisy:postdaisy:postscript:slow:/usr/lib/lp/postscript/postdaisy:P
AGES
*=-o*,COPIES *=-c*,MODES group=-n2,MODES group\=\\([2-9]\\\)= -n\\1,MODES
```

```
portrait=-pp,MODES landscape=-pl,MODES x\=\\(\\-*[\\.0-9]*\\)= -x\\1,MODES
y\=\\(\\-*[\\.0-9]*\\)=-y\\1,MODES magnify\=\\([\\.0-9]*\\)=-m\\1
```

The `lpfilter` command can be used to display this information about a particular printer in a more usable format as shown in the example below.

TRY THIS   Examine the Parameters of a Print Filter

```
# lpfilter -f postdaisy -l
Input types: daisy
Output types: postscript
Printer types: any
Printers: any
Filter type: slow
Command: /usr/lib/lp/postscript/postdaisy
Options: PAGES *=-o*
Options: COPIES *=-c*
Options: MODES group=-n2
Options: MODES group\=\([2-9]\)=-n\1
Options: MODES portrait=-pp
Options: MODES landscape=-pl
Options: MODES x\=\(\-*[\.0-9]*\)=-x\1
Options: MODES y\=\(\-*[\.0-9]*\)=-y\1
Options: MODES magnify\=\([\.0-9]*\)=-m\1
```

The `awk` command below lists the input and output types for all the filters contained in the `filter.table` file.

TRY THIS   List Input and Output Types for Filters

```
awk -F: '{print $4, $6}' filter.table
postscript postdown
postdown PS
postdown PS
troff postscript
daisy postscript
dmd postscript
matrix postscript
plot postscript
simple postscript
postscript,post postscript
tek4014 postscript
```

8.3.5   Preprinted forms

A *preprinted form* is just that. It is a form that can be used on a printer instead of a plain sheet of paper and is probably considerably more expensive. Company letterhead or transparencies are typical examples. When using preprinted forms, you want to ensure that jobs requiring them print when the form is mounted. You also want jobs not requiring the forms to wait. You wouldn't want Brett, the programmer, to print seven copies of his source code on either of these fairly expensive resources.

Printwheels, on the other hand, are replaceable printer parts that change the font on some impact printers. When using forms or printwheels, it is very useful to have a means of monitoring requests and ensuring that the right forms and printwheels are used with each print job. Print Service provides this control by allowing you to describe particular forms and printwheels, monitor requests for their use, mount and unmount them in response to queued jobs, and determine which printers and which users are allowed to use particular forms and printwheels.

Forms need to be created (described to the system), registered with Print Service, and made available to a particular printer. The systems administrator also needs to let Print Service know when a particular print form is mounted and ready for use so that print jobs requiring its use can be completed and print jobs not requiring the form will be held back or, if possible, sent to another printer.

8.3.5.1   Defining forms.

Defining a form involves setting the values of a set of characteristics that detail the overall size of the form along with several other variables that describe how closely the text and lines on the form are to be printed and whether a particular character set or print ribbon is required.

Print Service assists you in managing the use of preprinted forms and, using these descriptors, can determine how large print forms are and, consequently, when to eject a form. On the other hand, printing information into the correct boxes on a W-2 form or between the lines on a name and address label is up to you and your application software.

Forms management provides a means by which you will be notified when a print form is required by a print job. The type of alert that you will be sent and how often it will be sent are options that you select.

The parameters that you can include in a form description are explained below. Any of these parameters that are not included in your form description will assume the default (included within parentheses).

Page length	Number of lines on a page of a form, or length in inches or centimeters (66)
Page width	Number of characters, inches, or centimeters across the form
Number of pages	Number of pages in a form (1)
Line pitch	How closely the lines of a form are to each other in lines per inch or lines per centimeter

Character pitch	How closely characters in a line are to each other in lines per inch or lines per centimeter
Character set choice	A character set, printwheel, or font cartridge that should be used with this form
Ribbon color	Ribbon color with which the form should be printed
Comment	A description of the form for end users
Alignment pattern	Sample file used to align form in printer

An example is shown below.

```
# lpforms -f leave -l
page length: 20
page width: 80
number of pages: 1
line pitch: 6
character pitch: 10
character set choice: any
ribbon color: red
comment:
this is form for collecting inventory info
```

The `lpforms` command allows you to add, delete, or change a form already defined.

```
lpforms -f formname option
```

where option can be

-F	pathname to add a change and pathname is a form descriptor
-	to add or change a form from standard input
-x	to delete a form
-l	to list an existing form's attributes (shown above)
-A	alert to use (followed by alert options described below)

Some of this information is used in conjunction with the `terminfo` database by the interface program to initialize the printer for this form. When you define a form, you may want to specify how, when, and how often you will be notified when it is needed. This notification is called an *alert*. The command below is an example of defining an alert for the leave form.

```
lpforms -f leave -A mail -W 5

                    ^        ^        ^
                    |        |        |
                    |        |        +------- interval for alerts (minutes)
                    |        +--------------- type of alert (what to do)
                    +----------------------- form
```

Additional alert options include

write   Use the write command

quiet   Do nothing for current condition

none   Do nothing

shell   Run a shell command

list   Lists current alert

The command shown below lists the current alert associated with the specified form:

```
# lpforms -f leave -A list
When 2 are queued: mail to root every 1 minutes
```

Messages notifying you of the need to mount the form will look like this:

```
The form inventory needs to be mounted
on the printer(s):
scribe (2 requests).
4 print requests await this form.
Use the red ribbon.
Use the any printwheel.
```

If you use the -W option with your alerts, alerts will be sent out at the specified interval. If you use the -Q option, the alert is sent when that many requests are queued for the form.

If you set your -Q option, you can avoid excessive mounting and unmounting by requiring that some number of jobs requiring the form queue up before the system asks you to act on the request to mount the form.

Let's look at the alert after setting both -W and -Q.

```
# lpforms -f leave -A mail -Q 5 -W 1
# lpforms -f leave -A list
When 5 are queued: mail to root every 1 minutes
```

If alerts are being sent out every minute, you can use the quiet option to stop the alerts without affecting alerts for future request conditions; in this way, it is different from the none option.

8.3.5.2. Enabling and disabling the use of particular forms. The lpadmin command allows particular forms to be used or disallows their use on a particular printer. The format of this command is similar to the command for allowing users and hosts to access a printer, and the concepts of allow and deny lists are identical, as we shall see later.

This example allows use of the inventory and leave forms on the printer scribe, but disallows use of the form letterhead.

```
# lpadmin -p scribe -f allow:inventory,leave
# lpadmin -p scribe -f deny:letterhead
```

8.3.5.3 Creating user accesses to forms.

You can also build a list of users allowed to use or not allowed to use a particular form.

If an allow list is established, only those users included in the list will be permitted to use the form, and the deny list not even be consulted. If the allow list is empty, but a deny list exists, those users included in the deny list will be denied access to the form. The default (both lists empty) is for all users to have access to the form.

Allow and deny lists for forms are created with the commands shown below. User lists for forms access are formulated the same as user lists for printers. See Sec 8.5.1 for a more complete explanation of allow and deny lists.

```
# lpusers -f inventory -u allow:mrbill,greg
# lpusers -f leave -u allow:all
```

8.3.5.4 Mounting and unmounting forms.

Once you mount new forms on a printer, you need to tell Print Service that this has been done. The scheduler will then be able to send jobs waiting for the form to be printed. The two commands below show how to tell the system that a form is mounted and how to tell it that a form has been unmounted. To mount a different form after a form has been mounted, you do not need the second command; simply enter the `lpadmin` command to indicate the second form has been mounted.

```
lpadmin -p -M -f
lpadmin -p -M -f none
```

The printer should *not* be printing when you attempt to mount a form. Disable it first.

The `lpstat -f` command will list forms available for your use.

```
# lpstat -f
form inventory is available to you
form leave is available to you
```

8.3.6 Printwheels and character sets

The process of managing printwheels and character sets is very similar to that for tracking forms. Basically, you need a way to associate these printer capabilities with a particular printer so that the print services can identify and validate requests for these resources. For removable printwheels, you also need a mechanism for tracking requests, mounting the printwheels, and informing the system once they have been mounted.

If a printer has mountable printwheels, you need to create names for them and register these names with Print Service. It is also a good idea to label the printwheels if their identities are not obvious.

If a printer has selectable character sets without having a removable part, you need to list the names and associate each with a name or number that corresponds to a terminfo entry.

8.3.6.1 Printwheels. If a requested printwheel is not mounted, the system notifies root. The print job then waits in the queue until the printwheel has been mounted. You tell Print Service when you've mounted the printwheel.

Of course, you have to have specified ahead of time that the particular printer has printwheels. This information is not tied to the `terminfo` database. Print Service will assume that there are no alternative printwheels unless you register them with the following command.

```
lpadmin -p -S

# lpadmin -p diablo -S courier,helvetica
                        ^           ^
                        |           |
                        names of printwheels
                        or cartridges
```

This registers the names with Print Service and associates the printwheels with the particular printer. Print Service then "knows" that a user's request for a particular printwheel makes sense and can send an alert for you to mount it. You need to make this association on Print Service as well as on the print clients.

You can be alerted through e-mail, a message on your login terminal or console window, or a message crafted by a program that you select. You can even elect to receive no alerts, although this is seldom a good idea. The default is to send a message to your screen.

Printwheels are mounted and unmounted in the same manner as forms, and the same mechanisms are used to alert the systems administrator when a new printwheel is required. The commands below are used to mount and unmount a printwheel. As with forms, you do not need to unmount one printwheel to mount another.

```
lpadmin -p -M -S
lpadmin -p -M -S none
```

8.3.6.2 Character sets. Selectable character sets, unlike removable printwheels and font cartridges, are listed in the `terminfo` database. Character sets are, after all, among the capabilities of a printer which `terminfo` supports. Because character sets can be switched without human intervention, no alerts are required and there is no need for mount and unmount operations. It is necessary, however, to determine which character sets are available for a particular printer type and to inform Print Service if your users will be referring to any of these character sets by aliases. Print Service will assume that all character sets available for a particular printer type are available unless you tell it.

To determine what character sets are defined for a particular printer type, you can use the `tput` command to extract this information from `terminfo`. To fetch the name of each character set from `terminfo`, start with the zeroth entry and increment the character set number (`csnm`) until there is no response.

Notice that the response to each `tput` command is on the following line. In the example below (for the DEC LN03 printer type), there are 16 character sets numbered 0 to 15.

```
# tput -T ln03 csnm 0
usascii# tput -T ln03 csnm 1
english# tput -T ln03 csnm 2
finnish# tput -T ln03 csnm 3
japanese# tput -T ln03 csnm 4
norwegian# tput -T ln03 csnm 5
swedish# tput -T ln03 csnm 6
germanic# tput -T ln03 csnm 7
french# tput -T ln03 csnm 8
canadian_french# tput -T ln03 csnm 9
italian# tput -T ln03 csnm 10
spanish# tput -T ln03 csnm 11
line# tput -T ln03 csnm 12
security# tput -T ln03 csnm 13
ebcdic# tput -T ln03 csnm 14
apl# tput -T ln03 csnm 15
mosaic# tput -T ln03 csnm 16
```

When you issue the `lpadmin -p -S` command, you can substitute other names for any of the character sets as shown in the example below.

```
lpadmin -p printername -S charset1=alias1,charset2=alias2…
lpadmin -p magic -S usascii=american,english=british
```

You can list available character sets with the `lpstat -S` command.

```
# lpstat -S
character set
character set american
character set british
character set japanese
character set usascii
character set english
character set finnish
character set norwegian
character set swedish
character set germanic
character set french
character set canadian_french
character set italian
character set spanish
character set line
```

```
character set security
character set ebcdic
character set apl
character set mosaic
```

8.4   Configuring Printers

Configuring printers requires a number of steps to describe a printer and register its services. If you use AdminTool, many of the somewhat complicated steps required to install and configure a printer (e.g., setting up the listen services) are handled for you.

8.4.1   Using Printer Manager

The easiest way to install a printer in Solaris 2.x is to use the Print Manager tool available through AdminTool. Printer Manager will provide you with a form into which you can enter printer-specific information and select important printer configuration information such as printer type and content type. It also will invoke processes needed to support your printer, including the listen services for remote print requests.

Printer Manager is started by double-clicking on its button within AdminTool (see Fig. 8.3). Printer Manager, shown in Fig. 8.4, will list existing printers and provide you with pulldown menus to add a local printer or provide access to a remote printer. The `Goto` field at the top of the form permits you to operate on another host.

In Fig. 8.5, we have selected the option to add a local printer. Figure 8.6 displays the form in which we enter information pertaining to this printer. Some

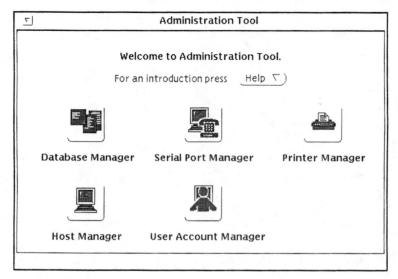

Figure 8.3   AdminTool.

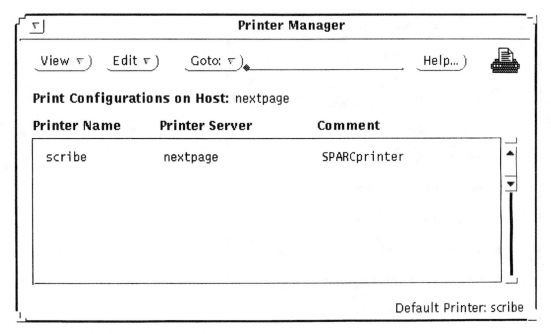

Figure 8.4 Printer Manager.

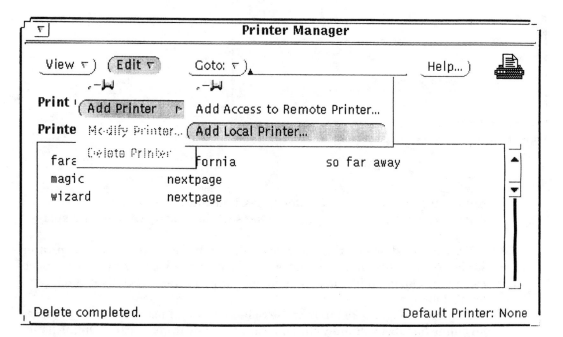

Figure 8.5 Adding a local printer.

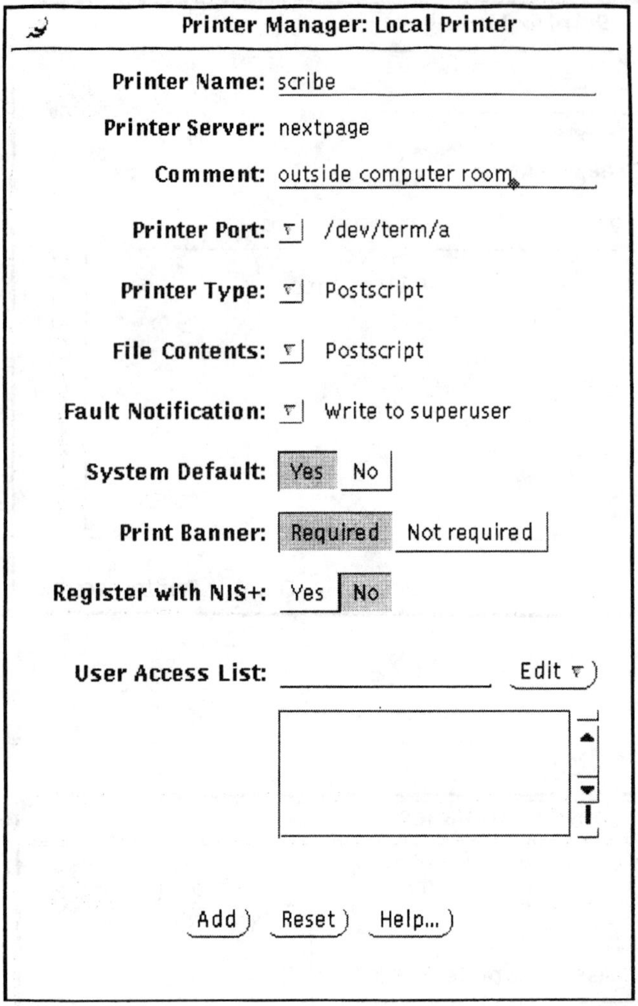

```
 ◡                Printer Manager: Local Printer

          Printer Name:  scribe
        Printer Server:  nextpage
               Comment:  outside computer room

          Printer Port:  ▽|  /dev/term/a
          Printer Type:  ▽|  Postscript
         File Contents:  ▽|  Postscript
     Fault Notification: ▽|  Write to superuser
        System Default:  | Yes | No |
          Print Banner:  | Required | Not required |
     Register with NIS+:   Yes | No |

       User Access List:  _____   Edit ▽ )

                          _____
                          |                    | ▲|
                          |                    | ▽|
                          |_____| |

              Add )   Reset )   Help... )
```

Figure 8.6 Describing a local printer.

printer information (e.g., printer types and content types) can be selected from a list that this form contains. One such list (printer types) is displayed in Fig. 8.7.

Figure 8.8 shows our printer list following the addition of the printer scribe. Notice the comment that was added in the local printer form. Such comments can simplify management of your printers, especially if you have a lot of them.

Printer Manager, like many of the Solaris 2.x administration tools, provides an online handbook. Simply click on the Help... key to get started. Online handbooks provide hypertext links to help you move speedily to the section or topic

```
┌─────────────────────────────────────────────────────────────┐
│  ↲          Printer Manager: Local Printer                   │
│  ═══════════════════════════════════════════════════════     │
│                                                               │
│      Printer Name: _____           │
│                                                               │
│    Printer Server: nextpage                                   │
│                                                               │
│         Comment: ▸_____            │
│                                                               │
│      Printer Port: ▽│ /dev/term/a                             │
│                                                               │
│      Printer Type: ▽   Postscript                             │
│                   ┌──────────────────────────┐                │
│     File Contents:│ Postscript               │                │
│                   │                          │                │
│                   │  Reverse Postscript      │                │
│  Fault Notification:│  Epson 2500            │                │
│                   │                          │                │
│    System Default:│  IBM ProPrinter          │                │
│                   │                          │                │
│                   │  Qume Sprint 5           │                │
│     Print Banner: │                          │                │
│                   │  Daisy                   │                │
│  Register with NIS+:│  Diablo                │                │
│                   │                          │                │
│                   │  Datagraphix             │                │
│                   │                          │  t ▽ )         │
│   User Access List:│  DEC LA100              │                │
│                   ├──────────────────────────┤  ┌──┐          │
│                   │  DEC LN03                │  │▲ │          │
│                   │                          │  ├──┤          │
│                   │  DECwriter               │  │▽ │          │
│                   │                          │  │T │          │
│                   │  Texas Instruments 800   │  └──┘          │
│                   │                          │                │
│                   │  Other...                │                │
│                   └──────────────────────────┘                │
│                                                               │
│        Add )   Reset )   Help... )                            │
│                                                               │
└─────────────────────────────────────────────────────────────┘
```

Figure 8.7 Listing printer types.

that you need. Double-click on any boxed text to move to the indicated topic (see Fig. 8.9). Figure 8.10 displays a help page for adding a printer.

8.4.2 Manual setup

Manual setup of Print Service involves a number of steps and requires that you understand the printer description information discussed earlier in this chapter. The particular sequence of commands that you will use to set up a printer and start Print Service will depend on whether you are running both Solaris 2.x and earlier versions of SunOS (4.1 and earlier) or other BSD UNIX systems or only Solaris 2.x. For example, configuring a SVR4 print client is different from configuring a BSD print client, as shown below:

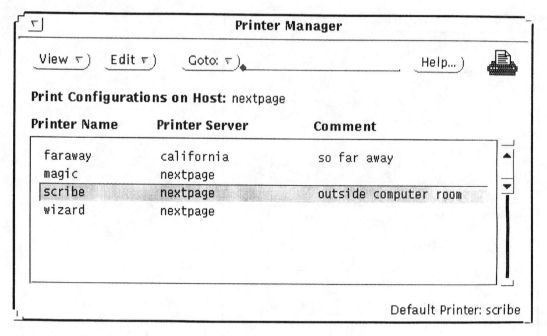

Figure 8.8 Listing printers.

8.4.2.1 Configuring a BSD print client.
Clients of BSD print servers should be set up with the following sequence of commands:

```
# lpsystem -t bsd farhost
# lpadmin -p localname -s farhost!farprinter
# lpadmin -p localname -T unknown -I any
# accept scribe
# enable scribe
```

The lpsystem command registers the print server name with Print Service. The two lpadmin commands add the remote printer to the system and associate a local name for the printer. The accept and enable commands allow print jobs to be queued up and printed.

8.4.2.2 Configuring an SVR4 print client.
Clients of SVR4 print servers are set up very similarly. Notice how we specify realistic values to our printer and content types; this was not the case for BSD print servers.

```
# lpsystem -t s5 <printserver>
# lpadmin -p faraway -s farhost!farprinter
# lpadmin -p faraway -T PS -I PS
# accept faraway
# enable faraway
```

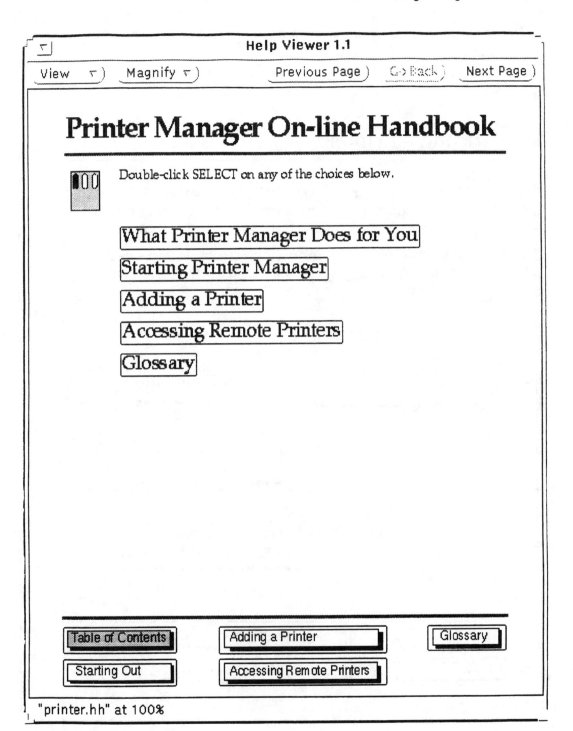

Figure 8.9   Printer manager on-line handbook.

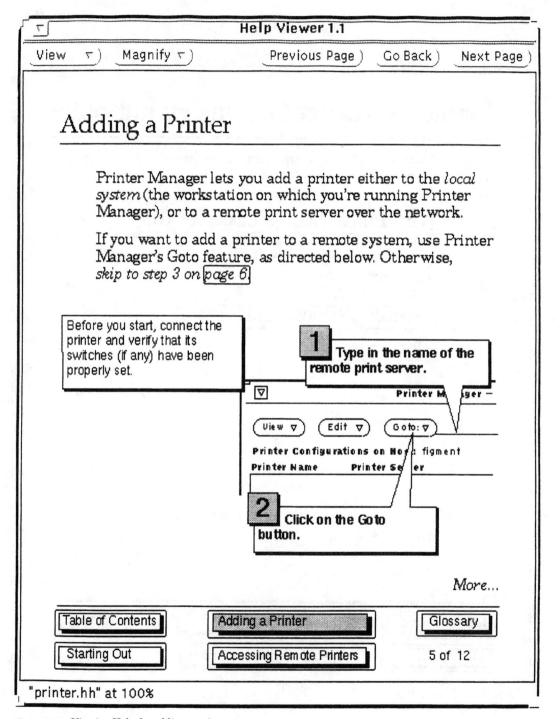

Figure 8.10   Viewing Help for adding a printer.

8.4.3   Printer alerts

Print Service provides a mechanism for detecting printer faults and reporting them. Errors ranging from simple problems (e.g., running out of paper) to serious printer malfunctioning (e.g., a printing breaking down and going offline) can be reported in any of several different ways.

As with alerts which notify you of the need to mount a form or printwheel, you have three choices on how to receive alerts concerning print problems: (1) you can be notified by mail, (2) a message is sent to your console or login terminal, or (3) you can execute a selected program. You can also elect to receive no alerts at all.

```
# lpadmin -p scribe -A mail -W 5
# lpadmin -p scribe -A write -W 5
# lpadmin -p scribe -A /usr/local/alert -W 5
# lpadmin -p scribe -A none
```

If you want alerts to be sent to other than root, you can add the username to the alert command as shown in the example below with the mail command.

```
# lpadmin -p scribe -A 'mail slee' -W 5
```

Once you've noted an alert and want to stop receiving further notices about the same problem, you can ask Print Service to stop sending the notices with the following command. The quiet command will only apply to the current problem and you will still be alerted if new problems crop up.

```
# lpadmin -p scribe -A quiet
```

Following correction of a printer fault, Print Service will recover in one of three ways. It will

- Continue with the top of the page that was printing when printing was interrupted by the fault.
- Restart with the beginning of the print job that was active when the printing was interrupted by the fault.
- Wait for the systems administrator to reenable printing.

The first of these options requires use of a filter which is capable of waiting for the fault to be cleared before printing starts again. The default printer does not have the detailed knowledge of printer control sequences needed to provide this capability. You can determine which of these recovery methods is used with a particular printer by using one of the following example lpadmin commands:

```
# lpadmin -p scribe -F continue
# lpadmin -p scribe -F beginning
# lpadmin -p scribe -F wait
```

Printer alerts, by the way, are for the systems administrator. Most errors in print requests result in immediate error messages which are provided to the requester. Users who request, for example, forms which they are not permitted to use or who send a print job to a printer that they are not authorized to print on are told right away.

8.5   Configuring Printer Usage for Users

There are several attributes of Print Service configuration that determine how and when your users are able to print. These include access lists which determine who can print where, print priorities which determine how quickly a print job will move to the top of a print queue, and the default printer which determines where print jobs not explicitly sent to a particular printer will be printed.

8.5.1   Maintaining Access Lists (Hosts and Users)

Access to printers can be finely controlled through access lists which determine which users, which host systems, or which users on which hosts are allowed or denied use of each individual printer. Files in the printer-specific subdirectory in /etc/lp/printers control these access. The two files (either or both may not exist) are users.allow and users.deny. We will discuss how these files are created and how they define and control printer access.

The allow and deny lists are created with the lpadmin command. The file users.allow is simply a list of users and hosts allowed to print to a particular printer. The file users.deny, on the other hand, is a list of users and hosts for whom access is denied. If you have both of these files, the access.deny file is ignored.

If neither file exists or the existing files are empty, everyone has access. The word all in the users.allow list has the same effect. The word all in the users.deny file will disallow everyone (unless the users.allow list contains a user list, in which case the users.deny file is ignored). In every case, if the users.allow list is not empty, *only* the allow list is used to determine access privilege. If the users.allow list is empty and the users.deny list is not, only those users in the deny list are refused.

```
users.allow        users.deny        effect

===========        ==========        ======

(empty)            (empty)           everyone can print

(empty)            alan              everyone but Alan can print

alan               (empty)           only Alan can print

alan               (anything)        only Alan can print

nextpage!all       (anything)        only users on host "nextpage" can print

(empty)            nextpage!all      only users on host "nextpage" cannot print
```

Before establishing allow or deny lists, you should determine whether you want to allow or deny a greater number of users and hosts and set up whichever of the two lists will be easiest to maintain. Keep in mind that you have three choices in setting up printer accesses:

- To maintain a list of users allowed to print
- To maintain a list of users denied access to a printer
- To maintain no lists at all (i.e., allow everyone to print)

and that you have these choices for each printer. If you maintain allow or deny lists, you will need to update them when new users are added to your system or when users leave your organization.

Access lists should be created on Print Service, but can also be set up on the print client. This allows Print Service to tell the user that access is denied before a response can be returned from the server. If you choose to maintain lists on both the server and the client, you must also be careful to keep them synchronized. Do not attempt to synchronize these lists by copying the files themselves. This will not work. On the other hand, it is easy to re-create the lists from a file. In the example below, we are setting up an allow list from a file copied from another system (using the C shell).

```
nextpage# foreach allowed (`cat users.allow-`)
? echo "adding " $allowed
? lpadmin -p scribe -u allow:$allowed
? end
adding nerdville!all
adding fred
adding all!slee
...
```

With the `lpadmin` command, you can set up allow or deny lists. You can set up both, but the deny list will not be consulted if the allow list exists. When you use allow lists, subsequent `lpadmin` requests to allow users will add these users to the existing list. The two `lpadmin` commands shown below will create both the `users.allow` and `users.deny` files in `/etc/lp/printers/scribe`, but only the former will be referenced. The single user listed in both commands will, therefore, be able to print on scribe.

```
# lpadmin -p scribe -u allow:all!slee,fred,vail
# lpadmin -p scribe -u deny:vail,earth!all
```

Printer Manager only sets up allow lists. When you set up a local printer, you can create a list of those users and systems allowed access.

In user lists for printer access, the user and host pairs can be formed using any of the host and username patterns shown below:

user	User on any system
system!user	User on particular host
system!all	All users on particular host

`all!userparticular`	User on any host
`all!all`	Any user on any host
`all`	Any user on any host

If there is only one part to the name, it is assumed to be the username. If the pattern contains a `!`, the left part is the system and the right part is the username. Either part (or both) can be `all`, representing all users or all hosts.

If you use an exclamation mark in your user list, you must have a username or the keyword `all` on the right side of it. In other words, the pattern, `system!` is not allowed.

`vail`	The user `vail` on any system
`happyday!joe`	The user `joe` on host `happyday`
`happyday!all`	Any user on host `happyday`
`all!vail`	The user `vail` on any host
`all`	Any user on any host

If you want all of your users to be able to access a printer, you can use the allow `lpadmin` keyword with the word `all` and your `users.allow` list will be replaced with an empty `users.deny` list.

TRY THIS   What is *Wrong* with this Command?

If you maintain no allow or deny lists on the print server to which the printer scribe is attached, and then you issue the command below to allow all users on a new host to print to scribe, what will happen?

```
lpadmin -p scribe -u allow:nerdville!all
```

This command sets up a `users.allow` file for scribe. It will contain the string `nerdville!all` allowing, as you intended, all users on that host to print. At the same time, all other users will be prevented from using scribe.

The moral of this exercise is this: If you want everyone to be able to use a particular printer, don't use `lpadmins -u` option at all.

Users who are not permitted to use a particular printer will get an error message like that shown below when they attempt to print:

```
UX:lp: ERROR: You are not allowed to use the destination
   "scribe".
TO FIX: Use the lpstat -p command to list all
   known printers; you can use those marked
   "available".
```

If they then issue the `lpstat -p` command as suggested, they will see which printers are available to them and which are not.

```
$ lpstat -p
printer scribe now printing scribe-10. enabled since Tue Mar 23 13:32:44 EST
1993. not available.
printer wizard is idle. enabled since Fri Apr 16 11:39:29 EDT 1993. available.
printer faraway is idle. enabled since Wed Apr 21 10:48:15 EDT 1993. available.
```

8.5.2   Print priorities

Print Service has a scheme for print job prioritization which supports the use of up to 40 different priority levels. Numbered 0 to 39, with 0 as the highest possible priority, print priorities allow critical print jobs to jump ahead of other jobs in the print queue.

Every print request has a priority. Most print requests will simply use the default priority. You can determine the default print priority as well as the highest priority than any users or particular users can request.

To change the system default priority, use the lpsystems command with the -d option as shown below. The default priority will be used any time a print job is submitted without specifying an explicit priority (i.e., most of the time). Initially, this systemwide default is 20. Here it is being reset to 15.

```
# lpusers -d 15
```

To establish the highest priority that a user can request, use the lpusers command with the -q option. In the command displayed below, two users are limited to requesting priorities of 10 or below (i.e., 10 to 39).

```
# lpusers -q 10 -u slee,Mary
```

The list of users can be expressed using the same name and host forms as with allow and deny lists. In other words, username, host, or host!username pairs and the keyword all can be used to construct your list. The command below limits all users on the host nextpage and Mary (wherever she is logged in) to priorities of 10 or lower.

```
# lpusers -q 10 -u nextpage!all,all!Mary
```

Without a user list, the command lpusers -q sets the priority for all users. The command lpusers -q 15 sets the highest priority level that all users not specifically given higher privilege with the lpusers -q 10 -u list command.

Users can request a particular priority when they make a print request. If the requested priority does not exceed what is allowed them, it will be accepted. Users can always print at the highest priority level established for them or at any lower (i.e., higher number) priority. Further, if no systemwide or user-specific limits are set, they can specify that a particular print job be run at the highest priority. The example below shows how an urgent print request assumed a position at the top of the queue.

```
# lp -q 0 urgent.notices
request id is scribe-23 (1 file(s))
# lpstat -o
scribe-23      slee      78 Apr 14 14:23 filtered
scribe-21      vail      113 Apr 9 07:58 filtered
scribe-10      vail      1460 Apr 5 14:41 on scribe
scribe-12      vail      225 Apr 5 15:08 filtered
scribe-15      slee      98 Apr 5 16:42 filtered
scribe-18      fred      954 Apr 6 17:45 filtered
scribe-19      fred      88 Apr 9 07:51 filtered
scribe-20      root      78 Apr 9 07:56 filtered
scribe-22      root      25560 Apr 9 08:00
```

You will probably not have to enforce priority limitations unless your users are prone to abuse the priority mechanism and play leapfrog with the print queue to the detriment of other users. If your print queues are usually backed up and your users are not particularly sensitive to each other's needs, you might be well advised to reserve the highest priority for particular individuals or particular situations in which you temporarily assign the highest priority to an individual user.

8.5.3   Default printer setup

You can determine which printer is used as the system default or is the default for a particular user. The lpadmin -d command sets up as the default printer for a particular system. For example, the command lpadmin -d scribe makes scribe the default printer for the system.

To set a particular user's default, use the LPDEST environment variable. When users each have their own workstations, which way you set the default printer may seem moot. On the other hand, most users can change their environment variable, but cannot change the systemwide setting unless they have root or lp privilege. If both the system and user environment variables are defined, the user's environment variable is used rather than the system-level default.

To set the system default, use

```
# lpadmin -d scribe
```

To set a particular user's default (Bourne and Korn shells), use

```
$ LPDEST=magic
$ export LPDEST
```

To set a particular user's default (C shell):

```
nextpage% setenv LPDEST magic
```

8.6 Managing Print Queues

One of the keys to successfully managing print queues is to know and use the commands that report on the status of Print Service. The `lpstat` command provides four options that you should use regularly.

```
lpstat options:
```
(none)	Show all print requests
-a	Show printers accepting requests
-c	Show class names and members
-d	Show system default printer
-f	Show forms
-o [list]	Show status of print requests; list can be a list of printer names, class names, or specific request IDs
-p [printers]	Show status of printers listed
-p [printers] -D	Show status of printers and descriptions
-p [printers] -l	Show status of printers and characteristics
-r	Show if scheduler is running
-R request	Show position of job in queue
-s	Show summary of Print Service status
-S	Show character sets
-t	Print all status information
-u [users]	Print status of print requests for users or listed users
-v [printers]	Print names of printers and pathnames for all printers or listed printers

Examples of some of these options and their results are included below.

```
# lpstat -r
scheduler is running

# lpstat -o
scribe-21    root       3 Apr 9 07:58 filtered
scribe-10    root       6 Apr 5 14:41 on scribe
...

# lpstat -a
scribe accepting requests since Tue Mar 23 13:32:43 EST 1993

# lpstat -t
scheduler is running
system default destination: scribe
device for scribe: /dev/term/a
scribe accepting requests since Tue Mar 23 13:32:43 EST 1993
printer scribe now printing scribe-10. enabled since Tue Mar 23 13:32:44 EST
```

```
1993. not available.
form inventory is available to you
form leave is available to you, mounted on scribe
character set
scribe-21    root         3 Apr 9 07:58 filtered
scribe-10    root         6 Apr 5 14:41 on scribe
...

# lpstat -p -D -l
printer scribe now printing scribe-10. enabled since Wed Apr 14 15:40:26 EDT
1993. not available.
  Form mounted: leave
  Content types: postscript
  Printer types: PS
  Description: SPARCprinter
  Connection: direct
  Interface: /usr/lib/1p/model/standard
  On fault: mail to root every 1 minutes
  After fault: continue
  Users allowed:
   pointhope!all
   slee
   munchkin!naomi
   nerdville!all
  Forms allowed:
   leave
  Banner not required
  Character sets:

  Default pitch:
  Default page size: 80 wide 66 long
  Default port settings:
```

8.6.1 Canceling print requests

The cancel command allows you to cancel a single print request or a group of print requests. Your users can only cancel their own requests. The syntax of the command is a simple `cancel`. For example, the command `cancel scribe-10` cancels the single print job, `scribe-10`. Similarly, the command `cancel scribe-10 scribe-20` cancels two print jobs. You can cancel print jobs sent to other printers and for specific users. To cancel all print jobs for slee on the printer scribe, enter `cancel -u slee scribe`.

You will see a list of cancellation confirmations, for example

```
request "scribe-10" canceled
request "scribe-20" canceled
```

You can also cancel all print requests for a given list of users. To cancel all print jobs for slee, type `cancel -u slee`. To cancel all print jobs in the queue for slee on the printer scribe, enter `cancel -u slee scribe`.

The command `cancel scribe` will cancel the current print job on printer scribe.

8.6.2 Changing priorities

Print priorities can be changed after submission of the print request with the `lp` command's `-i` option:

```
lp -i -<jobid>
-q<new-
priority
% lp -i scribe-10 -q 10
```

Individual users will not be able to reprioritize their print jobs at a higher priority than is allowed them through the limits that you set.

8.6.3 Rerouting print jobs

The `lpmove` will move a print job that is queued up for one printer to another. If options of the print job cannot be handled by the new destination, `lpmove` will reject the move request

```
lpmove <jobs> <dest>

# lpmove scribe-10 magic
```

You can move a print job from a class to a specific printer in that or another class (provided the print job is compatible with the new destination).

The command `lpmove <dest 1> <dest 2>` will move all jobs in the first queue to the second. Following this command, `lp` will also reject further requests for the first destination.

```
# lpmove magic scribe
destination magic is not accepting requests
move in progress…
total of 1 requests moved from magic to scribe
```

When you use the `lpstat -t` command, you will also see that the printer is no longer accepting requests.

```
# lpstat -t
…
magic not accepting requests since Mon Apr 19 18:02:44 EDT 1993 -
   requests moved to scribe
…
```

The `request-ids` of the old jobs are not changed so that users can track their print jobs even in the new print queue.

```
# lpstat -o scribe
…
scribe-51    root      78 Apr 19 15:40 filtered
magic-54     root       3 Apr 19 18:02 filtered
```

8.7   Managing Print Service

There are times when you will need to stop the queuing of print jobs or take a printer out of service. Print Service provides commands to control whether print jobs can be added to a print queue and whether jobs in the print queue will be printed.

8.7.1   Accepting and rejecting requests

The accept and reject commands control whether print jobs can be added to the print queue. Accept allows new print requests to be added to the queue. Reject disallows new print jobs from being added to the queue. Print Service confirms your request as shown below.

```
# accept scribe
destination "scribe" now accepting requests
# reject scribe
destination "scribe" will no longer accept requests
```

8.7.2   Enabling and disabling printing

Enabling and disabling printing controls whether a printer will actually print jobs in the queue. A disabled printer can still accept further requests.

8.7.3   Taking a printer out of service

If you want to take a printer out of service, you should disallow queuing of further print jobs, disable printing, and reroute the print jobs waiting in the queue to another printer. In the following sequence of steps, we have done all these things and added a message that will make it clear to users when the printer is no longer in service.

```
# reject -r "Printer scribe going out of service" scribe
destination "scribe" will no longer accept requests
```

Some time may pass between this step and the next. We may, after all, want to allow the currently queued jobs to print.

```
# disable -W -r "Printer scribe out of service, jobs rerouted to magic" scribe
printer "scribe" now disabled
```

Users' print jobs will then be rejected and the following message will be displayed when they try to print on scribe.

```
UX:lp: ERROR: Requests for destination "scribe" aren't
    being accepted.
   TO FIX: Use the "lpstat -a" command to see why
    this destination is not accepting
    requests.
```

When they use the `lpstat -a` command as suggested, your message will be displayed.

```
# lpstat -a
scribe not accepting requests since Wed Apr 14 15:33:45 EDT 1993 -
   Printer scribe out of service, jobs rerouted to magic
```

It is important to emphasize the difference between the `reject` and `disable` commands. The `reject` command prevents new print jobs from being added to the queue. The `disable` command, on the other hand, stops printing altogether. After entering the `reject` command and before entering the `disable`, the remaining print jobs will still be printed.

If there are still jobs in the queue when you disable the printer (as suggested by the message we have posted for users in the preceding command sequence), you can reroute them to a different printer with the `lpmove` command. In the scenario above, we would issue the command `lpmove scribe magic` to route the print jobs to the printer magic. The `lpmove` command is explained further in Sec. 8.6.3.

8.8 The Life and Legacy of a Print Job

Print requests are stored in spool directories while awaiting printing. In the print scenario we follow in this section, we will follow two print requests as Print Service sets up the print job. One is a request to print a regular file, the other simply takes its output from standard input. You will see how the print jobs are set up in the spool directories in an example below.

TRY THIS **Follow a Print Job**

You might want to turn your printer off so that the print jobs you will submit in this exercise will be around long enough for you to examine the files that result from your request. Find a time (or a printer) that will not impact your users.

```
# lp myfile                  <-- print a file
# echo hello | lp            <-- pipe to printer
# ls -1 /var/spool/lp/requests/nextpage
total 4
-rw-rw---- 1 lp    lp      42 Mar 23 15:04 1-0 <-- the print jobs
-rw-rw---- 1 lp    lp      39 Mar 23 15:30 2-0
```

Below, the contents of one of these files has clearly captured some of the key parameters of the print request.

```
# cd /var/spool/lp/request/nextpage
# more 1-0                          <-- print request
scribe-1                           <-- printer
0                                  <-- userid of submitter
root                               <-- submitter
1                                  <-- groupid of submitter
4225                               <-- size of file
732917051                          <-- time of submission
nextpage                           <-- requesting host
```

If we then take a look at another of the spool directories, we can see that a number of files have been set up for each of the print jobs. The files starting with a capital *F* contain the filtered output of the print request (i.e., the file content after filtering).

```
# cd /var/spool/lp/tmp/nextpage
# ls -1
total 52
-rw-------  1 root      root          0 Mar 23 15:04 1
-rw-------  1 lp        lp           83 Mar 23 15:04 1-0
-rw-------  1 root      root          0 Mar 23 15:30 2
-rw-------  1 lp        lp           76 Mar 23 15:30 2-0
-rw-------  1 root      other         6 Mar 23 15:30 2-1
-rw-------  1 root      other     13649 Mar 23 15:04 F1-1
-rw-------  1 root      other      8784 Mar 23 15:30 F2-1
```

The contents of a file after filtering will usually look very different. The output of postscript filters, for example, is rendered in the PostScript language and even a small amount of text will be turned into a fairly substantial page description.

Other files within this directory capture other information about the print requests.

```
# more 2-0
C 1                                <-- # copies
D scribe                           <-- destination printer
F /var/spool/lp/tmp/nextpage/2-1   <-- specifies input file
P 20                               <-- priority
t simple                           <-- content type (before filtering)
U root                             <-- submitter
s 0x0000                           <-- outcome of print request
# more 2-1                         <-- input file
hello
# lpstat -0
scribe-1          root             4225 Mar 23 15:04 on scribe
scribe-2          root                6 Mar 23 15:30 filtered
```

In this exercise, you can see how the files are set up to support printing. The last `lpstat` command lists the two print jobs in the print queue. The second job (`scribe-2`) is annotated as `filtered`. This indicates that the word `hello` that we piped to the print command `lp` was filtered through a PostScript filter so that it could be printed on scribe, a PostScript printer.

8.9 Using Printer Log Statistics

The printer log files contain useful information on the activity of your printers and on the files which are being printed. Generating reports on the number of print jobs by user group might help you determine which group most needs an additional printer or, depending on your environment, who should pay for it.

An example of a log file entry is shown below. Each of the lines contains a single piece of information except for the first, which includes five pieces of information about the print job.

```
=any-4, uid 0, gid 1, size 4390, Mon Apr 5 13:52:42 EDT 1993
x /usr/lib/lp/postscript/dpost
y /usr/lib/lp/postscript/download -pscribe|/usr/lib/lp/postscript/postio
2>>$ERRFILE -L/var/tmp/scribe.log
z scribe
C 1
D any
F /apps/maps/file.1
P 20
t troff
U slee
s 0x0010
```

In order to extract information from the log files, you need to know what each of the lines represents. Codes used in the file are listed below.

=	Separator line, contains information about submitter and time submitted
C	Number of copies
D	Printer and class destination
F	Name of file to be printed
f	Name of form used
H	Resume, hold, or immediate indicators
N	Type of alert to use
O	-o options used in request
P	Priority
p	List of pages printed
r	If requester specified "raw"
S	Character set or printwheel
s	Outcome of request (e.g., successful printing)

T   Title for banner page

t   Type of content

U   Submitter

x   Slow filter used

y   Special modes for print filter

z   Printer used (may be different from destination)

The format of the requests log file is easy to decipher and consistent. This gives you a lot of flexibility in extracting statistics from it. As an example, the awk command shown below will create a list of the users who have requested print jobs since the current requests log was initiated (usually the current day, since these files are usually cycled by lp's cron file during the night).

```
awk ' ~ /^U$/ {print $2}' /var/lp/logs/requests
```

If you add a sort and a uniq command, you can list each user once.

```
awk ' ~ /^U$/ {print $2}' /var/lp/logs/requests | sort | uniq
```

Replace the U with a D to display a list of the requested destinations or an F for a list of printed files.

TRY THIS   **Count Jobs by Printer (Using** awk**)**

```
#     by_printer
#
$0 ~ /^z scribe$/     {++scribe}
$0 ~ /^z magic$/      {++magic}
END {
     print "scribe:", scribe
     print "magic: ", magic
}
# awk -f by_printer /var/spool/lp/logs/requests
scribe: 30
magic: 10
```

In this awk script, we have explicitly listed two printers and we increment a count each time one of the lines z scribe or z magic appears in the requests file. You can invoke this script with the command

```
awk -f by-printer /var/lp/logs/request
    for (x = 1; x <= ix; ++x)
        if (user[x] == $2) {
            ++prints[x]
            found = TRUE
        }
```

```
            if (found == FALSE) {
                ++ix
                user[ix] = $2
                ++prints[ix]
            }
            USER = FALSE
        }
    }
END {
        for (x = 1; x <= ix; ++x)
            print user [x], prints[x]
    }
----------------------------------------
# awk -f by_user request
kless 34
mrbill 62
slee 8
root 9
fred 3
vail 1
```

In this awk script, we create two arrays which correspond to a list of the users encountered in the requests file and the count of jobs they've printed. These two arrays are built as print requests are encountered in the file. The benefit of this is that we don't need to identify the users ahead of time (i.e., we don't need to explicitly include them in the script). At the end, we list the users and the number of print jobs each has requested.

You might also be interested in the completion statistics for a particular log file. In the awk script below, we match the more important completion states reported in the log file and print counts by type. Notice how we evaluate a hexadecimal string to determine whether particular digits are set. The string [0-9A-F] in awk represents any hex value between 0 and F.

8.10   Debugging Print Problems

Although Print Service provides considerable control over printing, and includes tools and commands to facilitate management of printers, there will still be occasions when you will have to investigate printer problems.

8.10.1   Checking the hardware connection

One good technique along the lines of divide and conquer is to separate printer problems from queuing problems as quickly as possible. Often, you can determine whether hardware is responsible for a printing problem by sending data directly to a printer (i.e., bypassing the queue). If your data prints when sent directly to the printer but jobs in the queue never do, you can generally assume that the physical connection and the printer itself is all right. For most printers, you can run this test by using the echo command and directing its output to the port to which the printer is attached.

```
#echo "yo,printer">/dev/term/a &
```

If the printer is a PostScript printer, you should use the cat command to send a PostScript file to the printer port as shown below.

```
# cat /usr/openwin/share/images/PostScript/parrot.ps>/dev/term/a &
```

If you do not get any output, chances are your problem is physical. Don't overlook "simple, stupid" problems. A printer may have been inadvertently turned off. If the printer serves more than one system or has just been added to your print server, make sure which physical switches may set the baud rate or determine which port on the printer is being used.

Examine the cable connecting the printer to the server. Make sure it is solidly connected and that no pins in the connectors are broken.

8.10.2   Look for evidence

Once you have determined that the problem is not a hardware problem (i.e., your message or file prints correctly), you should look for a problem with Print Service. Don't overlook the log files. Read your mail. Print Service notifies you of many problems that it detects.

Another extremely important question to ask yourself is whether the problem affects the print server, print clients, or both. Check the print queue on both client and server.

```
# lpstat -o
```

If print requests are hanging on the local system, look into problems with the scheduler on the local system.

8.10.3   Starting the scheduler

One of the first things to check is whether the scheduler is running and that the printer is enabled and accepting print jobs. To check if lpsched is running:

```
# lpstat -r              # lpstat -r
scheduler is running     scheduler is not running
```

If you do not get this response, restart the scheduler and check it again with the command sequence shown below:

```
# /bin/sh /etc/init.d/lp start
Print services started.
# lpstat -r #                            lpstat -r
scheduler is running               scheduler is not running
```

If the scheduler is still not running, take a look in lpsched's log file. You might be accumulating error indicators that will help you to determine the problem, like that shown below:

```
Fri Apr 23 11:03:16 1993: Received unexpected signal 11; terminating.
```

Sometimes the scheduler will not start because of problems it encounters with log files or spool directory files which it checks on startup. If there is a SCHED-LOCK file in /var/spool/lp, remove it and try again. If you're still unable to get the scheduler started, try cleaning out the spool directories for the printer and try again. This is somewhat drastic since print jobs in the queue will be lost, but your options are limited if the scheduler will not start or stay up. It is not a bad idea to try to salvage spooled jobs and log files by copying the files to another directory; sometimes these files will be difficult to re-create and it will be worth your while to copy them before cleaning out the print queue. Look at the directory containing print requests and spool files:

```
/var/spool/lp/tmp/nextpage
```

for files with names like 58-1 and F58-1. These files contain user data before and after filtering. Copying them to a "safe" place before removing the contents of the two directories indicated below may save someone a lot of work.

8.10.4   Ensuring the printer is accepting requests

If the problem is that new print jobs are being refused, make sure that the printer is accepting requests and that the users requesting printing are authorized to use the particular printer.

To check if printer is accepting requests:

```
# lpstat -a
scribe accepting requests since Wed Apr 21 12:44:13 EDT 1993
```

If the printer is not accepting requests, use the accept command:

```
# accept scribe
```

8.10.5   Check user accesses

If you maintain printer access lists, check to see if the user is included in the /etc/lp/printers/scribe/users.allow file. If you, instead, maintain a list of users and hosts denied access to a printer, check the deny list maintained in /etc/lp/printers/scribe/users.deny. You can also ask your users if they receive an error message like the one shown below.

```
UX:lp: ERROR: You are not allowed to use the destination
    "scribe".
  TO FIX: Use the lpstat -p command to list all
    known printers; you can use those marked
    "available".
```

Keep in mind that access lists on print servers and print clients can be out of sync.

8.10.6 Make sure the printer is enabled

Your problem may be that the printer has been disabled. To make sure the printer is enabled:

```
# lpstat -p printer
printer scribe now printing scribe-57. enabled since Wed Apr 21 12:44:13 EDT
1993. available.
```

If the printer is not enabled, enable it with the command `enable scribe`. Make sure you check the print server and the client.

8.10.7 Check the serial port

To check the serial port, find out which port the printer is attached to and make sure it is set up with the correct ownership and permissions.

```
# lpstat -t | grep device
device for scribe: /dev/term/a      <-- Note printer port
# ls -l /dev/term/a
lrwxrwxrwx  1 root      root     29 Feb 2 17:27 /dev/term/a ->
../../devices/zs@1,f1000000:a
```

As you can see, /dev/term/a is a symbolic link. Check the ownership and permissions on the file it points to. If they are not as shown below, use the chown and chmod commands that follow.

```
# ls -l /devices/zs@1,f1000000:a
crw-----  1 lp     sys     29, 0 Apr 23 12:07 /devices/zs@1,f1000000:a
# chown lp /dev/term/a              <-- Make sure you use correct port here
# chmod 600 /dev/term/a             <-- Make sure you use correct port here
```

You might also check running processes to make sure the port is not expecting a login process. In the second example below, this is the case. The word "passwd" is the giveaway. If this is the case, cancel the current print job and use the command

```
# lpadmin -p scribe -h
```

to indicate that the device associated with the printer is hardwired and, therefore, will not support login.

```
# ps -ef | grep term
   root    519     518 80 11:36:24 term/a      0:00 /bin/sh -c /etc/lp/in-
terfaces/scribe scribe-57 nextpage!slee "' 1"" /var/spool

#ps -ef |grep term
   root    519     518 80 11:36:24 term/a      0:00 /bin/sh -c /etc/lp/in-
terfaces/scribe scribe-57 nextpage!slee "passwd\n##
```

8.10.8   Examine the printer configuration

There is a lot of information available to you on the printer's configuration. Examine the output from the `lpsat` command show below. Maybe a form is mounted on your printer that no jobs in the queue require. Did you miss an alert? Has a filtering operation failed? Take a look at the printer configuration for clues.

```
#lpstat -p scribe -1

printer scribe now printing scribe-57. enabled since Wed Apr 21 12:44:13 EDT
1993

Form mounted:

Content types: PS

Printer types: PS

Description: outside computer room

Connection: direct

Interface: /use/lib/lp/model/standard

On fault: write to root once

After fault: continue

Users denied:

slee

Forms allowed:

(none)

Banner not required

Character sets:

Default pitch:

Default page size: 80 wide 66 long

Default port settings:
```

8.10.9   Checking network printing

If the printing problem appears to be a problem with remote print requests, check if `lpnet` is running:

```
# ps -ef | grep lpNet
root      574      569      15      11:38:36 ?       0:00 lpNewt
root      668      246      7       12:24:53 pts/2  0:00 grep lpNet
```

Check `/var/lp/logs/lpNet` for messages like "could not connect" and make sure listen services are running on the server for whichever types of print clients, SVR4, or BSD you have. You can run sacadm -1 on the print server to check the status of the port monitor. As you can see here, the listen service is running.

```
# sacadm -1

PMTAG     PNMTYPE    FLGS    RCNT    STATUS     COMMAND

tcp       listen     -       999     ENABLED    /usr/lib/saf/listen tcp #

zsmon     ttymon     -       0       ENABLED    /usr/lib/saf/ttymon #
```

You can also use the pmadm -1 command to make sure the print monitor is listening for requests from the lp print service as shown here.

```
# pmadm -1

PMTAG    PMTYPE    SVCTAG    FLGHS    ID      <PMSPECIFIC>

tcp      listen    lp        -        root    - - p - /var/spool/lp/fifos/listenS5 #
```

Check the file /etc/lp/Systems for remote hosts added by the lpsystem command. The entries should look like this:

```
farhostbsd:x:-:bsd:-:n:10:-:-:
```

If you do not find an entry for the particular host, use the lpsystem command to add it. Examples for both types of print clients are shown below.

```
# lpsystem -t bsd pointhope
# lpsystem -t s5 barrow
```

8.10.10   Check for printer faults

It may be that your printer stopped because of a fault. If its fault recovery option specifies to wait, you must enable the printer to get it to print again.

If, after repairing the problem, you realize that you might have had a much easier time if printer alerts had been sent to the right person, use the lpadmin command to reset the alert. Mail to root might not be as effective as a console message. Determine what works best for you.

```
# lpadmin -p scribe -A 'write root'
# lpadmin -p scribe -A 'mail slee' -W 5
```

8.11   Summary

Most of what the system administrator needs to do to configure and manage printers can be done through Print Manager within AdminTool. At the same time, it is important for systems administrators to have a basic understanding of the print subsystem and the files and directories that it uses.

9

Managing
Resource
Sharing

One of the primary advantages of a network is the opportunity that it presents for sharing a wide variety of resources, including data, applications, and peripherals, among a group of users.

The network-based file systems available in Solaris 2.x include both NFS and RFS. Both are implemented as file system types. Although NFS, the network file system, and RFS, for remote file sharing, both have very similar functionality, they differ in some respects and each has its own advantages. We will not discuss RFS per se in this chapter. Instead, we will discuss the common set of commands for administering both NFS and RFS resources; this is called the *distributed file system* (DFS; not to be confused with DCE DFS).

NFS has become a standard for sharing file systems over a network and runs on a variety of systems. RFS also allows sharing of resources, including files, devices, and named pipes between different computers on the network. For both these file system types, the administrator of a particular host can select what is to be shared and then add it to a list of shared resources. At many sites, the system administrator will manage this sharing of resources for the entire network. From the point of view of each host, you can select from these shared resources what you want to use from other systems.

In order to avoid the complexities of having system administrators learn two separate command sets for the two different file system types, DFS was developed. DFS provides a single set of commands that works with both NFS and RFS.

DFS allows you to access remote resources and to share resources from your local disk. You may elect to share files using NFS, RFS, or both in order to take advantage of different services that each provides.

9.1   Sharing Files

In order to share files with other users, you both need to share the files and to advertise that this sharing has been enabled. Instead of the `exportfs` and `adv` commands that prior versions of NFS and RFS use, a single command `share` makes a resource available to other systems.

The command `share /usr/local` is an example of the simplest type of share command. This command allows the `/usr/local` file system to be mounted by any host. It uses the default file system type which, in most cases will be NFS and places no restrictions on the mount, which means that it can be mounted read/write. The corresponding mount command on the host taking advantage of this shared resource is `mount boson:/usr/local /usr/local`.

To mount a shared file system, you need to be superuser and to have a mount point (i.e., a directory) as shown in the example below. Once a file system is mounted, whether it is NFS or RFS, it will look and act as though it is a local file system. In this example, we also unmount the file system, leaving only an empty file which identifies the directory as a mount point.

```
fermion# mkdir /usr/local
fermion# touch /usr/local/"File system is not mounted"
fermion# mount boson:/usr/local /usr/local
...
fermion# unmount /usr/local
fermion# ls /usr/local
File system is not mounted
```

The `share` command can also be issued with restrictions limiting which hosts you will share the directory with and whether the hosts which mount the shared resource will have read-only or read/write access. An optional description field is also available with the share command for those less-than-obvious directory names:

```
boson# share -F nfs -o rw /usr/local/forsale -d "items for sale"
```

Options to the `share` command include

`rw`	Mountable read/write by any host
`ro`	Mountable read-only by any host
`rw=boson: fermion`	To be shared only with specified hosts; these can mount the resource read/write
`ro=boson: fermion`	To be shared only with specified hosts; these can mount the resource read-only
`ro, rw=boson`	Mountable read-only by all hosts, but mountable read/write by boson
`root=boson: fermion`	Only root from the specified hosts will have root access (others treated as nobody)

anon=UID	UID becomes effective UID assigned to root from unknown hosts
secure	Hosts must use AUTH_DES authentication to mount
kerberos	Hosts must use kerberos authentication to mount

The share command, without any arguments, will show you what file systems and directories are being shared. If you are sharing a file system already, you do not need to further share directories within it since subscribers can elect to mount the entire directory or only part of it.

```
boson# share
- /usr/local rw " "
```

The unshare command turns sharing off. This command, however, requires an argument. You can unshare a specific resource with unshare as in the following command. As you can see from the example below, once the resource is unshared, nothing is shared:

```
boson# unshare /usr/local
boson# share
boson#
```

File systems that you wish to share on a "permanent" basis can be included in the /etc/dfs/dfstab file and will be automatically shared when your system boots or, more specifically, when it enters run level 3 (or run level 2 for NFS).

The shareall command can be used to share all file systems specified in the dfstab file or in any file with the same format. If, for example, you have a set of directories that you mount whenever you produce your monthly accounting, you can include the mount commands for these in a file that is formatted like the dfstab file and mount them with a shareall command that looks like the following:

```
boson# shareall acctgfiles
```

where acctgfiles contains the share commands:

```
share -F rfs -o ro /usr/acctg/statements
share -F nfs -o ro /usr/acctg/data
```

The shareall command can also be used to selectively mount file systems by type from the dfstab or dfstab-like files. When you specify a file system type with the shareall command, it will mount only file systems of that type from the specified file.

The command boson# shareall -F nfs acctgfiles would mount the data directory only from the above example. Without the specified file, the command would mount all nfs files listed in dfstab.

The unshare command corresponding to the `shareall` command is `unshareall`. Like `shareall`, this command can be limited to unsharing file systems of a given type. The commands below illustrate this difference:

```
boson# unshareall
boson# unshareall -F nfs
```

9.2   DFS Files

Files that are used by the distributed file sharing system include the following:

`/etc/dfs/fstypes`	Registers the distributed file system packages that are installed on your system
`/etc/dfs/dfstab`	Lists the resources that you want to automatically share
`/etc/vfstab`	Lists the resources that you mount, automatically or on demand
`/etc/dfs/sharetab`	List the currently shared resources from your host
`/etc/mnttab`	Lists the currently mounted resources on your host

9.3   DFS Commands

All the DFS commands have a very similar and simple syntax, which is:

```
dfscommand -F type -o options arguments
```

The DFS commands are organized into pairs of opposites.

`share`	Share a resource, with restrictions if needed
`unshare`	Stop sharing a resource
`shareall`	Share all resources specified in `/etc/dfs/dfstab` or a specified file
`unshareall`	Stop sharing all resources, by `fstype` if specified
`mount`	Mount a specific resource
`umount`	Umount a specific resource
`mountall`	Mount all resources specified in `/etc/vfstab` or a file in `vfstab` file format
`umountall`	Umount all mounted file systems, by `fstype` if specified
`dfshares`	List available shared resources from remote or local systems
`dfmounts`	Lists the local resources that are shared along with the clients of this resource sharing

9.4   Automounter

Automatic mounting of file systems in Solaris 2.3 and later makes use of a new kernel virtual file system called `autofs`. Together with the automount daemon, `automountd`, `autofs` provides a responsive and dynamic automatic file system.

Users will not need to differentiate automounted file systems from statically mounted or local file systems.

The automounter mounts file systems in the background as they are needed and subsequently unmounts them when they have not been used for some period of time (the default is 5 min). Without requiring anything more than move into a particular directory, Automounter simplifies the system administrator's task of keeping file systems available for users on their network. Automounting also saves network resources by reducing the NFS overhead. File systems are not mounted when they are not required. As a consequence, the overall NFS load is significantly reduced.

When home directories are mounted using automounting, they will not unmount automatically as long as the user is logged in, even if he is idle for days. This is because his login "occupies" the mount. As with mounting through the /etc/vfstab file, file systems that are automounted will not unmount if they are busy.

Automounter is best suited to mounting file systems that are needed only occasionally on a particular system. Home directories are an ideal candidate for automounting. If your users log into different hosts, their homes will be mounted whenever and wherever they log in. You might also automount application file systems, data partitions, and mail and calendar files. Operating system partitions (e.g., /, /usr, /usr/kvm, /usr/share), on the other hand, should always be mounted through the /etc/vfstab file.

Let's examine a typical interaction with automount. First let's list the contents of local home directory, /export/home:

```
# ls /export/home
aeasley johng lost+found slee
```

We see that there are three directories, plus the lost+found directory (used by fsck) which identifies that this is the base of a file system. Next we look at the mount point /home and see that there is nothing mounted there:

```
# ls /home
#
```

Next, we invoke a mount simply by issuing a command to change directories and see that the home partition from the host named hbar is mounted.

```
# cd /home/hbar
# ls
fred      mom          onowa    steve    vail
james     lost+found   pete     tom
```

If we issue a change directory command to switch to /home/boson, we will see that the local home partition is also available at this location.

```
# cd /home/boson
```

```
# ls
aeasley    johng     lost+found     slee
# ls /home
boson hbar
```

Unlike earlier versions of Automounter, the somewhat confusing /tmp_mnt convention is no longer used as a base for automounted file systems. Instead, file systems are mounted "in place"; their pathnames look the same as if they were local.

9.4.1   Configuring Automounter

In maintaining the automounting database, you may have to create new maps, modify maps as you add or remove hosts and users, and share and unshare partitions to adjust to new and changing automounting requirements. How you update Automounter depends on whether you are running NIS+, running NIS, or using the /etc files. For NIS and /etc files, you will use an editor, and for NIS, you will follow this with a cd /var/yp and make auto.home. For NIS+, you will likely use AdminTool or the nistbladm command.

Automounting specifications come from a series of maps. These can be NIS+ or NIS maps or /etc files. The master map contains a list of the other maps. Automounter comes preconfigured to mount home directories. A list of maps and a list of home directories are derived from NIS+ or NIS. As shown below by the + entry, the default /etc/auto_master file specifies that the list of maps will be augmented by the contents of the NIS+ or NIS master map, if such a map exists. The format of each subsequent line of this file is

```
mount-point map-name [ mount options ]
```

The /net and /home lines refer to mount points and the map associated with each mount point. The /net map, for example, uses the host's map and provides an automatic way to mount anything from any host provided your host has the proper access to mount it (the partitions may be shared with a restricted set of clients).

```
# Master map for automounter
#
+auto_master
/net      -hosts         -nosuid
/home     auto_home
```

If we are running NIS+ and our auto_master map contains a reference to an additional automount map which we have created (e.g., auto_data1), the /data1 autofs mount point will be created along with the /net and /home mount points.

In the niscat example shown below, this is the case. The /etc/auto_master file on the NIS+ master would contain these same lines, while the clients would likely contain only the default entries.

```
# niscat auto_master.org_dir
+auto_master
/net        -hosts          -nosuid
/home       auto_home
/data1      auto_data1
```

If we are running NIS, we have a very similar setup. We would use the `ypcat auto.master` command to list the master map.

9.4.1.1 Automounting home directories.

Automounter can be used to mount home partitions, as was shown on p. 167, or individual home directories. Thus, you have control on whether to mount an individual's files. Automount entries for home directories and individual users will be different as shown in the lines below.

```
boson       boson:/export/home
hbar        hbar:/export/home
sor         sor:/export/home
fred        hbar:/export/home/&
johng       hbar:/export/home/&
jones       sor:/export/home/&
slee        boson:/export/home/&
```

The difference between the two approaches is whether the entire home partition is mounted or simply the individual's home. If user jones logs onto `boson`, we will either mount `sor:/export/home` or `sor:/export/home/jones` depending on which approach we take in configuring our automount maps. Further, Jones's home directory will either be mounted as `/home/sor/jones` or as `/home/jones` in accordance with the particular approach (since the key is used in creating the mount point).

Clearly, mounting individual home directories requires more work on your part, since each user will need an automount map entry. On the other hand, you can easily fold this requirement into any script that you use to create and remove home directories. If you use admintool, there is a check box for auto-home setup.

9.4.1.2 Automounting shared directories.

Invoking a mount within `/net` is the same as invoking an automount of a home directory. We change directories into a directory which will require mounting:

```
boson# cd /net/hbar
boson# ls
cdrom       export       scratch       usr       var
boson#
boson# ls export
data1       exec        home
```

```
boson# ls scratch
bentley    jackal       letters     netstats    traffic
gmj        lost+found   monotony    steve
```

All the exported partitions which we are allowed to mount are now mounted. If we were to compare this list of directories with a sorted list of file systems exported from the referenced host, we would see that it corresponds:

```
hbar# more /etc/exports | sort | awk '{print $1}'
#
/cdrom
/export/data1
/export/exec/kvm/sun4c.sunos.4.1.3
/export/exec/kvm/sun4m.sunos.4.1.3
/export/exec/sun4.sunos.4.1.3
/export/home
/scratch
/usr
/usr/X11R5
/usr/lang
/usr/local
/var/spool/calendar
/var/spool/mail
```

In fact, autofs follows a similar procedure when you access a /net directory. It first pings the specific host. It then requests a list of the shared-file systems, sorts the resultant list, and proceeds down the sorted list mounting each file system. Even if we use only one of the file systems on hbar, all of them are mounted. For this reason, a mount through /net is less efficient than a mount through a more specific automount map, unless, of course, you require a good portion of the directories which are mounted.

9.4.2 Types of automount maps

There are two basic types of automount maps—direct and indirect. Lines in either type of map have the same general syntax:

```
key [ mount options ] location
```

but the look of the key field is quite different with direct and indirect maps. For direct maps, the key field is the full pathname of the mount point. For indirect maps, it is a simple name representing the autofs mount point.

The auto_home map is an example of an indirect map. The simple keys like fred and boson give this away. Direct maps, on the other hand, have keys like /usr/X11R5 or /var/spool/news. The difference is also expressed in the way the file systems are mounted. Indirect mounts generally reflect the mapname.

Our `auto_data1` map, for example, which was defined with the `auto_master` entry:

```
/data1 auto_data1
```

is used to mount file systems it contains as `/data1/boson`, `/data1/hbar`, and so forth. Direct maps, on the other hand, are used to mount file systems using whatever pathnames are specified. Most applications and data files are mounted using direct maps.

If you make changes to a master map or a direct map, you have to run the automount command to effect the changes. Changes to indirect maps, however, will occur right away.

9.4.3   Alternate-source specifications

Automounter maps can specify alternate locations for a given file system. This can be a valuable feature when you are designing a network for reliability. An alternate source for application or data files, for example, can provide continuous service when the primary source is unavailable. Alternate sources for file systems do not make a lot of sense when applied to file systems which your users will update; they would not know, at any particular time, where their files were being written.

Alternate mount locations are specified as a list of locations, each of which consists of a hostname and pathname. If all of the hosts store the mountable files in the same location, that location can be specified once with the alternate hosts specified in a comma-separated strong. An example of this syntax is

```
/usr/local -ro hbar,boson,sor,gauss:/usr/local
```

Additionally, a weight can be specified so that preferred mounts are attempted first. The syntax above lists equally likely mounts. The syntax

```
/usr/local -ro hbar,boson,sor(1),gauss(2):/usr/local
```

on the other hand, gives highest priority (priority 0 is the default and is highest) to `hbar` and `boson` with descending priority to `sor` and `gauss`. Regardless of assigned weighting, however, the proximity of the server to the host determines the actual priority. NFS will attempt to use the nearest location on the network. Your assigned weights will be used only if the servers are about the same distance in network time from the client. Servers which are separated from the client by bridges or gateways, for example, will not be selected if a server on the same subnet is available.

9.4.4   Multiple mounts

You can also ensure that several mounts occur together by joining them into a single map entry. This can be important, for example, if you are mounting an applications directory and certain collections of data or configuration files will be needed for the application to work.

Multiple mounts are best expressed using the continuation character \ to separate each entry in the multiple mount entry. An example of this syntax is

```
/apps/maps -ro \
   /rasters         hbar:/export/data1/images \
   /mapicons        boson:/export/data1/mapicons \
   /xmap            boson:/usr/local/bin/xmap
```

This example specifies three separate mounts that are required to occur together. The three resultant mounts, /apps/maps/raster, /apps/maps/mapicons, and /apps/maps/xmap, are read-only and are derived from two servers. If you wanted different mount options for the three mounts, you could put the mount options on the three separate lines rather than the first one.

```
/apps/maps -ro \
   /rasters         hbar,boson:/export/data1/images \
   /mapicons        hbar,boson:/export/data1/mapicons \
   /xmap            hbar,boson:/usr/local/bin/xmap
```

Here, we have almost the same situation, except that the file systems will be mounted from whichever host is nearest and responds first.

9.4.5   Automount map variables

You can create automount map entries that use variables to substitute for a number of architecture- or OS-specific differences to help in the mixed environment. For example, if you maintain two versions of an application, one for your sun4 systems and one for your sun4m systems, your automount map entry could use the ARCH variable so that each client mounts the correct version. That entry might look like this:

```
/apps/sigproc/bin -ro hbar:/apps/sigproc/bin/$ARCH
```

Other automount map variables include CPU, HOST, OSNAME, OSREL, and OSVERS. Each of these is derived from the associated uname command. The ARCH variable is derived from /usr/kvm/arch.

9.4.6   Starting and stopping automount

Automounter starts automatically at boot time (when you enter run level 2) and can also be started on the command line. The startup file, /etc/init.d/autofs, is a shell script and can be run with start and stop arguments. If you want to change the default timeout for unmounting automounted file systems, this is the place to do it. The command /usr/sbin/automount has an optional -t as well as a verbose option -v.

The `/etc/auto_master` file is read at boot time when all the `autofs` mount points specified within this file and in the referenced NIS+ or NIS `auto_master` map are created. The mount points created by automount look like traditional mount points (i.e., empty directories). However, the kernel recognizes them as mount points and will not permit you to remove them with a `rmdir` command. If you remove the references to these mount points through your automount files and maps and run the automount command, Automounter will remove the mount points that are no longer required.

9.4.7   When file systems won't mount

A user who attempts to use an automounted directory that doesn't exist, is not shared (or exported) with that user's system, or is not included in the automount map, will get a `No such file or directory` message as shown below.

```
boson# cd /data1/seren
boson# ls
3c273        lilly1        n1068        vflatEs.hhd
vflatEs_4.r6d
gtopar       lost+found    n5548        vflatEs.hhh
vflatEs_4.r6h
boson# cd /data1/dipity
/data1/dipity: No such file or directory
```

Therefore, if a few of your users complain that a directory they believe they should be seeing is not mounting, the following commands should pinpoint the problem. In this example, `data1` is the automount map and `dipity` is the name of the host.

1. Does the file system exist?

```
dipity# ls -ld /dipity/data1
drwxr-xr-x 18 root 512 Nov 4 15:36 /dipity/data1
```

2. Is the file system included in the automount map?

For NIS+:

```
boson# niscat auto_data1.org_dir | grep dipity
dipity dipity:/dipity/data1
```

For NIS:

```
boson# ypcat -k auto.data1 | grep dipity
dipity dipity:/dipity/data1
```

3. Does the client have permission to mount it?

For Solaris 2.x servers:

```
dipity# share | grep data1
/dipity/data1 ro=hbar:gauss "data files"
```

For SunOS 4.1.x servers:

```
dipity# exportfs | grep data1
/export/data1 -access=dept
```

4. Check if the automount daemon is running.

```
boson# ps -ef | grep auto
root 126 1 80 Jan 01? 0:06 /usr/lib/autofs/automountd
boson# ps -aux | grep auto
root 139 0.0 0.6 296 200 ? S Nov 26 25:29 automount /net -hosts
```

9.4.8 References

Consult the man pages for these commands:

```
automount
automountd
```

Search Answerbook using the following terms:

```
autofs
automount
```

9.5 Summary

As Sun used to say, "The Network *is* the Computer." Considering Solaris 2.x's utilities for mounting file systems over networks with increasingly less user intervention, this statement is becoming increasingly true. The mount commands, Automounter, and Volume Manager (discussed in Chap. 3) allow you to manage these shared resources.

10

Managing Backup

Backing up file systems is one of the most common and the most boring tasks that a system administrator is responsible for. Backups preserve the hard work of your users and are, therefore, very important. In truth, however, backups are rarely used. The best strategy for doing backups is to do them regularly, but implement them so that they take as little effort as possible.

Today's peripherals have made possible a giant step toward this goal. With a number of fairly inexpensive tape devices that can store tens of gigabytes of data, most of the manual labor of doing backups is gone. In addition, modern backup software provides an easy-to-use interface to most of the backup commands, often permitting end users to help desk attendees retrieve backed up files without the need for a UNIX wizard.

10.1 Backup Issues

In addition to the concern that backups not require a lot of manual intervention, there are a number of other concerns that you should weigh in planning your backup strategy. Changing media, even if only once a day or once a week, means training yourself to act like cron. In addition, you need to label media or develop some type of cataloging technique so that you know what's on each backup. If you are sequencing through a series of tapes to meet your monthly backup schedule, it is easy to overwrite one backup with another simply by forgetting to change the tape or inserting the wrong tape in the drive.

Another concern is that backing up a mounted partition introduces a risk that some files will be incorrectly backed up because they are volatile while in use. At the same time, unmounting systems to avoid this risk means that you must tolerate some system downtime while backups are in progress.

Backups and restores are also slow. Fetching a file that was inadvertently removed might require loading several tapes and spending considerable time looking through the contents to find the latest copy of the lost file.

We will address some of these issues as we get into the Solaris 2.x backup commands and some of the features of modern backup software.

10.2   Tape Device Names

The device naming scheme for tapes in Solaris 2.x includes a logical device number, optional density, and optional features (e.g., to rewind or not). Without a density indicator, high density is assumed.

The naming scheme for tape devices follows this format:

```
/dev/rmt/#do
```

where

\#   The logical devices number

d   The optional density

o   An optional feature

The device `/dev/rmt/0` is the first tape device and is equivalent to saying `/dev/rmt/0h`. Adding an n would invoke the no-rewind option. Preceding this name with a hostname, as in `boson:/dev/rmt/0n`, specifies a tape drive on a remote host.

These naming conventions apply whether the tape is a nine-track, QIC cartridge, or an 8-mm exabyte drive.

10.3   The `ufsdump` Command

The `ufsdump` command backs up a complete file system. Like the `dump` command in 4.x systems, `ufsdump` is best run when the file system to be backed up is not in use. Otherwise, there is some risk that files will be in a state of change when they are being backed up and some corruption can ensue. To reduce the likelihood of this, you can change the run state of the system with the `init` command. The command `init 0` or `init s` puts the system in single-user mode. Clearly, you should provide warnings to any users who may be logged in or using the system before doing this.

The `ufsdump` command can be used to make full backups (i.e., all files) or can create incremental backups. The dump level ranges from 0 to 9. A level 0 dump will back up a file system in its entirety, regardless of any previous dumps. Dump levels 1 to 9, on the other hand, will dump all files which have been modified since the last dump at a lower level. Notice that these dump levels have meaning only in relationship to other dumps; this point can be confusing.

If you make a 0 level dump of your server's home partition every Sunday night and then a level 5 dump every Monday through Friday night, each of these level 5 dumps will contain an increasingly large collection of files—namely, all files which have been modified since the backup on Sunday.

The monthly dump schedule which is most frequently suggested, and is contained in the man page for the `ufsdump` command, is shown below. Each level 3 dump contains all of the files modified since the full (level 0) dump on the first Sunday of the month. Similarly, each level 5 dump contains all files modified since the full dump or the preceding level 3 dump. Using this scheme means that you will have "extra" copies of files on the level 3 and level 5 dumps. For example, a file modified on the Monday following the full dump will be contained in the subsequent four dumps regardless of whether it is further modified. However, the schedule also reduces the number of dumps that you will have to use to restore a file. Any file removed during the week will be available on the previous day's dump.

	Sun	Mon	Tue	Wed	Thu	Fri
Week 1	Full	5	5	5	5	3
Week 2		5	5	5	5	3
Week 3		5	5	5	5	3
Week 4		5	5	5	5	5

Each dump (Monday through Friday) in the weekly schedule shown below, on the other hand, would contain only those files modified since the previous day's backup.

	Sun	Mon	Tue	Wed	Thu	Fri
Week X	Full	5	6	7	8	9

The dumps would be significantly smaller, but you might have to look through several day's dumps to find a file removed during the week.

The format of the `ufsdump` command is

```
ufsdump [0-9][abcdDflnosStuvwW] /dev/rmt/# /dev/dsk/c#t#d#s#
```

where you select a number from 0 to 9 to indicate the backup level (0 is highest) and # represents a number. The string of options includes some that are mutually exclusive—the c and D commands, which represent cartridge and diskette, respectively, are clear examples. A likely dump command is

```
ufsdump 0cuf /dev/rmt/0 /dev/dsk/c0t0d0s7
```

If you are following standard disk partitioning, this command will do a complete backup of your /export/home file system to a cartridge tape. The u causes the /etc/dumpdates file to be updated; this is a very useful option since it keeps the most recent dump dates for each file system at each dump level. The f indicates that the following argument is the tape device to be used.

The `ufsdump` command will require manual intervention if there are errors or the end of the media volume is encountered. The `ufsdump` command also checkpoints at the start of each subsequent tape volume so that it can be restarted if one tape in a series is defective. Multivolume dumps are less common as higher-density devices are used for backup. However, `ufsdump` is capable of using as many volumes as are required to dump a file system and checkpoints in between to minimize the volumes that must be redone if media fail.

Files backed up with the `ufsdump` command are restored with `ufsrestore`. This command can restore entire dumps or can be used interactively. Interactively, the command provides a directory structure that you can navigate with `cd` and `add`, `delete`, and `extract` commands to select the files you want to restore and begin the process.

10.4   Backing Up with `tar` and `cpio`

The `tar` and `cpio` commands can also be used to back up and restore files. These commands are generally used on select sets of files rather than complete file systems. Of these, the tar command is more appropriate for copying files and subdirectories from a single location. The `cpio` command, on the other hand, is better when you are selecting random files and packs the files more efficiently. It is also able to skip over bad spots in the media. The `cpio` command is also able to create headers in several other formats, notably `bar`, `crc`, `odc`, `tar`, and `ustart`; this feature is important if you are creating tapes for vastly different systems.

10.4.1   The `tar` Command

To back up a set of files with tar, a command like the following is used. This command will back up all files in the current directory:

```
boson% tar cvf /dev/rmt/0 .
```

The `c` option specifies that we are creating the tape. The `v` specifies verbose mode and causes the `tar` command to provide a line for each file that it writes to the tape. The `tar` command can also be used with wildcards or a series of filenames. The commands `tar cvf /dev/rmt/0 data*` and `tar cvf /dev/rmt/0 .login .cshrc .logout` back up all files and directories starting with `data` and local `CShell` configuration files respectively.

The `tar` command can also be used to extract from tape. Replacing the `c` option with an `x` reads the same files off the backup. With no files specified, `tar` reads the entire tape.

The `tar` command does not have to be used with an actual tape device. It can be used to read and write files to or from an online `tarfile` by using a filename in place of the device name. As an example, the command `tar cvf data.tar data*` creates a `tarfile` called `data.tar` containing all files beginning with `data`. If you then compress the resultant `tarfile`, you have a fairly efficient way for your users to back up their personal files in their own file space. Clearly this doesn't guard against unlikely disk failures, but it safeguards against inadvertent overwrites of currently volatile files.

The `tar` command also provides one of the more convenient ways to copy groups of files or entire directories from place to place on your system or between systems. The benefit of this approach over `copy` or `move` commands is that original ownership and permissions of the files are retained. In addition, symbolic links do not resolve into the files that they point to, but are copied as

symbolic links. The command (cd ../data; tar cpBf - *) | tar xvpBf
- copies all files from a sister directory called data into the current directory.
Unlike the ufsdump command, tar does not read or write multiple volumes.

10.4.2 The cpio Command

The cpio command is very similar to tar, but provides the ability to span volumes, prompting for additional volumes as needed. Typically, cpio is used to
read a file list from standard input, although you can specify a list of files on
the command line. The command ls data* | cpio -oc>savedata copies all
files beginning with data to the file savedata. To store these same files on
tape, the command would be ls data* | -oc>/dev/rmt/0.

The c in these commands, by the way, is not the same as the c used with tar.
The cpio command reads or writes according to the direction of your I/O redirect. To extract files backed up with cpio and to verify correct operation of a
cpio backup, you simply reverse the direction of the I/O. To verify correct operation of the cpio command, add the t option (table of contents).

```
boson% cpio -civt < savedata
```

10.5 Tricks Using Find

Both the tar and cpio commands lend themselves to being cleverly used to
back up files. The command below looks for files which have changed within
the last day and backs them up to a file called find . -atime -1 -print /
cpio -oc > data.cpio.

Another use of find with cpio is to copy directory trees much as we did with
the tar command a couple sections earlier. A sample command to copy files in
the current directory (including subdirectories) into a sister directory called
savedata is find . -print -depth | cpio -pd ../savedata.

10.6 Using TapeTool

The OpenWindows TapeTool allows you to easily read or to list files which have
been written to tape using the tar command. It also simplifies creation of tar
backups since it allows the user to drag files from File Manager into the
TapeTool window to back them up.

The List..., Read, Write, and Props... buttons take the place of command options. List... performs a tar -t operation. You can then select files with your
mouse and use the menu under the Read button to read selected files or everything on the tape. The tool also allows you to type in filenames in the File to
Write: field or to drag them into the tool. The Write button will be enabled
(i.e., darkened) when you have selected files to write using one of these techniques.

The Props... button brings up a form which allows you to select the particular tape device to use as well as a hostname for copying remote files. It also includes additional options for the write request, including the ability to strip

the path of all files or files from certain directories so that these files can be read back into any directory. The Props... form also allows you to exclude SCCS and SCCS+ directories, specify a blocking factor, follow symbolic links so that the actual files are backed up, display errors when such links cannot be resolved, and suppress information related to ownership and file permissions (for portability).

The Props... form also provides some options related to reading files. You can choose to ignore checksum errors, prevent the read from changing the file modification times of files it reads, and restore files to their original permissions despite current umask settings.

Finally, the Props... form Other: settings allow you to specify that the tape operation exits on the first error, and the exclude setting lets you specify a file that contains a list of files and/or directories to be excluded from the read operation.

10.7   Features of Good Backup Software

Solaris 2.x commands to backup and retrieve file systems and files are powerful and extremely versatile. At the same time, they require a good degree of expertise to use successfully. Modern backup software with pushbutton interfaces provide clear advantages for the casual user. The TapeTool answers some of these objections by providing menus and buttons as well as a drag and drop operation to facilitate reading and writing files. For most applications, the default settings are fine and users will not even have to delve into the possible options at their disposal.

Modern backup software for system-level backups, on the other hand, should include these options as well as the ability to do incremental backups and safeguard against accidental overwrites. It should keep fairly detailed and useful indexes of your backups to provide accurate and easy to understand views into your backed up files.

Good backup software should work over your network allowing you to easily back up file systems from any network host to the tape drive of your choice, whether this is a single-cartridge tape or a unit with multiple 8-mm drives. It should be able to run unmanned under most circumstances, requiring only the swapping of media and minor labeling. It should also provide some means of version control so that you can differentiate versions of backed up files and restore the one that meets your requirement.

10.8   Summary

We've examined in this chapter some of the features of good backup software and Solaris 2.x commands backing up and restoring files. The man (manual) pages for the tar, ufsdump, and cpio commands contain additional information. Look for information on TapeTool in AnswerBook.

11

Administering
Software
Packages

All bundled and unbundled software for Solaris 2.x is distributed in the form of software packages. Software packages are groupings of files which represent a particular function or application. The man pages, for example, are implemented as a software package and all files which constitute the man pages are loaded when you add this package to a system.

Software packaging offers several significant advantages over traditional software installation strategies by enhancing the system administrator's control over what software is loaded on their systems. In addition, this software packaging, which provides commands for configuring, listing, installing, and deinstalling software, is common across the installed base of SVR4 UNIX systems.

To cite examples of the benefits of software packaging is easy. Most system administrators will remember having installed software and finding out that there was no way to tell later on where all its files went. Just as likely, they will remember wondering where all files located within a particular directory came from. System and application software was difficult, if not impossible, to deinstall reliably for these reasons. Further, determining what software was installed on a given system was generally a matter of elaborate record keeping, mental notes, or guesswork. Software packaging has done away with this entire class of problems.

Package administration maintains a view of what software is loaded and where it is loaded by keeping extensive logs that can be queried by the systems administrator and the package administration commands. These logs also detail file ownership and permissions and can be used to determine when permissions have changed, sometimes a great aid in diagnosing problems with applications.

In Solaris 2.x, software packages are loaded, deinstalled, and queried through a series of commands or tools built specifically to make the job of managing software packages extremely straightforward.

11.1   Configuration Clusters

Solaris 2.x contains over 70 software packages. These packages are organized into four configuration clusters to facilitate installing systems at one of four levels of basic functionality. These four clusters are not mutually exclusive but progressively inclusive as illustrated in Fig. 11.1. The four configuration clusters, in ascending order of completeness, are

Core—enough software to boot the system and run Solaris

End user—software most needed by end users, e.g., OpenWindows and Deskset

Developer—developer support except for unbundled compiler and developer tools

Entire distribution—everything

You have a choice during installation to install any of these four clusters. Depending on the size of the disk, the intended use and user, and availability of software from other systems on your network, you can elect to install anywhere from just the basics to the entire distribution. You can also, within each of these categories, elect to omit selected packages. For example, you might want most of the software distribution but know that you will never be using uucp. You can select, during installation, to omit the packages that make up uucp, or you can selectively remove them later.

A general scheme for software package configuration is illustrated in Fig. 11.2.

11.2   Software Categories

Software packages are grouped into categories of related software. All the Solaris software related to graphics, for example, is grouped into a category called *graphics*. Software categories, unlike configuration clusters, are mutually exclusive. Do the Try This exercise to list the software categories which are represented on your system. The pkginfo command will be covered in Sec. 11.4.1.

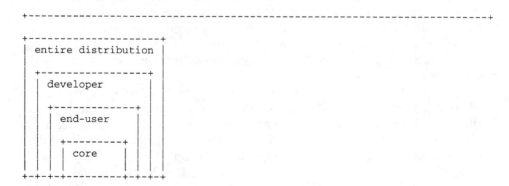

Figure 11.1   Configuration clusters.

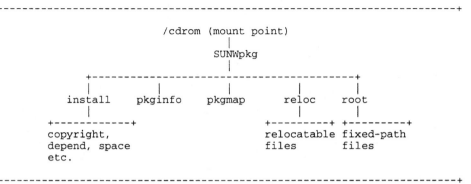

Figure 11.2 Software package configuration.

TRY THIS   List Software Categories

```
# pkginfo | awk '{print $1}' | sort | uniq
```

SPARCompile

Application

Graphics

Library

System

In this example, we are listing software packages, selecting only the first column of output, sorting on this column (the category), and then printing the name of each software category ($1) that is encountered only once (uniq). The number of software categories you will see depends on how your system was installed and how much application software has been added since.

It is important, at this point, to reemphasize the distinction between package categories and configuration clusters. The software categories which we just listed in the Try This exercise represent major system functionality with a very coarse granularity, while configuration clusters represent four major levels of functionality. Any software package will belong to a single software category but may be included in anywhere from one to all four configuration clusters.

TRY THIS   Count Software Packages by Category

In this exercise, create an awk procedure by entering the lines above the dashes into a file (it doesn't need to be executable). Below the dashes, we display the command that you should use to invoke the script and the results on a sample system.

```
# count: count groups of lines with same first field
#
```

```
BEGIN {PREV = ""
COUNT=0}
{
if (($1 !=PREV) && (NR>1)) {
print PREV, COUNT
COUNT=1
}
else
++COUNT
PREV=$1
}
END { print PREV, COUNT }
------
# pkginfo | sort | awk -f count
SPARCompile 5
application 7
graphics 6
library 1
system 60
```

You can see from the preceding Try This that most of the software packages which comprise Solaris are in the "system" category. Each of the other four categories has broken out a separate functionality, such as the packaging of graphics routines into a graphics category. You can also see that the system on which this command was executed has an unbundled compiler which has added packages to both the SPARCompile and application categories.

The awk script, which depends on sorted input, simply counts the number of entries beginning with the same first field (the software category).

11.3 The Solaris Software Package

A software package in Solaris 2.x is the collection of files and directories that comprise a particular function or application. Some system utilities are separated into a number of packages. The uucp utility, for example, is made up of two software packages, one which includes the configuration files that belong in the root file system (the /etc/uucp files), and another which includes the uucp commands and scripts (the /usr/lib/uucp files). There are two formats that a software package will assume with regard to distribution media, each of which is appropriate to the particular medium on which it is distributed. Packages distributed on tape or diskette use a datastream format while software packages distributed on CD-ROM are usually stored in a fixed directory structure format that is a ufs file system.

Software packaging also implies a certain directory and file structure that supports its uniform installation and deinstallation. The pkgadd command, discussed in Sec. 11.4, is able to transfer efficiently the contents of a software package from the distribution media to a system and later deinstall it, because the regular configuration of the software on the distribution media facilitates installation and deinstallation.

To understand the concept of a software package, it is useful to have a picture of the directory structure with which a package is constructed. Each software package includes a number of subdirectories, some of which are optional. Figure 11.2 illustrates a typical software package layout.

11.3.1 The `install` directory

The `install` directory contains optional files and scripts that are used during installation of the software package. Examples of such files are the copyright notice, the space file which details additional space requirements for the software, and the depend file which contains lines which specify what other software the package requires, is incompatible with, or which depends on it. Scripts you might find included in the install directory might include request scripts which request installer input, class-action scripts that define what happens with a group of objects (files), and procedure scripts that define what should be done during different stages in the installation process. Changes in the ownership and permissions of files are likely to be found in procedure scripts. In the lines below, three files, which have been located in their new home (referred to by the variable $ABHOME), are subsequently given the correct ownership and permissions.

```
chmod 755 $ABHOME/answerbook
chown bin $ABHOME/answerbook
chgrp bin $ABHOME/answerbook
```

11.3.1.1 The `depend` file. The `depend` file will list software package dependencies. This information is used during software installation and removal. For example, if you are about to remove software that is required by another package, the `pkgrm` command will warn you about this problem. The `depend` file will contain lines such as

```
P SUNWowrqd OpenWindows required core package
P SUNWowoft OpenWindows optional fonts
```

In this example, the P indicates a software prerequisite. An I would indicate incompatible software, and an R would indicate a reverse dependency (other software depends on this software).

11.3.1.2 The `copyright` file. The `copyright` file contains the copyright notice for the software and is usually displayed during installation.

11.3.1.3 The `response` file. Some software packages might be supplied with their own `response` file to support optional noninteractive installation. If you want to take advantage of the `response` file provided with a software package, use the -r option with the pkgadd command as shown below. In this example, the software package is on CD ROM.

```
# pkgadd -d /cdrom -r /cdrom/SUNW pkg/install/response SUNW pkg
```

The process of creating response files is discussed in Sec. 11.4.7.

11.3.1.4 Other files. Various other files may also be included in the install directory. Often scripts executed after installation or removal are included. Space requirements for additional files may appear. As mentioned earlier, a request script may be provided.

TRY THIS   List Contents of a Software Package install Directory

```
# ls -l /cdrom/SUNWpkg/install
total 390
-rw-r—r— 1 sys sys 2582 Nov 5 16:14 copyright
-rw-r—r— 1 sys sys 1007 Nov 5 16:14 depend
-rw-r—r— 1 sys sys 4405 Nov 5 16:17 postinstall
-rw-r—r— 1 sys sys 751 Nov 5 16:17 postremove
-rw-r—r— 1 sys sys 7158 Nov 5 16:17 request
```

11.3.2   The pkginfo file

The pkginfo file included in each package identifies the software package in considerable detail. You can see the kind of information that is included in this file in Fig. 11.3.

```
+--------------------------------------------------------------------------+
# more /cdrom/SUNWpkg/pkginfo
PKG=SUNWpkg
NAME=The Generic Solaris 2.X Software Package
ARCH=sparc
VERSION=2.4.8
CATEGORY=application
PRODNAME=Generic Solaris 2.X Application Software
PRODVERS=2.4
DESC=Generic Solaris 2.X Application -- i.e., Good Stuff
BASEDIR=/opt
CLASSES=NULL
VENDOR=The Next Page, Inc.
HOTLINE=Please call us right away
EMAIL=
MAXINST=1000
PSTAMP=abcxyz012345678901

+--------------------------------------------------------------------------+
```

Figure 11.3 Sample pkginfo file.

Package information will include the software abbreviation, full name, version, and architecture along with a lot of other information which describes the software package. The pkginfo file should not be confused with the pkginfo command.

11.3.3 The pkgmap file

The pkgmap file contains information about files belonging to the particular software application. This information is used to check the accuracy of a software package. The lines in the pkgmap file describe particular files in the software package. An example of such an entry, shown in Fig. 11.4, details a file that is intended for the bin directory of an application directory and is called getmap. The intended permissions (0644), owner and group, size, checksum, and modification time are also included.

Entries for devices files will look somewhat different and include major and minor device numbers. Refer to the man(ual) page for pkgmap for additional information on the content of this file.

11.3.4 The root and reloc directories

The root and reloc directories, if they exist, will contain object files which are loaded in a specific directory or can be relocated anywhere in the system.

Most software packages that you install, aside from the Solaris system, will contain predominantly relocatable code. Within the base directory in which you install them, they will probably have a fixed directory structure. You will have a choice, however, to load them in /opt or in another file system. Many packages will have both fixed and relocatable executables. It is not uncommon, for example, for an application to install some executables in /usr/bin or /usr/local/bin while allowing you to choose where to install the bulk of its files.

If a package is relocatable, you will be prompted during the installation for the location where you want it installed. There are some options which determine prompting during installation which will be discussed later in this chapter.

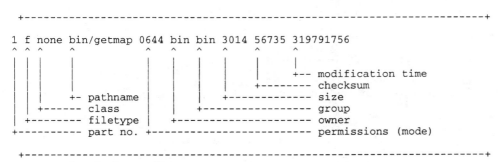

Figure 11.4 Sample pkgmap file.

11.4   Package Administration Commands

Solaris provides a series of commands that you can use to install, deinstall, and query software packages, and configure installation parameters to facilitate later installation. There is also a set of commands for software package creation.

Solaris also provides two tools which further facilitate administration of software by organizing the functionality of these commands into a single menu-oriented or graphics-user interface (GUI)-based front end. Whether the individual commands or one or the other of the tools is best for you will depend, in part, on whether you use the commands within scripts that you create (in which case, you will use the commands) or on a character-based terminal (in which case you will not use the GUI-based tool).

The software package administration commands are listed in Fig. 11.5 along with the commands for package creation and the software management tools.

11.4.1   The pkginfo command

The pkginfo command provides information in varying detail on the software that is installed on your system or resides on media which you have mounted. Combining pkginfo with UNIX utilities such as grep and awk, you can selectively retrieve a lot of valuable information from pkginfo. If you're not sure of the name of a software package, for example, you can retrieve it easily with pkginfo, grep, and a good guess.

To view packages which have been loaded on your system, use the pkginfo command. In the example below, we have piped the output of this command through more. You can see that several columns of information are provided. The first is the software category name, the second is the package name or package identifier, and the third is a textual description of the particular package.

```
+------------------------------------------------------------------------------+
Software Package Administration Commands:
pkginfo - display information about software packages
pkgchk -  validate software package
pkgadd  - transfer package to system
pkgrm   - removes a software package from the system
pkgparam- display parameters for package
pkgask  - store answers for later non-interactive installations

Software Package Creation Commands:
pkgmk   - create an installable package
pkgproto- generate prototype file entries for pkgmk
pkgtrans- translate package format, datastream <-> file system format
installf- add a file to the software installation database
removef - remove a file from the software installation database

Software Administration Tools:
swm     - a menu-oriented tool for administering software packages
swmtool - a GUI-based tool for administering software packages
+------------------------------------------------------------------------------+
```

Figure 11.5 Software administration tools and commands.

TRY THIS   List Software Packages

```
# pkginfo | more
application SUNWabe Solaris 2.1 End Use AnswerBook
system SUNWaccr System Accounting, (Root)
system SUNWaccu System Accounting, (Usr)
system SUNWadmap System & Network Administration Applications
system SUNWadmfw System & Network Administration Framework
system SUNWadmr System & Network Administration Root
system SUNWarc Archive Libraries
system SUNWast Automated Security Enhancement Tools
system SUNWaudio Audio applications
system SUNWaudmo Audio demo programs
system SUNWbcp Binary Compatibility
system SUNWbnur Networking UUCP Utilities, (Root)
system SUNWbnuu Networking UUCP Utilities, (Usr)
system SUNWbtool SPARCompilers 2.0.1 Bundled tools
system SUNWcar Core Architecture, (Root)
graphics SUNWcg12 GS (cg12) Device Driver
graphics SUNWcg12u GS (cg12) Run-time support software
system SUNWcg6 GX (cg6) Device Driver
...
```

TRY THIS   Find Package Information for UUCP

```
# pkginfo | grep UUCP
system SUNWbnur Networking UUCP Utilities, (Root)
system SUNWbnuu Networking UUCP Utilities, (Usr)
```

The pkginfo command can give you information about packages on CD as well as those already loaded on your system.

TRY THIS   Locate the Package Name for the man Pages

```
# pkginfo | grep man
system      SUNWfac      Framed Access Command Environment
system      SUNWman      On-Line Manual Pages
system      SUNWowman    OpenWindows online user man pages
system      SUNWowpmn    OpenWindows online programmers man pages
```

If you add a -d option to the pkginfo command, you can direct it to report on a particular device. The most common use of this option is illustrated below.

Here, we are requesting a list of the packages included on a CD ROM mounted on the mount point `/cdrom`. In this example, we can see that the AnswerBook CD for Solaris 2.1 is mounted.

TRY THIS   List Packages on a Mounted CD ROM

```
# pkginfo -d /cdrom
application SUNWpkg Generic Solaris 2.1 Software Application
```

The `pkginfo` command has a `-c` option which confines the response to a particular software category.

TRY THIS   List All Packages That Are Part of the Graphics Category

```
# pkginfo -c graphics
graphics SUNWcg12 GS (cg12) Device Driver
graphics SUNWcg12u GS (cg12) Run-time support software
graphics SUNWdial Buttons/Dials (bd) Streams Module
graphics SUNWdialh Buttons/Dials (bd) Header Files
graphics SUNWgt GT Device Drivers
graphics SUNWgtu GT Run-time support software
# pkginfo -c graphics | grep buttons
graphics SUNWdial Buttons/Dials (bd) Streams Module
graphics SUNWdialh Buttons/Dials (bd) Header Files
```

The `pkginfo` command has a number of other parameters. The `-l` option provides a long listing and gives the most detail on the software package. As you can see, there are a number of parameters which describe software packages which we have not yet looked at.

Refer to the man page to get a description of other `pkginfo` options.

TRY THIS   Show All Parameters Associated with a Particular Software Package

```
# pkginfo -l    SUNWman
PKGINST:        SUNWman
NAME:           On-Line Manual Pages
CATEGORY:       system
ARCH:           all
VERSION:        23.0
BASEDIR:        /usr
VENDOR:         Sun Microsystems, Inc.
DESC:           System Reference Manual Pages
PSTAMP:         windmill921020212042
```

```
INSTDATE:        Feb 02 1993 04:52
HOTLINE:         Please contact your local service provider
STATUS:          completely installed
FILES:           3223 installed pathnames
                 3 shared pathnames
                 32 directories
                 16584 blocks used (approx)
```

TRY THIS   Check for Partially Installed Software Packages (Most Likely, You Will Not Encounter Any)

```
# pkginfo -p
#
```

11.4.2   The software installation database

The package administration commands and tools maintain a database of software packages that are installed on your system. The database is stored within the /var/sadm directory. In /var/sadm/install, the contents file includes a reference to every file belonging to every software package. This file can be used in many ways to query the configuration of your system. The subdirectory /var/sadm/pkg contains a subdirectory for each package that is installed on your system. Within each of these subdirectories, you will find two directories and two files.

The install directory will usually contain the copyright notice and a copy of the depend file that we described earlier. There may be some additional files (e.g., scripts) stored here as well.

The save directory will usually be empty. The pkginfo file, which we discussed when we outlined the architecture of a software package, is stored here for later use by commands such as pkginfo.

TRY THIS   Compare Entries in contents and pkgmap Files

```
# grep banner.1 /var/sadm/install/contents
/usr/share/man/man1/banner.1 f none 0444 bin bin 456 34674 718651004
SUNWman
# grep banner.1 /var/sadm/pkg/SUNWman/pkgmap
1 f none share/man/man1/banner.1 0444 bin bin 456 34674 718651004
```

You can see that the information in each of these files is roughly the same for any particular entry. The pkgmap file, of course, contains information only concerning files for the particular software package, in this case the man pages, SUNWman. The contents file, on the other hand, contains information on files belonging to every installed application.

11.4.2.1 The contents files. The file /var/sadm/install/contents keeps
track of installed files and provides a sophisticated means of managing your
software configuration. This file is kept in sorted order; don't expect to see what
you last added at the tail end of this file. You should also be careful to take good
care of this file, since it is the repository of information about all software packages and all files belonging to these packages. It would be extremely difficult
to recreate this file without reloading your software.

If you elect to back this file up, you should be careful to back it up again every
time you add or remove a package from your hosts so that your system's software and this file are always synchronized.

The contents file will have two types of entries; one of each type is shown
below. The first represents a regular file, the second a symbolic link. The name
following the = sign in the second line is the name of the file that the symbolic
link will point to.

```
/usr/snadm/classes/database.2.0/get_aliases_entry=./method s none SUNWadmap
/usr/snadm/classes/database.2.0/get_aliases_entry is pointer to ./method
```

By examining this file, you can determine the origins of a particular file.

TRY THIS   Determine Which Package /etc/aliases File Belongs to

```
# grep aliases /var/sadm/install/contents
/etc/aliases=./mail/aliases s none SUNWcsr
/etc/mail/aliases f none 0644 root bin 1201 33769 720808907 SUNWcsr
```

You will see a lot of lines containing the string aliases. The two that are displayed in the box above, among these, represent the entry for the /etc/aliases
file. As you can see from the entries, the /etc/aliases file is a symbolic link to
/etc/mail/aliases and is derived from the SUNWcsr package.

TRY THIS   Determine Which Package the Uutry Script Belongs to

```
# grep Uutry contents
/usr/lib/uucp/Uutry f none 0555 uucp uucp 1813 8044 720794102 SUNWbnuu
/usr/share/man/man1m/Uutry.1m f none 0444 bin bin 1327 44878 718652462
SUNWman
```

The Uutry script belongs to the SUNWbnuu package. We can also see that there
is a man page for Uutry. The man page is part of the SUNWman package.

You can list files that are contained in a given package by using grep
against the contents file. For example, if we want to count files included in
the AnswerBook package, we can grep on SUNWabsso in /var/sadm/in-
stall/contents.

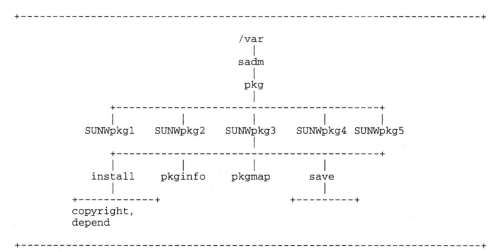

Figure 11.6   Software installation database directory.

```
# grep SUNWabsso /var/sadm/install/contents
```

The command that follows tells us that there are 3768 lines in the contents file associated with this package.

```
# grep SUNWman /var/sadm/install/contents | wc -l
3768
```

It is also possible to use the contents file to list files which are not part of any software package (e.g., data files). The script shown in Fig. 11.6 checks each file in or below the current directory and prints the names of those it does not find in the /var/sadm/install/contents file. As an example, this script has been run in /usr/lib/uucp and finds a couple of extra files which have been added.

11.4.2.2 The /var/sadm/pkg files.   The software package files stored within /var/sadm/pkg detail a lot of information on a package-by-package basis. The pkginfo files within these directories (e.g., /var/sadm/pkg/SUNWman/pkginfo) provide data for the long listing of the pkginfo command pkginfo -l. The pkgmap file, very similar to the contents file, provides information of individual files belonging to a particular software application.

TRY THIS   Take a Look at a pkgmap file

```
# more pkgmap
: 1 56948
1 i copyright 2582 32260 716575668
1 i depend 1085 25001 714381825
```

```
1 s none man=./share/man
1 i pkginfo 321 25555 719616051
1 d none share 0755 root sys
1 d none share/man 0755 bin bin
1 v none share/man/man.cf 0644 bin bin 157 11592 718650891
1 d none share/man/man1 0755 bin bin
```

11.4.3   The pkgchk Command

The pkgchk command is used to verify the installation of software. If, for example, you believe that permissions have changed on application files or you suspect that a file has been inadvertently deleted, the pkgchk command will verify the files belonging to software packages by comparing the contents file to what is actually loaded on your disk.

TRY THIS   Change the Permissions on a File and Find Change with pkgchk

```
#chmod 444 /usr/Solaris_2.1_AB/bookinfo
#pkgchk SUNWabsso
ERROR: /usr/Solaris_2.1_AB/bookinfo
permissions <0755> expected <0444> actual
```

(*Note:* Make sure you put the file back and fix its permissions.)

The message expected tells you that the permissions have been changed since installation. You would, of course, get this same message if the contents file had been modified, but this should not be the case since no one should ever edit this file.

TRY THIS   Move a File to a Safe Place to Determine Whether It Has Been Moved Using the pkgchk Command

```
# mv bookinfo woops
# pkgchk SUNWabsso
ERROR: /usr/Solaris_2.1_AB/bookinfo
pathname does not exist
```

(*Note:* Make sure you put the file back and fix its permissions.)

The pkgchk command cannot tell you if a file has been added where it does not belong. Nevertheless, it is possible to extract this information using the awk script provided in Fig. 11.7.

The pkgchk command will help you to monitor what is loaded on your system and repair any permissions problems that might crop up. Of course, like

```
+-------------------------------------------------------------------+
#!/bin/csh
#                find_new
#
set DIR = `pwd`
foreach FILE (`ls -R`)
        set FOUNDF = `grep "$DIR/$FILE " /var/sadm/install/contents | wc -l`
        set FOUNDL = `grep "$DIR/$FILE=" /var/sadm/install/contents | wc -l`
        set FOUND = `expr $FOUNDF + $FOUNDL`
        if ($FOUND == 0) then
                echo "New file: " $DIR/$FILE
        endif
end
+-------------------------------------------------------------------+
# /export/home/slee/book/packages/find_new      <-- execute this
New file:  /usr/lib/uucp/contents
New file:  /usr/lib/uucp/fix.uucp
New file:  /usr/lib/uucp/set.uucp

+-------------------------------------------------------------------+
```

Figure 11.7 The find_new script.

many UNIX commands, pkgchk will not provide any output if it finds no inconsistencies with what it is expecting. No news is good news.

One word of caution: The pkgchk command can generate errors which should be considered bogus; that is, many changes in the status of a file since the time it was installed are normal and natural. Take, as an example, the core package for root, SUNWcsr. This package contains many files which detail configuration information and, therefore, are always modified when the system is set up; examples include such files as /etc/passwd, /etc/shadow, /etc/mail/aliases, /etc/inet/hosts, and /etc/mnttab (which notes currently mounted file systems). Since these files are modified as you configure your system and during normal operation, size and checksum differences detected by pkgchk should not be of any concern.

In addition, a significant number of ownership and permissions errors may indicate nothing beyond normal differences between the installation and normal state of your system.

TRY THIS   Compare the State of Your Core Root Package with Its Installation State

    pkgchk SUNWcsr

Most likely, you will get a considerable number of errors, most referring to changes in the file size and the related checksum. You can capture the error messages that pkgchk generates by directing standard error to a file as shown here.

TRY THIS   Save and Examine Your Errors

    pkgchk SUNWcsr 2>SUNWcsr.errors

These errors will look like those shown below:

```
ERROR: /etc/inet/hosts
file size <46> expected <78> actual
file cksum <3463> expected <5728> actual
ERROR: /etc/passwd
permissions <0644> expected <0444> actual
file size <478> expected <640> actual
file cksum <36706> expected <50416> actual
```

Size and checksum errors should be ignored for files which are expected to be volatile. Permissions and ownership changes may indicate problems worth investigating. In the example of the passwd file as shown in the example, the modification of privileges probably occurred sometime during system setup. Since the new privileges are reduced and root (the owner) can overwrite the file when necessary, these permissions are not a problem.

In addition, you might sometimes run into a message such as

```
# pkgchk SUNWspro
WARNING: no pathnames were associated with
```

The no pathnames were associated message indicates that the file or software package cannot be found on the system.

You can also check the completeness of an installation by providing the full pathname for a specific file using the -p option:

```
/usr/sbin/pkgchk -p
```

TRY THIS   Check Integrity of Specific File

```
pkgchk -p /etc/uucp/Systems
ERROR: /etc/uucp/systems
group name <uucp> expected <other> actual
file size <825> expected <972> actual
file cksum <1247> expected <12754> actual
```

You can check the accuracy of file attributes only by using the -a option.

TRY THIS   Check File Attributes for a Software Package

```
# /usr/sbin/pkgchk -a SUNWcsr
ERROR: /etc/rc2.d/S82mkdtab
pathname does not exist
pathname not properly linked to
ERROR: /etc/skel/local.cshrc <../../etc/init.d/mkdtab>
pathname does not exist
```

```
ERROR: /etc/skel/local.login
pathname does not exist
ERROR: /etc/skel/local.profile
pathname does not exist
ERROR: /proc
permissions <0755> expected <0555> actual
group name <sys> expected <root> actual
ERROR: /tmp
group name <sys> expected <root> actual
owner name <sys> expected <root> actual
```

Some of the file checking options can be used in conjunction with each other.

TRY THIS   Combine Package Check Parameters

```
# pkgchk -c -p /etc/uucp/Systems
ERROR: /etc/uucp/Systems
file size <825> expected <972> actual
file cksum <1247> expected <12754> actual
```

In this example, we only have errors related to the file contents (size and check-sum) because we used the -c option. We only get output related to the uucp Systems file because we used the -p option and provided a specific pathname to that file.

TRY THIS   Generate and Repair a Permissions Problem:

```
# cd /usr/man/man3
# chmod 600 * (now, only root can read this portion of the man pages)
# chown slee s* (substitute user on your system for "slee")
# pkgchk SUNWman 2>SUNWman.errors
```

Take a look at the SUNWman.errors file. It will contain lines like those shown in Fig. 11.8.

In this case, since all your "errors" are in one location, it is fairly simple to go back to /usr/man/man3 and make the needed repairs. Figure 11.9 contains an awk script which will generate the chmod, chown, and chgrp commands needed to repair these types of errors from the error listing itself.

Here is an example of how to use this script:

1. # pkgchk SUNWman 2>SUNWman.errors

2. # cat SUNWman.errors | awk -f pkgfix>fixes

3. # more fixes (look at generated commands)

```
+--------------------------------------------------------------------------+
ERROR: /usr/share/man/man3/qfconvert.3
     permissions <0444> expected <0400> actual
ERROR: /usr/share/man/man3/qgconvert.3
     permissions <0444> expected <0400> actual
ERROR: /usr/share/man/man3/quadruple_to_decimal.3
     permissions <0444> expected <0400> actual
ERROR: /usr/share/man/man3/seconvert.3
     permissions <0444> expected <0400> actual
     owner name <bin> expected <slee> actual
ERROR: /usr/share/man/man3/setlogmask.3
     permissions <0444> expected <0400> actual
     owner name <bin> expected <slee> actual
ERROR: /usr/share/man/man3/sfconvert.3
     permissions <0444> expected <0400> actual
     owner name <bin> expected <slee> actual
ERROR: /usr/share/man/man3/sgconvert.3
     permissions <0444> expected <0400> actual
     owner name <bin> expected <slee> actual

+--------------------------------------------------------------------------+
```

Figure 11.8 pkgchk errors.

```
+--------------------------------------------------------------------------+
#       pkgfix:  awk script which will generate chmod, chown, and chgrp
#                commands to fix errors found by pkgchk
{
if ($1 == "ERROR:") {
        FILE = $2
        }
else if ($1 == "permissions") {
        PERMS = substr($2,2,4)
        print "chmod", PERMS, FILE
        }
else if ($1 == "owner") {
        ix = index($3,">")
        OWNER = substr($3,2,(ix-2))
        print "chown", OWNER, FILE
        }
else if ($1 == "group") {
        ix = index($3,">")
        GROUP = substr($3,2,(ix-2))
        print "chgrp", GROUP, FILE
        }
PREVFILE = FILE
}

+--------------------------------------------------------------------------+
```

Figure 11.9 The pkgfix awk script.

4. # chmod 744 fixes

5. # fixes

6. # pkgchk SUNWman

The file generated in step 2 will look like the lines included in Fig. 11.10. Step 4 makes the file containing these commands executable, and step 5 invokes the changes. When you enter the command shown in step 6, the permissions, ownership, and group errors should be gone.

```
+-------------------------------------------------------------------------+
chmod 0444 /usr/share/man/man3/qfconvert.3
chmod 0444 /usr/share/man/man3/qgconvert.3
chmod 0444 /usr/share/man/man3/quadruple_to_decimal.3
chmod 0444 /usr/share/man/man3/seconvert.3
chown bin /usr/share/man/man3/seconvert.3
chmod 0444 /usr/share/man/man3/setlogmask.3
chown bin /usr/share/man/man3/setlogmask.3
chmod 0444 /usr/share/man/man3/sfconvert.3
chown bin /usr/share/man/man3/sfconvert.3
chmod 0444 /usr/share/man/man3/sgconvert.3
chown bin /usr/share/man/man3/sgconvert.3
+-------------------------------------------------------------------------+
```

Figure 11.10 Repair commands from `pkgfix`.

11.4.4 The `pkgadd` command

The `pkgadd` command loads software packages. Interactive by default, `pkgadd` can be used noninteractively by using answers previously stored in a file called a `response` file. In Sec. 11.4.7 we will see how a response file is created. When used noninteractively, the `pkgadd` command uses both response files (providing answers to prompts so that the installer does not have to answer the questions during installation) and `admin` files (providing alternatives for handling problems that arise during installation).

When run interactively, the `pkgadd` command will walk you through the installation, requesting, when needed, additional information about what you are loading or where you want to load it. When the `pkgadd` command is run interactively, you can deal with problems as they are encountered, and provide answers to installation queries. The `pkgadd` command allows you to specify more than one package on the command line, and it will run through each in order. If it runs into a problem at some point, it will ask if you want to continue the installation. You can say yes, no, or quit. If you say quit, subsequent packages will not be installed. If you say no, the current package will not be installed, but `pkgadd` will proceed with the next.

The `-n` option instructs `pkgadd` to run noninteractively. Some packages may not support noninteractive installation. Others may come with preset response files. The `-d` instructs `pkgadd` to look to a certain device to find its files. Without this option, `pkgadd` will look in `/var/spool/pkg`.

```
/usr/sbin/pkgadd -d /cdrom -n <package>
/usr/sbin/pkgadd -d /cdrom -n -r <response file> <package>
```

This and other `pkgadd` options which determine how it is run and from where it gets answers and software are listed below. See the man page for `pkgadd` for a full description of these options.

```
-a specify alternate admin file. Otherwise, it uses /var/sadm/install/admin/de-
   fault
-n noninteractive mode
-d device where installation medium is located
-R root-path (an alternate base directory for the installation)
```

```
-r response, uses response file created from pkgask
-s spool, reads the package into the specified directory rather than installing it
```

The pkgadd command is sophisticated and handles many contingencies that can occur when you are loading software. If you do not have enough room for the software that you want to load, for example, some action must be taken. Depending on whether you are using pkgadd interactively or using a prepared response file, you will be prompted for what to do or the action specified in the default or a selected admin file will be used. Figure 11.11 illustrates the use of the pkgadd command.

The pkgadd command

Requests that media be inserted if it isn't already

Mounts the device if needed

Determines whether the device is appropriate for SVR4

Determines what packages are on the media

Checks sequencing if the installation media is multivolume

Compares the target machine with the current

Checks software dependencies (i.e., some packages require others)

Determines whether the run state of the system is appropriate for installation

Determines whether the software is already installed

Checks the history of prior installations

Picks up where a prior installation, if not run to completion, left off

Composes the target directory name (as we saw somewhere above)

Ensures that disk space is adequate

Checks whether files of the same names will be overwritten by installation of this software (uses pkgmap)

Checks for files which might have setuid or setgid bits set

Moves files to temporary storage prior to install

Installs the package in destination location if all is well

```
+-------------------------------------------------------------------------+
boson# pkgadd -d /cdrom/solaris_2_3_ab

The following packages are available:
   1  SUNWaadm       Solaris 2.3 System Administrator AnswerBook
                     (sparc) 47.1.8
   2  SUNWabhdw      Solaris 2.3 on Sun Hardware AnswerBook
                     (sparc) 28.2.7
   3  SUNWaman       Solaris 2.3 Reference Manual AnswerBook
                     (sparc) 40.1.7

Select package(s) you wish to process (or 'all' to process
all packages). (default: all) [?,??,q]:
+-------------------------------------------------------------------------+
```

Figure 11.11 Starting up installation with pkgadd.

```
+-------------------------------------------------------------------------+
you have mail
# mail
From root Thu Feb 11 17:03 EST 1994
Date: Thu, 11 Feb 94 17:03:46 EST
From: root (Solaris 2.3 System Software AnswerBook)
Message-Id: <9302112203.AA00881@boson.>
Content-Length: 116

Installation of Solaris 2.3 System Software AnswerBook on boson as
package instance <SUNWabsso> was successful.


?

+-------------------------------------------------------------------------+
```
Figure 11.12 Mail from `pkgadd`.

The `pkgadd` command should be run as root and when the system is in run
state 3. It will send mail to root (or whomever is specified in the `admin` file)
when installation is complete (see Fig. 11.12).

11.4.5 The `pkgrm` command

The `pkgrm` command removes a package from the system, whether fully or partially installed. If the `pkgrm` command determines that other software depends
on the software package being removed, it will refer to the `admin` file to determine what to do. The `pkgrm` command can be run interactively or noninteractively. The -R option should be used if the root path for the installed package is
different from /; in this case, all files, including the /var/sadm files, are relocated to a different directory.

The `pkgrm` uses information from the software installation database to remove software packages.

If the optional package ID is provided, `pkgrm` removes that package, or else
it prompts for whether to remove each package within a given directory.

11.4.6 The `pkgparam` command

The `pkgparam` command displays parameters which are associated with a software package. These are taken from the `pkginfo` file that is delivered with the
package or a file that you can refer to with the -f option.

You can request a particular parameter by including it in the request or all
parameters by entering the command without parameters.

TRY THIS   Request Hotline Information for a Package

```
# pkgparam SUNWman HOTLINE
Please contact your local service provider
# pkgparam INFOP HOTLINE
Call Vail on extension 1234
```

Here, we show two possible responses to the hotline request for a software package. Depending on the `pkginfo` file that is included with your software package and possible customization (i.e., you can decide to replace `HOTLINE` entries with specific names and phone numbers), you may get more or less useful information from this query.

TRY THIS   Determine Version for a Software Package

```
# pkgparam SPROcc VERSION
1.13
```

You might be calling in a problem with a software package and need the version number. The `pkgparam` command will provide this easily as seen in the example above.

TRY THIS   Retrieve All Parameters for a Package

```
# pkgparam SUNWman
none
US/Eastern
/sbin:/usr/sbin:/usr/bin:oz`
/usr/sadm/sysadm
SunOS
mars-beta1.2.1
SunWman
On-Line Manual Pages
all
23.0
system
/usr
System Reference Manual Pages
Sun Microsystems, Inc.
Please contact your local service provider
s 1 2 3
1000
windmill921020212042
SUNWman
/var/sadm/pkg/SUNWman/save
/a
/usr
Feb 02 1993 04:52
```

Compare the output of the `pkgparam` command with that of the `pkginfo -l` command for the same package. You will see considerable overlap in the information presented. The `pkginfo` command provides a very different format; that is, parameters are labeled rather than simply listed as in the example above. Another, possibly more important distinction, is that the `pkginfo` command uses a number of its options (e.g., architecture, version, and category) as selection criteria to select all packages with a certain value in common. The `pkgparam` command, on the other hand, uses parameter names to determine what to display from the `pkginfo` file associated with a particular package.

11.4.7 The `pkgask` command

The `pkgask` command stores answers for an interactive software package so that it can be installed noninteractively at a later time. The answers collected when `pkgask` is run are stored in what is called a `response` file. Using a `response` file is very convenient when you will be installing software repetitively.

The `pkgadd` command will use the stored `response` file if requested with the `-r` option. If, however, `pkgadd` encounters any problems during a noninteractive installation, and cannot find a resolution in the `admin` file or the `response` file, it will terminate the installation.

Building a `response` file with `pkgask` is a simple process. You will interact with the installation script much the same as you would if you were actually installing the software. Your answers will be stored in a file. Figure 11.13 (with many lines deleted to save space) illustrates the process of building a response file for AnswerBook. If you've ever installed AnswerBook, you will recognize the interactions with the install script. Keep in mind as you look at this example, that the `-d` option specifies that the software to be installed is on CD ROM (mounted on `/cdrom`), and the response file is specified with the `-r` option. Look at the file that this interchange created. Notice how the responses provided while running `pkgask` are stored.

The next request for input asks you to specify the parent directory of AnswerBook. Make sure to choose a parent directory on a file system big enough to accommodate all the files to be moved for the INSTALL OPTION you selected.

The `response` file built from this interaction with the `pkgask` script is displayed in Fig. 11.14. Notice how the answers provided by the installer are included. Notice also the additional information that is provided here describing the package. This response script could not be absent-mindedly used to install the wrong software.

11.4.8 The `admin` files

The `admin` files provide default actions to take whenever a package installation runs into problems. For example, you may not have enough disk space to install the software. You might have existing files which would be overwritten by files belonging to the new software. You might find that the software you are installing requires additional software which is not installed on the system or that software you are removing is required by some other package. The `response` files determine reactions to these conditions. You can use a default response file for all software installations and removals, or you can build one

```
+---------------------------------------------------------------------------------+
# pkgask -d /cdrom/solaris_2_3_ab -r /var/sadm/pkg/SUNWaadm/response SUNWaadm

Processing package instance <SUNWaadm> from </cdrom/solaris_2_3_ab>

Solaris 2.3 System Administrator AnswerBook
(sparc) 47.1.8

      Copyright 1993 Sun Microsystems, Inc. All Rights Reserved.
            Printed in the United States of America.
2550 Garcia Avenue, Mountain View, California, 94043-1100 U.S.A.

This product and related documentation is protected by
copyright and distributed under licenses restricting its use, copying,

   .
   .
   .

The X Window System is a product of the Massachusetts Institute of Technology.

This product incorporates technology used under license from Fulcrum
Technologies, Inc.

The installation options are as follows:
Option: Description:
---------------------------------------------
1. nil:    less than 1 Megabyte disk space required [slowest performance].
2. heavy:  37.91 Megabytes disk space required [best performance].
Enter the number of an installation option from the list above (1 or 2).


Select an installation option: 1

Specify the parent of the AnswerBook home directory:  /opt

Response file </export/home/slee/book/packages/SUNWabsso.resp> was created.

Processing of request script was successful.
+---------------------------------------------------------------------------------+
```

Figure 11.13 Using pkgask.

```
+----------------------------------------------------------------------------+
CLASSES=none
Distrib=/cdrom/solaris_2_3_ab
ABHOME=/opt/SUNWaadm
ABTOP=/opt
INSTALL_CASE=nil
ABrelease=47
ABissue=1
AB_OS=5
AB_Type=UBAB
AB_Install_Type=UBAB
AB_Pkg_Name=SUNWaadm
AB_Name=SUNWaadm
noneDEST=
IndexDEST=/cdrom/solaris_2_3_ab/SUNWaadm/reloc/IndexDEST
ContentsDBDEST=/cdrom/solaris_2_3_ab/SUNWaadm/reloc/ContentsDBDEST
PostScriptDEST=/cdrom/solaris_2_3_ab/SUNWaadm/reloc/PostScriptDEST

+----------------------------------------------------------------------------+
```

Figure 11.14 The response file.

for installing and removing a particular package. Both the pkgadd and pkgrm commands provide a -a option for specifying an alternate admin file. The default admin file, /var/sadm/install/admin/default, is used if you do not specify an alternative. You should edit this file if you want to change your options globally.

There are 11 parameters that you can set in your admin files. The default setting for most of the parameters is ask; i.e., if there is a problem during installation, ask the installer what to do. The ask default should not be used for non-interactive installations since this makes little sense and will cause the installation to abort if there are problems during installation. Ask is also not a valid value for the mail parameter.

Other options for problem resolution include nocheck, quit, abort, nochange, and overwrite. Use of these options depends on the particular parameter; overwrite, for example, has relevance only when there is a conflict between files with the same name.

abort	Abort the entire installation
nochange	Leave as is
nocheck	Don't check if condition exists
overwrite	Overwrite existing file(s)
quit	Quit the current installation (proceed to other packages if additional installations are requested)
unique	Do not overwrite software, create new instance

An admin file does not need to include a value for all 11 parameters. If pkgadd runs into a conflict and finds that no value has been set for the particular parameter, the default value ask is used.

basedir	The base directory where relocatable packages will be installed
mail	To whom mail should be sent when software is installed or removed
runlevel	Run level OK for install; nocheck and quit are options to this parameter and say not to check software configuration and to abort if configuration conditions not met
conflict	What to do if there are conflicts in file names; options are nocheck (overwrite other files), quit (abort), nochange (omit conflicting files from installation)
setuid	Check for setuid and setgid files. Options include nocheck (don't bother), quit (abort install), and nochange (install without these bits set).
action	Determine whether possible security problems may result from software installation. Options include nocheck (ignore security impact) and quit (abort installation if detect security problems).
partial	Check whether there is a partially installed version of the software. Options include nocheck (don't check) and quit (abort if detect).
instance	What to do if there is a previous instance of the package. Options include quit (abort without installing), overwrite (overwrite existing package, if more than one, that which is same architecture as what is being installed), unique (do not overwrite software but create new instance of package).
idepend	What to do if package dependencies are not met. Options include nocheck (don't check), quit (abort).
rdepend	Controls dependencies for software removal so that you will not unintentionally remove a software package that is a prerequisite of another.

Options include nocheck (don't check), quit (abort removal).

space   What to do if there is inadequate space; nocheck (don't check—installation will fail if and when it runs out of space), quit (abort)

Valid values for each of these 11 parameters include the following:

basedir	Any directory
mail	Any user(s), comma-separated
runlevel	nocheck quit
conflict	nocheck quit nochange
setuid	nocheck quit nochange
action	nocheck quit
partial	nocheck quit
instance	quit overwrite unique
idepend	nocheck quit
rdepend	nocheck quit
space	nocheck quit

An example admin file is shown in Fig. 11.15.

11.5   Software Administration for Clients

So far we've ignored the issue of diskless and dataless clients. There are some situations in which the client type has an important impact on the way software is installed on a server for that client's use.

If you are installing software for a server's own use or installing software completely within file systems which will simply be mounted by other hosts (e.g., software packages completely installed in /usr or /opt), there are no additional steps and software installation proceeds as described earlier in this chapter.

On the other hand, when software being installed on the server for use by a client impacts that client's root partition (e.g., software containing a device driver), or when the client's /usr partition is not the same as the server's, the situation is a bit more complex.

```
+--------------------------------------------------------------------------+
#ident   "@(#)mydefaults"                    /* SVr4.0  1.5.2.1      */
mail=root,slee
instance=unique
partial=ask
runlevel=ask
idepend=ask
rdepend=ask
space=ask
setuid=ask
conflict=ask
action=ask
basedir=default
+--------------------------------------------------------------------------+
```

Figure 11.15   A sample admin file.

When installing software for use by clients, you must differentiate between diskless and dataless clients. Both get their /usr and shared partitions from the server. Their root partitions, on the other hand, are stored on the server in one case and on the local disk in the other. When installing software that affects the root partition, therefore, it is important to make sure that the correct root partition is being updated.

If you are adding a package which needs to update the root partition on a diskless client, you use the -R option of the pkgadd command. This option specifies the pathname for the client's root partition. Using this option, you can be sure to update the client's root (e.g., /export/root/kelvin) rather than root on the server.

```
# /usr/sbin/pkgadd -R /export/root/kelvin \
-d /cdrom/solaris_2_3/s0/Solaris_2.3 \
-s /var/tmp/spooldir \
SUNWpkg
```

If you are adding a package which needs to update the root partition on a dataless client, on the other hand, you need to mount that client's root partition before using pkgadd with the -R option. This also works with standalone systems. The client's root partition must be shared read/write with the server, of course, before this will work.

```
# mkdir /ROOT
# /etc/mount kelvin:/ /ROOT
# /usr/sbin/pkgadd -R /ROOT \
  -d /cdrom/solaris_2_3/s0/Solaris_2.3 \
  -s /var/tmp/spooldir \
  SUNpkg
```

If you are installing software for a client of architecture different from that of the server, you will need to be sure that the correct /export/exec directory is updated. Basically, the aim is to make the environment for the package installation look like you are installing the software from the client's perspective. Using a series of loopback mounts to attach the client's partitions to the proper location for the installation, you can then use pkgadd with the -R option to specify the alternate pathname to be used as the base for the install. The loopback mounts permit you to mount file systems that are already mounted, making them accessible from a different perspective. Keep in mind that the -R pathname will determine both the root and /usr partitions. Since this operation takes a number of commands to ensure that, for the purposes of the installation, root and /usr files are all in the proper place, it is a good idea to create a script to manage this process for you. Sample scripts for setting up the installation environment for installing software for a diskless client and dataless client where both the root and /usr partitions might be affected are included as Figs. 11.16 and 11.17.

These scripts require that the user provide the client name and the OS indicator for the client architecture (the directory under /export/exec which sup-

```
+------------------------------------------------------------------------+
#!/bin/sh
# setup_diskless
#
if test $# -ne 2
then
        echo "Usage:   setup_dataless <CLIENT> <OS>"
        exit
else
        CLIENT=$1
        OS=$2
fi
# loopback mount client's file systems
/bin/mkdir /$CLIENT /$CLIENT/usr /$CLIENT/usr/kvm
/etc/mount -F lofs -o rw /export/root/$CLIENT /$CLIENT
/etc/mount -F lofs -o rw /export/exec/$OS/usr /$CLIENT/usr
/etc/mount -F lofs -o rw /export/exec/kvm/$OS/usr/kvm /$CLIENT/usr/kvm
+------------------------------------------------------------------------+
```

Figure 11.16 setup_diskless script.

```
+------------------------------------------------------------------------+
#!/bin/sh
# setup_dataless
#
if test $# -ne 2
then
        echo "Usage:   setup_dataless <CLIENT> <OS>"
        exit
else
        CLIENT=$1
        OS=$2
fi
# mount and loopback mount client's file systems
/bin/mkdir /$CLIENT /$CLIENT/usr /$CLIENT/usr/kvm
/etc/mount -F nfs -o rw $CLIENT:/ /$CLIENT
/etc/mount -F lofs -o rw /export/exec/$OS/usr /$CLIENT/usr
/etc/mount -F lofs -o rw /export/exec/kvm/$OS/usr/kvm /$CLIENT/usr/kvm
+------------------------------------------------------------------------+
```

Figure 11.17 setup_dataless script.

ports the client). The subsequent pkgadd with a -R option must specify
/$CLIENT (e.g., kelvin) as the base directory.

After the software installation is complete, you should unmount the file systems in the reverse order of how they were mounted and then remove mount points. An example script for doing this is shown in Fig. 11.18.

11.6 Package Administration Tools

Solaris 2.1 and later versions provide two tools for further simplifying software administration by organizing the package installation, removing, and configuration commands within an easy-to-use framework of utility software tools. The menu-based swm and the GUI-based swmtool both provide similar func-

```
+------------------------------------------------------------------------+
#!/bin/sh
# unmount_client
#
if test $# -ne 1
then
        echo "Usage:   unmount_diskless <CLIENT>"
        exit
else
        CLIENT=$1
        PKG=$2
        OS=$3
fi
# umount client's file systems
/etc/umount /$CLIENT/usr/kvm
/etc/umount /$CLIENT/usr
/etc/umount /$CLIENT
/bin/rmdir /$CLIENT
+------------------------------------------------------------------------+
```

Figure 11.18 unmount-client script.

tionality. Your choice of which of these tools will probably depend on familiarity and whether or not you are working with a bitmapped monitor or a character-based terminal.

Both of these tools provide easy selection of software, choice of installing or removing, as well as setting up configuration parameters for software installation. They even provide a way to mount media inside control of the tool itself.

11.6.1 swm

The Software Manager, swm, provides a simple menu-choice interface software management. You can see from Figs. 11.16 to 11.20 that software installation, deinstallation, and setup of admin files can all be accomplished within the framework of this character-based tool.

When you start up swm, it will run off and check what software packages are loaded on your system.

Figure 11.19 displays the main menu of swm. The first option, [a], allows you to set the configuration parameters which were described in Sec. 11.4.8. For the parameters on the configuration properties menu, displayed in Fig. 11.20, we have included the name of the admin file equivalent (where applicable) on the right. Of the 11 parameters included in the admin file, all except basedir are included in this menu. The base directory is set within swm in the installation media selection menu, through option [c] from the main menu.

In Fig. 11.20, we can see the parameters that you can set that determine what will happen when a software installation runs into problems. We've added some comments on the side of the form to correlate the menu items to the parameters as you use them in admin files. As you can note from this form, using ? followed by any of the other listed option designators will provide you with an explanation of the particular parameter. When you elect to change one of the parameters, you can use the scroll bar to cycle through a list of options, making this tool very easy to use.

```
+-----------------------------------------------------------------------+
|                                                                       |
|                                                                       |
|                                                                       |
|              *** Software Manager Main Menu ***                       |
|                                                                       |
|         Choose a function:                                            |
|                                                                       |
|             [a] Edit configuration properties                         |
|             [b] Select target hosts for software installation/removal |
|                                                                       |
|             [c] Load software distribution media                      |
|             [d] Select software products for installation             |
|             [e] Install selected software products                    |
|                                                                       |
|             [f] Select software products for removal                  |
|             [g] Remove selected software products                     |
|                                                                       |
|             [q] Exit swm                                              |
|                                                                       |
|                                                                       |
|                                                                       |
|                                                                       |
|         Type any bracketed letter to select that function:            |
|                                                                       |
+-----------------------------------------------------------------------+
```

Figure 11.19 Main menu (swm).

```
+-----------------------------------------------------------------------+
|              *** Configuration Properties Menu ***                    |
|                                                                       |
|      [a] Incorrect Run Level:     ask          <-- runlevel           |
|      [b] Existing Targets:        ask          <-- conflict           |
|      [c] Setuid/setgid Targets:   ask          <-- setuid             |
|      [d] Setuid/setgid Scripts:   ask          <-- action             |
|      [e] Partial Installations:   ask          <-- partial            |
|      [f] Existing Packages:       unique       <-- instance           |
|      [g] Installation Dependencies: ask        <-- idepend            |
|      [h] Removal Dependencies:    ask          <-- rdepend            |
|      [i] Insufficient Space:      ask          <-- space              |
|      [j] Show Copyrights:         yes                                 |
|      [k] Allow user interaction:  yes                                 |
|      [l] Host List:               boson                               |
|      [m] Mail Recipients:         root         <-- mail               |
|                                                                       |
|      (configuration not saved)                                        |
|                                                                       |
|                                                                       |
|                                                                       |
|      Type  [a-m] to modify the associated value                       |
|        or ?[a-m] for information about a particular property          |
|        or  [Esc] to restore previously-saved values                   |
|        or  [s] to save properties to a file                           |
|        or  [Return] to use these values and return to main menu.      |
|      Select an option:                                                |
+-----------------------------------------------------------------------+
```

Figure 11.20 Configuration properties menu (swm).

The menu also provides options which determine whether to display copyright notices and whether to run the installation with or without user interaction.

The host list, which defines candidate hosts for the software installation, is manipulated through option [b]. These hosts may not "trust" the current host and the software installation may not proceed. The target host selection menu shown in Fig. 11.21 also displays the determination that swm has made about the status of a particular system. We can see from this figure that boson is a standalone or server, while hbar is a diskless client.

The target host selection menu allows you to add and remove hosts from the intended target list for the software you are about to install or remove. With swm, you can perform installations on remote systems. This menu allows you to mount or unmount and eject CD ROMs. Notice the device address for option [a] and the mount point in [b]. Item [c] is like the -d option in pkgadd and lets you select the source for the installation software.

As you can see, a list of software which you can elect to install or remove (Figs. 11.22 and 11.23) is provided from the software installation database on your system or the mounted media. This list also includes the size in megabytes

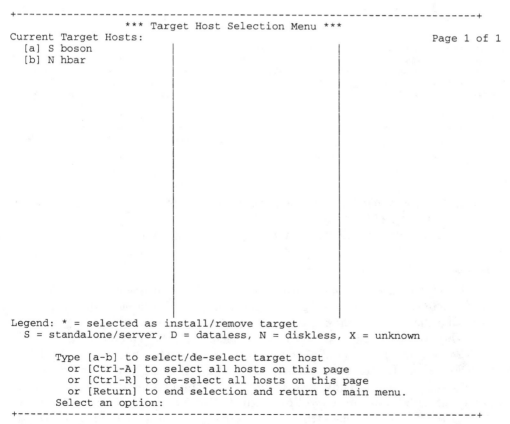

```
+-----------------------------------------------------------------------+
                   *** Target Host Selection Menu ***
Current Target Hosts:                                    Page 1 of 1
   [a] S boson           |                       |
   [b] N hbar            |                       |
                         |                       |
                         |                       |
                         |                       |
                         |                       |
                         |                       |
                         |                       |
                         |                       |
                         |                       |
                         |                       |
                         |                       |
                         |                       |
                         |                       |
                         |                       |
                         |                       |
Legend: * = selected as install/remove target
   S = standalone/server, D = dataless, N = diskless, X = unknown

     Type [a-b] to select/de-select target host
        or [Ctrl-A] to select all hosts on this page
        or [Ctrl-R] to de-select all hosts on this page
        or [Return] to end selection and return to main menu.
     Select an option:
+-----------------------------------------------------------------------+
```

Figure 11.21 Target host selection menu (swm).

```
+-----------------------------------------------------------------------+




          *** Installation Media Selection Menu ***

     Current Media Parameters:

          [a] CD-ROM Device:                  /dev/dsk/c0t6d0s2

          [b] CD-ROM Mount Point:             /cdrom

          [c] Software Source Directory:      /cdrom

          [d] Default Base Directory:         <none>



     Selecting software from CD-ROM volume: Seagate IPI ZBR Elite cyl 1893






     Type [a-d] to modify the associated value
       or [l] to mount and load software from the specified CD-ROM
       or [u] to unload and eject the specified CD-ROM
       or [Return] to use these values and return to main menu.
     Select an option:


+-----------------------------------------------------------------------+
```

Figure 11.22 Installation media selection.

of each software package and the overall disk space free and available on your
system (lower right corner of Fig. 11.23).

The swm software will unmount and eject the cdrom on exiting.

11.6.2 swmtool

The GUI-based Software Manager Tool, swmtool, provides an easy-to-use interface to the software management functions, but the same basic functionality that the software administration commands and swm provides.

When you first start the Software Manager Tool, the window shown in Fig.
11.24 appears. In Fig. 11.25, you can see we are trying to mount a local CD
ROM. As Fig. 11.26 illustrates, however, we have run into a small snag because
the CD ROM has already been mounted by Volume Manager. In Figs. 11.27
through 11.30, you can see we specify the CD as a mounted directory. Until we
enter the full pathname for the mount, /cdrom/solaris_2_3/s0, we don't get
anything in our software selection window.

```
+---------------------------------------------------------------------+
  Software Available for Removal:                            Page 1 of 4
    [a]  P  4.1* Heterogeneous Install Software..........................0.24 Mb
    [b]  P  Archive Libraries............................................12.29 Mb
    [c]  P  Audio applications...........................................0.80 Mb
    [d]  P  Audio demo programs..........................................4.20 Mb
    [e]  P  Automated Security Enhancement Tools.........................0.26 Mb
    [f]  P  Binary Compatibility.........................................1.78 Mb
    [g]  P  Buttons/Dials (bd) Header Files..............................0.23 Mb
    [h]  P  Buttons/Dials (bd) Streams Module............................0.03 Mb
    [i]  P  Core Architecture, (Kvm).....................................0.68 Mb
    [j]  P  Core Architecture, (Root)....................................3.44 Mb
    [k]  P  Core Sparc, (Root)...........................................9.76 Mb
    [l]  P  Core Sparc, (Usr)............................................22.47 Mb
    [m]  P  Core Sparc Devices...........................................0.05 Mb
    [n]  P  Documentation Tools..........................................1.62 Mb
    [o]  P  Dumb Frame Buffer Device Drivers.............................0.14 Mb
    [p]  P  Dumb Frame Buffer Header Files...............................0.14 Mb
    [q]  P  Extended System Utilities....................................2.19 Mb
    [r]  P  FileMerge....................................................1.25 Mb
    [s]  P  Framed Access Command Environment............................0.81 Mb
    [t]  P  GS (cg12) Device Driver......................................1.21 Mb
    [u]  P  GS (cg12) Run-time support software..........................0.90 Mb
    [v]  P  GT Device Drivers............................................1.70 Mb
    [w]  P  GT Run-time support software.................................1.65 Mb
    [x]  P  GX (cg6) Device Driver.......................................0.06 Mb
  Legend: * = selected for removal
     P = package, C = product cluster

                                        +-------------------------------+
  Type  [a-x] to select/de-select software  |          (required)    (free) |
     or  ?[a-x] to view software properties  | /         14.07 Mb    2.72 Mb |
     or  [Ctrl-N/Ctrl-P] to show next/prev page  | /usr   142.27 Mb   16.79 Mb |
     or  [Return] to complete selecting software. | /opt   34.94 Mb    1.50 Mb |
  Select an option:                         +-------------------------------+

+---------------------------------------------------------------------+
```

Figure 11.23 Selection of software for removal.

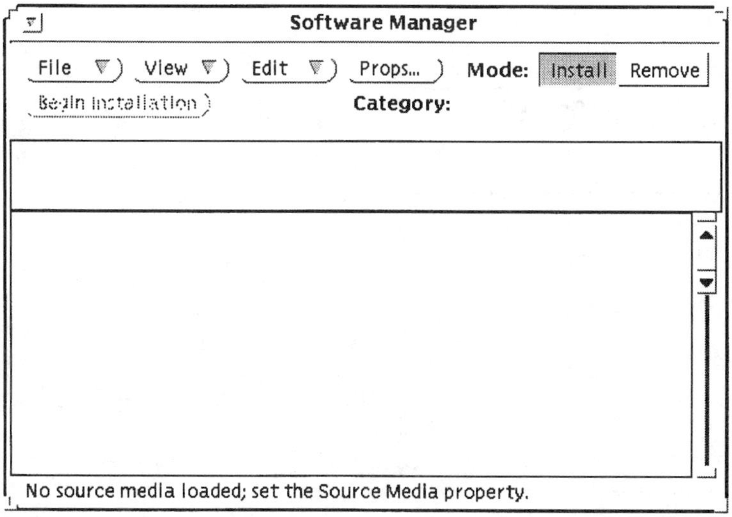

Figure 11.24 Software Manager.

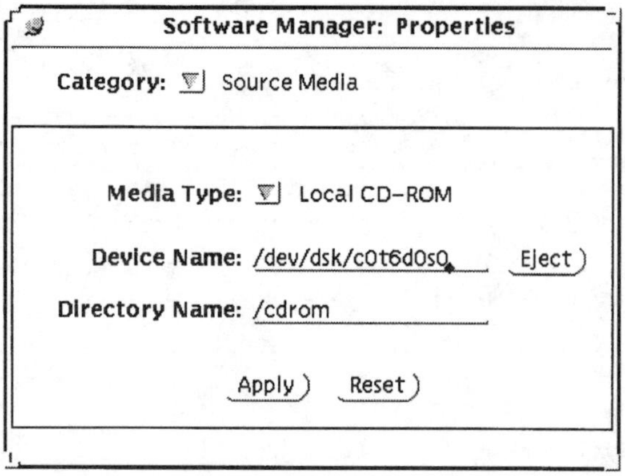

Software Manager: Properties

Category: ▽ Source Media

Media Type: ▽ Local CD-ROM

Device Name: /dev/dsk/c0t6d0s0   Eject)

Directory Name: /cdrom

Apply)   Reset)

Figure 11.25   Specifying source media.

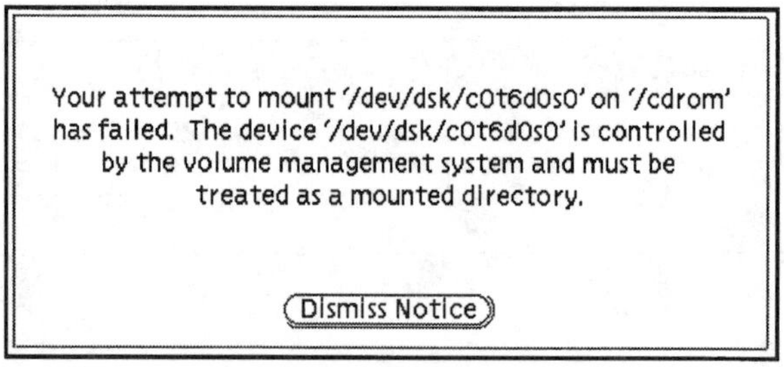

Your attempt to mount '/dev/dsk/c0t6d0s0' on '/cdrom'
has failed. The device '/dev/dsk/c0t6d0s0' is controlled
by the volume management system and must be
treated as a mounted directory.

(Dismiss Notice)

Figure 11.26   Mount notice.

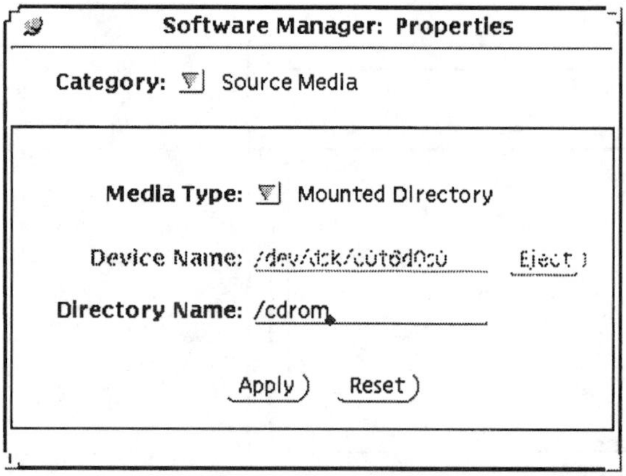

Software Manager: Properties

Category: ▽ Source Media

Media Type: ▽ Mounted Directory

Device Name: /dev/dsk/c0t6d0s0   Eject)

Directory Name: /cdrom

Apply)   Reset)

Figure 11.27   Specifying mount point.

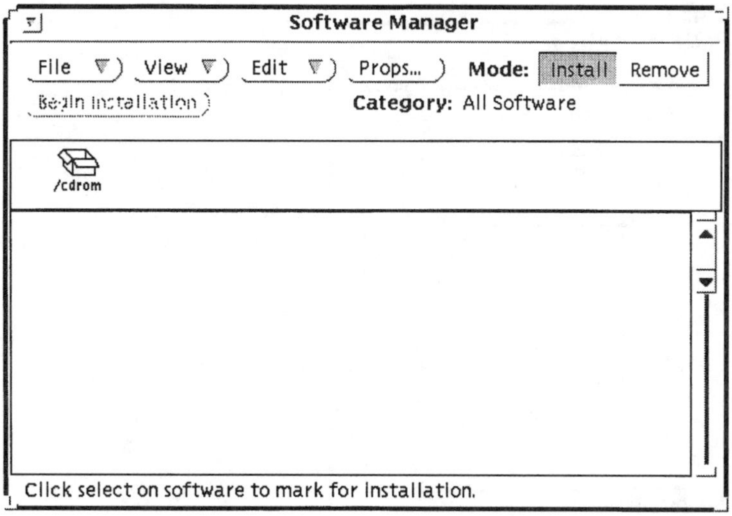

Figure 11.28   Selecting installation.

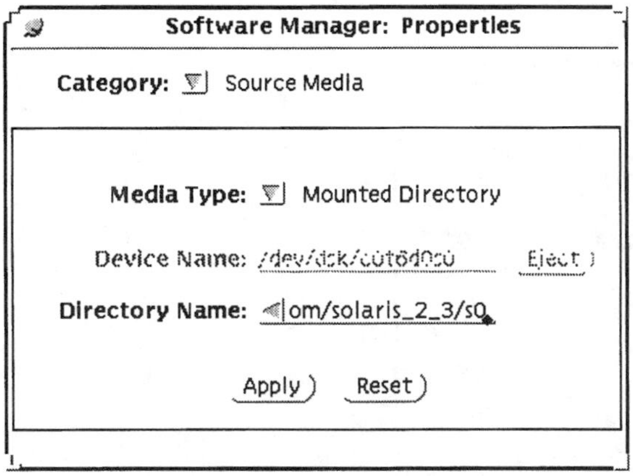

Figure 11.29   Selecting directory.

Figure 11.31 illustrates the space meter. The measurements indicated will change as you select and deselect software, and will show negative measurements if you do not have enough room to install what you have selected.

Figure 11.32 displays the software that the tool has found on the CD ROM. It lists the package names and the amount of space that each requires. Once you select a package or a number of packages, you can begin the installation using the `Begin installation` button in the upper left-hand corner. Be sure that you have not left all the packages selected if you are installing one or two. The command window which then appears is used to control the execution of the script. In Fig. 11.33, you can see the script for loading the online man pages.

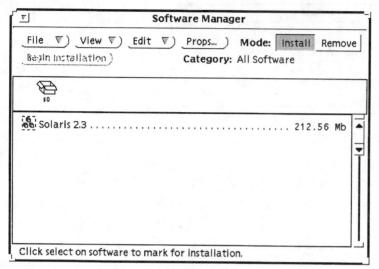

Figure 11.30 Viewing Solaris 2.3.

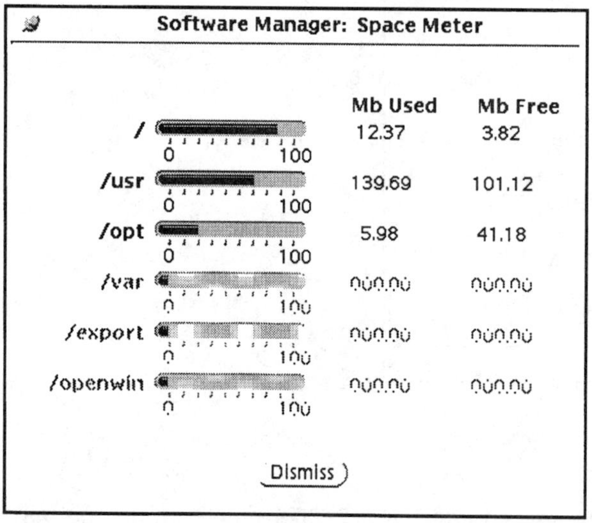

Figure 11.31 Space meter.

TRY THIS   **Examine the Menus in** swmtool

Pull down each menu of swmtool and examine the options that it provides. Try
selecting and deselecting software packages. Switch to iconic viewing mode by
using the Display...form found under the Props menu.

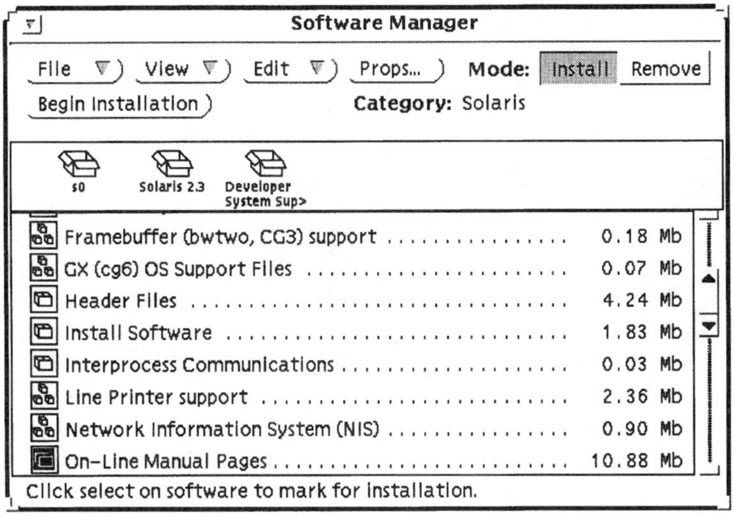

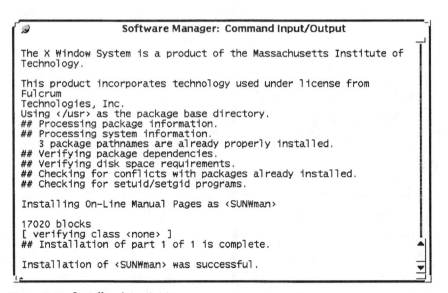

Figure 11.32 Selecting software packages.

Figure 11.33 Install script output.

TRY THIS   Install and Remove Software

Try installing and removing software on a system (Fig. 11.34). If you are not using the man pages, install and remove them. If you use them, remove and reinstall them. Become familiar with the swmtool and its various options.

The package control options displayed in Fig. 11.35 are the same as those provided by swm, but appear in a different order. Compare this form with the

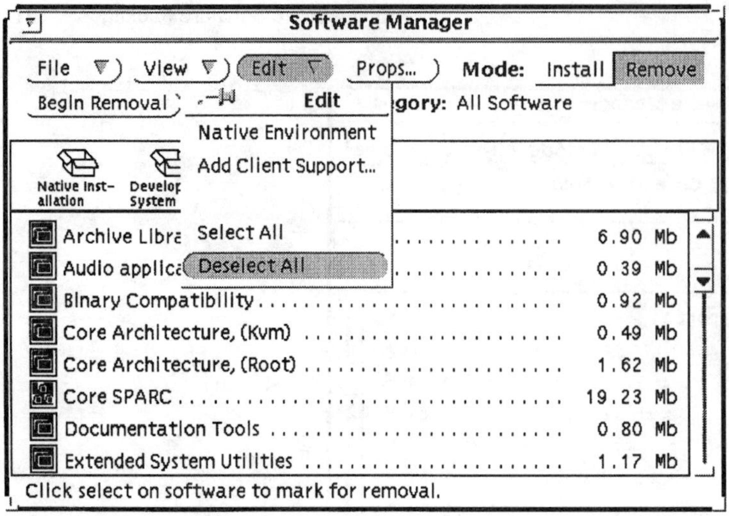

Figure 11.34 Deselecting packages.

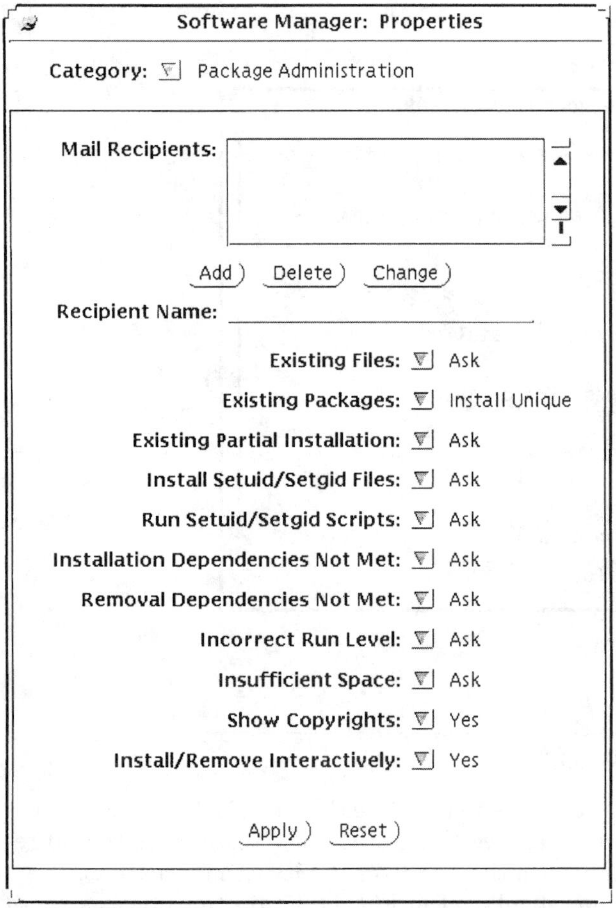

Figure 11.35 Selecting options.

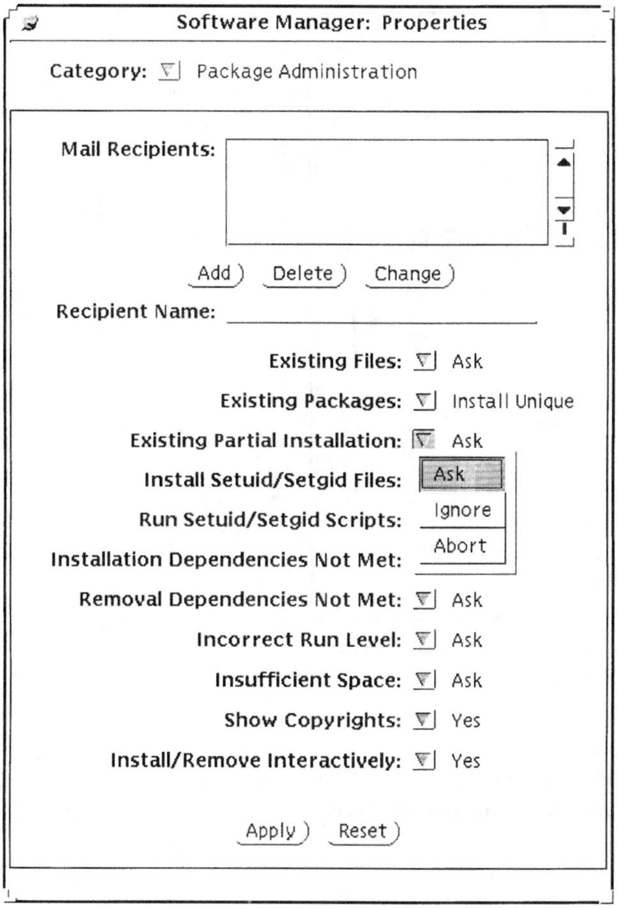

Figure 11.36 Selecting remote hosts for installation.

configuration properties menu from swm displayed in Fig. 11.20. Note how easily the options can be selected within this form in Fig. 11.36.

The form for managing target hosts for the installation is shown in Fig. 11.37. Like swm, swmtool allows you to create a list of hosts to receive the software that is being installed or from which the software should be removed. As with swm, the ability to install and remove software from remote hosts depends on having established trust between these hosts ahead of time so that the remote host will accept the commands issued from the local host. You need to know the root password of the remote host or have your host included in that host's /.rhosts file. When you add a remote host to the list, it will have one of four symbols to the left of its name in the list. In Fig. 11.37, three of these symbols are shown. The triangle indicates that the host is up. If there is an upside-down triangle, the host is down. The not symbol (circle with crossbar) indicates one of two things: (1) that the host is known, but that Software Manager on the

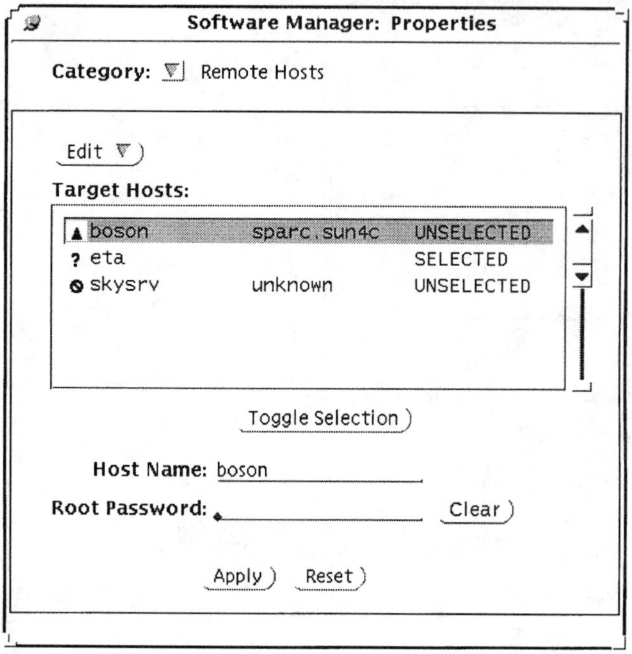

Figure 11.37   Selecting Browser display options.

install host does not have permission to add software; or (2) that the host is unknown. The question mark indicates that the host is not a Solaris 2.x system.

11.7   Summary

Both Sun and third-party software for Solaris 2.x is distributed in package
form allowing easy installation and deinstallation through the tools `swm` and
`swmtool`. AnswerBook coverage of these tools augments what is covered in this
chapter.

Advanced Administration

12

Security

Introduction

Solaris 2.x has added many enhanced security features for both the user and the administrator. Some of these have been in previous releases as options, some have been available as unbundled products. This chapter will describe the major features that have been incorporated in Solaris 2.x. The features detailed here will include basic systems security and Automated Security Enhancement Tool (ASET). There are other security features, which are discussed in other sections of the book such as Kerberos network authentication, NIS+ authenticated users, and AdminTool security features. Be sure to reference the appropriate section for those topics.

In Solaris 2.x most of the security features from previous releases have been included. The most notable exception to this is the C2 package that had been included in previous releases. Some of the features of C2 security, such as the /etc/shadow file and password aging, have been included. The C2 security package will be available as an unbundled product.

Added to the default system security is the use of a shadow password file, restricted shells, and password aging. Also incorporated into Solaris 2.x is the previously unbundled security package ASET, which provides a set of accounting and logging features to help detect unauthorized use of systems.

12.1 Password Security

In the past one of the security holes was the password file, /etc/passwd, which contained the encrypted password for each user. This file was readable by all users of the systems, and thus passwords could be decrypted and used to gain unauthorized access to a system. With Solaris 2.0 a new file has been added: /etc/shadow. The encrypted passwords are no longer kept in the /etc/passwd file. The field in the /etc/passwd file, where the password would have been stored has been replaced with an x and the encrypted passwords have been moved to the /etc/shadow file. The /etc/passwd file is still readable by all users, but the /etc/shadow file is readable by only the superuser, thus preventing users from obtaining encrypted passwords and decoding them.

12.2 Password Aging

A feature that has been previously optional is now incorporated into Solaris 2.x. Password aging is now a standard feature and is built into the /etc/shadow file format. Password aging makes a system more secure by forcing users to change their passwords every so often. That way even if an unauthorized user learns a password it will be of limited value because the user will be changing that password in the near future.

Password aging is implemented by using some of the fields of the lines in the /etc/shadow file. Those fields and the format of the /etc/shadow file are discussed below. In general, the fields specify the following:

- The minimum number of days between password changes. This means once a password has been changed, it may not be changed again for this number of days.
- The date of the last password change.
- The maximum number of days a password is valid. If a password has not been changed in this number of days, the user will be prompted for a new password at the next login session.
- A warning date. This is the number of days before the maximum time that a user will be warned to change the password on the account.
- The number of inactive days. A user who has not logged or accessed this account in the number of days specified will be prompted for a new password.
- An expiration date. This is an absolute date after which this account may no longer be used.

12.3 Format of `/etc/passwd` file

The format of the /etc/passwd file remains unchanged from previous releases of the operating system. The file contains a line for each user of the system, and each line consists of seven fields separated by colons (see Fig. 12.1).

The seven fields of an /etc/passwd line are as follows:

Username.   The user's login name. This name must be unique in eight characters.

Password.   This will be empty for no password or contain an x when the password is added to the shadow file.

Userid (UID).   A unique integer value between 1 and 65526. UID 0 is reserved for root.

```
# cat /etc/passwd
root:x:0:1:0000-Admin(0000):/:/bin/csh
daemon:x:1:1:0000-Admin(0000):/:
bin:x:2:2:0000-Admin(0000):/usr/bin:
sys:x:3:3:0000-Admin(0000):/:
adm:x:4:4:0000-Admin(0000):/var/adm:
lp:x:71:8:0000-lp(0000):/usr/spool/lp:
smtp:x:0:0:mail daemon user:/:
uucp:x:5:5:0000-uucp(0000):/usr/lib/uucp:
nuucp:x:9:9:0000-
uucp(0000):/var/spool/uucppublic:/usr/lib/uucp/uucico
listen:x:37:4:Network Admin:/usr/net/nls:
nobody:x:60001:60001:uid no body:/:
noaccess:x:60002:60002:uid no access:/:
js:x:1000:1:John Smith: /home/john
```

Figure 12.1 Sample password file.

Group ID (GID).   An integer value that must correspond to one of the group IDs listed in the /etc/group file.

Comment.   A short description of who this user is; perhaps the real name of the user.

Home directory.   The fully qualified pathname of the directory which the user will use for the home directory.

Login shell.   This will be the default shell the user will have started on login or the process that will be started on login.

If a user is added with the useradd utility (discussed below), the password field of this file will contain *LK*. This means that the user password is locked and the account will be locked until the superuser issues a password.

12.4   Format of the /etc/shadow file

The format of the /etc/shadow is very similar to that of the /etc/passwd file. The file contains one line for each user of the system, and each line consists of seven fields separated by colons. An example of an /etc/passwd file is presented in Fig. 12.2.

The seven fields of an /etc/shadow line are as follows:

Username.   The user's login name. This name must correspond to a name already in the /etc/passwd file.

Password.   This field will contain the 13-character encrypted password after the user has executed the passwd command. (More on this field later.)

Lastchanged.   The date, expressed as the number of days since January 1, 1970, when the password was last changed.

Minimum.   This is the minimum number of days required between password changes.

```
# cat /etc/shadow
root::6445::::::
daemon:NP:6445:::::::
bin:NP:6445::::::
sys:NP:6445::::::
adm:NP:6445::::::
lp:NP:6445::::::
smtp:NP:6445::::::
uucp:NP:6445::::::
nuucp:NP:6445::::::
listen:*LK*::::::
nobody:NP:6445::::::
noaccess:NP:6445::::::
jrg:k0BfRPkUSMpzk:8639::::::
foo:*LK*:::::::
```

Figure 12.2   Sample /etc/shadow file.

Maximum.   This is the maximum number of days that a password is valid.

Warn.   This is the number of days before the password expires that a user will be warned to change the password on the account.

Inactive.   This is the number of days of inactivity that is allowed for this user. If the account has not been accessed in this number of days, the user will be prompted for a new password on logging in.

Expiration.   This is the date that an account will no longer be accessible. This date is expressed as the number of days from January 1, 1970.

12.5   Password Synchronization

In the past, updates to the password file by hand were relatively easy because there was only the /etc/passwd file to deal with. With the use of the shadow file, manual update of user account is a little more difficult. The issue is that there must be a one-to-one correspondence for the user entries between the two files, /etc/passwd and /etc/shadow. Two new utilities aid in the update of the files and keep them in synchronization: useradd and pwconv.

If you choose not to use AdminTool to add or modify user entries, useradd is the proper way to add users. This command takes as parameters all of the options that would be specified in a password file entry such as UID, GID, comment, or home directory, as well as the password aging field that go into the /etc/shadow file. The only required parameter to the useradd command is the username. All other fields will use default values. To find the default values issue the command

```
# useradd -D
group=other, 1 basedir=/home skel=/etc/skel
shell=/sbin/sh inactive=0 expire=
```

A sample command to add a user looks as follows:

```
# useradd -u 1007 -g other -s /bin/csh -c newguy -m -k /etc/skel fred
or
# useradd fred
```

The useradd command correctly updates both the passwd and the shadow files. Other related commands are userdel to delete a user; and usermod, to modify a user entry. Again, both of these commands will correctly update the passwd and shadow files.

The pwconv command creates and updates the /etc/shadow files using information found in the /etc/passwd file. It is recommended that users be added using the useradd command or the AdminTool facility for two reasons.

- Editing the /etc/shadow and /etc/passwd files by hand increases the potential for errors.

- Editing the passwd file manually does not lock the user password and leaves the account vulnerable if you forget to assign the new user a password.

If you do use an editor (or the vipw command) to manipulate the files and an error does occur the pwconv utility is a way to reconcile the files. The pwconv command does the following.

- If the shadow file does not exist, it will create the shadow file using information in the passwd file.

- If the passwd file contains aging attributes, these will be transferred to the shadow file.

- If there are user entries in the passwd file that do not appear in shadow file, new entries will be made in the shadow file.

- If there are entries in the shadow file that do not appear in the passwd file, those entries will be deleted from the shadow file.

12.6   Security Features in the /etc/default Directory

There is a new directory in the Solaris 2.x environment, /etc/default. This directory contains three files: login, passwd, and su. These are ASCII files which control default policies for such events as remote logins, logfiles, and password control. These files are discussed below.

12.6.1   /etc/default/login

The /etc/default/login file (Fig. 12.3) controls system login policies. One of the primary issues controlled by this file is root access to a specific device.

There are almost no security restraints for any program run by root (UID=0). The system administrator can restrict logins by root to a specific device. In the /etc/default/login file, the restraint CONSOLE=/dev/console is used to restrict the root logins to the device specified. Leaving the line uncommented will restrict root logins to the console device.

```
#ident "@(#) login.dfl 1.7 93/08/20 SMI" /* SVr4.0
1.1.1.1 */
# Set the TZ environment variable of the shell.
# TIMEZONE=EST5EDT

# Set the HZ environment variable of the shell.
# HZ=100

# ULIMIT sets the file size limit for the login. Units are disk blocks.
# The default of zero means no limit.
# ULIMIT=0

# If CONSOLE is set, root can only login on that device.
# Comment this line out to allow remote login by root.
# CONSOLE=/dev/console

# PASSREQ determines if login requires a password.
# PASSREQ=YES

# ALTSHELL determines if the SHELL environment variable should be set.
# ALTSHELL=YES

# PATH sets the initial shell PATH variable.
# PATH=/usr/bin:

# SUPATH sets the initial shell PATH variable for root.
# SUPATH=/usr/sbin:/usr/bin

# TIMEOUT sets the number of seconds (between 0 and 900) to wait before aban-
  doning a login session.
# TIMEOUT=300

# UMASK sets the initial shell file creation mode mask. See umask(1).
# UMASK=022

# SYSLOG determines whether the syslog(3) LOG_AUTH facility should be used to
  log all root logins at level LOG_NOTICE and multiple failed login attempts
  at LOG_CRIT.
# SYSLOG=YES
```

Figure 12.3 Sample /etc/default/login file.

12.6.2 /etc/default/passwd

The /etc/default/passwd file contains parameters that control password parameters including password aging. The default is to set a minimum length for the password at six characters and no password aging. A sample /etc/default/passwd file is shown in Fig. 12.4.

12.6.3 /etc/default/su

The /etc/default/su file controls how root logins via su are logged. The default is to display the login message to the system console and to make an entry in the /var/adm/sulog file entry every time a user tries to gain root access from a remote system. A sample su file is presented in Fig. 12.5.

12.7 Restricted Shells

It is common to allow a guest login on systems to permit the occasional outside user access to the system. This can lead to a security problem if the guest login

```
# cat /etc/default/passwd
#ident "@(#)passwd.dfl 1.3 92/07/14 SMI"
MAXWEEKS=
MINWEEKS=
PASSLENGTH=6
```

Figure 12.4   Sample /etc/default/passwd file.

```
# cat /etc/default/su
#ident "@(#)su.dfl 1.5 92/07/14 SMI" /* SVr4.0
1.2 */
SULOG=/var/adm/sulog
CONSOLE=/dev/console
```

Figure 12.5   Sample /etc/default/su file.

is allowed use of the normal shell programs. Solaris 2.x provides a restricted shell, /usr/lib/rsh (do not confuse with remote shell, /usr/sbin/rsh), to limit the activities of logins. The restricted shell is different from the normal shells in the following ways:

- The user is limited to the home directory (cd is not allowed).
- The user cannot change the PATH variable. PATH is set up by the system administrator.
- The user cannot access commands or files by specifying complete path names.
- The user cannot redirect output with >> or >.

The restricted shell would be useful for a guest login whose primary task would be to rlogin to their home system. It is not completely secure, however, and should be used with caution.

Another note is that rsh is a restricted Bourne shell. There is a restricted version of the Korn shell, rksh.

There is no restricted version of C shell.

12.8   Automated Security Enhancement Tool

The Automated Security Enhancement Tool (ASET) aids the systems administrator with system security by automating functions that would normally be done by hand. This module will describe the features of ASET and how to customize ASET to serve your needs.

12.8.1   Introduction to ASET

ASET is a security package that provides automated tools to enable you to monitor system security by specifying a security level: high, medium, or low. For each security level, ASET will increase system security monitoring and reduce the risk of improper system access.

ASET performs seven basic system checks:

- File permissions
- System files contents
- User and group checks
- Configuration files contents
- Environmental file checks
- eeprom checks
- Router firewalls

For each of these checks, ASET will generate a report which will pinpoint weaknesses or changes to any of the critical portions of the system. When the ASET tools are installed, there is a set of master files in the directory /usr/aset which are used for comparison to system files. This directory is also where the report files are stored.

ASET is a disk-intensive operation and can have an impact on overall system performance. System administrators can reduce this impact by using cron to schedule ASET to run when system activity is lowest and only once each day or on alternate days.

12.8.2   ASET security levels

ASET allows three levels of security control: high, medium, and low. Each level changes the ASET activity on the system files. Activities at each level are outlined as follows:

Low security.   At the lowest security level, ASET compares the designated system files with the master copies kept in the /usr/aset directory and reports on potential weaknesses in the system due to changes in the system files. At this level ASET will take no action; it will simply report. System services will not be interrupted, and files will not be modified.

Medium security.   The medium security level should prove to be adequate for most installations. At this level, the same files are checked as the low security setting but some of the more important files may be modified. ASET will report any discovered weaknesses and any changes made to the system files. However, system services will not be interrupted at the medium security level.

High security.   At the highest security setting ASET will adjust the permissions and contents of many system and configuration files. Applications and commands will continue to run normally; however, if ASET discovers a security weakness, the processes used to repair the flaw and generate the report will take precedence over other system activities.

12.8.3 The /usr/aset directory

Figure 12.6 is a listing of the files in the /usr/aset directory.

Under the reports subdirectory are subdirectories for each report aset has generated. The names for these files are in the form monthdate_hour:minute. The /usr/aset/reports/latest entry is a symbolic link to the last report directory generated. The masters subdirectory contains three files: tune, alias, and checklist. The tune files, tune.low, tune.med and tune.high, specify the desired attributes for the system files. The alias file, uid_alias, is used to report on multiple accounts that use the same user identification (UID).

The checklist files are generated the first time ASET is run or when you change the security level that ASET is using. ASET will take a picture of the system files and use the picture to compare file attributes and make modifications as needed. The following system files are checked:

- /etc/default/login
- /etc/hosts.equiv
- /etc/inetd.conf
- /etc/aliases
- /var/adm/utmp
- /var/adm/utmpx
- /.rhosts
- /etc/vfstab
- /etc/dfs/dfstab
- /etc/ftpusers

```
total 42
drwx——       2 root      bin          512   May 12 09:11   archives
-rwx——       1 root      bin         7242   Sep 27 1993    aset
-rwx——       1 root      bin         2312   Sep 27 1993    aset.restore
-rwx——       1 root      bin         3231   Sep 27 1993    asetenv
drwx——       2 root      bin          512   May 12 09:14   masters
drwx——       3 root      bin          512   May 12 09:11   reports
drwx——       2 root      bin          512   Mar 10 20:29   tasks
drwx——       2 root      bin          512   May 12 09:14   tmp
drwx——       2 root      bin          512   Mar 10 20:29   util
```

Figure 12.6 The /usr/aset directory.

12.9 Summary

This chapter has examined some of the security features of the Solaris product including ASET, restricted shells, password aging, and password security. The following manual pages should be consulted for further information:

```
passwd (1)
rsh (1M)
useradd(1M), userdel (1M)
groupadd (1M), groupdel (1M)
pwconv (1M)
files:
  /etc/passwd
  /etc/shadow
  /etc/default/*
  /etc/skel/*
```

There is also a very good section on these topics in the AnswerBook.

13

Administering
NIS+

Any network with more than a handful of hosts will store information about its
hosts, users, and services in a network information service of some kind. Long
gone are the days when copies of host files were copied from system to system
to keep them communicating. Even with modern tools to facilitate synchronization of files over a network, the services provided by a network information
service are far advanced and much preferred.

Arriving with Solaris 2.x, NIS+ incorporates the best features of its predecessor, NIS, and the advanced naming conventions of DNS. With distributed
management, robust algorithms for synchronizing network information between servers, and good performance, NIS+ allows both large and small organizations to structure their network information to simplify its administration.

13.1   Introducing NIS+

NIS+ is a network information service which provides naming services similar to the Domain Name System (DNS) but, in other ways, is more like its predecessor, NIS. Like DNS, NIS+ provides a hierarchical namespace which provides for addresses which include information about specific hosts and their
position within the organizational hierarchy of which they are a member. Like
NIS, NIS+ provides much more than a mapping between hosts and numeric
addresses but the means to simplify network administration by providing distributed control over many types of network information.

NIS+ is more versatile and secure than NIS and provides much faster updates. As a consequence, it is also more complicated to set up and to administer.
However, its advantages far outweigh the costs associated with understanding
and managing this additional complexity. Very large organizations who need
distributed control without sacrificing overall performance and "seamless" con-
nectivity will find the advantages of NIS+ irresistible.

NIS+ provides the system administrator with a hierarchical namespace so that the addresses on the network resemble the structure of the organization. In addition, management of this information in a large organization can be delegated to administrators at various levels who have timely access to network changes occurring at that level.

NIS+ also provides a much more efficient mechanism for updating information in the network information service files. Changes to NIS+ are propagated incrementally and are automatically propagated, unlike NIS, which required the administrator to intentionally send out new copies of entire maps by using a make command.

Another advantage of NIS+ is its much enhanced security. By supporting the establishment and passing of credentials between clients and servers, opportunities for hosts to "spoof" have been eliminated. Credentials establish the authenticity of the machines making the connection.

NIS+ files are called *tables,* rather than *maps* as in NIS, and information within them (unlike with NIS) can be accessed from any column. With NIS, this information could be accessed only using the "key."

NIS+ can also be run in NIS-compatibility mode. This permits an NIS+ server to respond to requests from NIS clients. No changes to the NIS clients need to be made to run in this mode as the NIS+ server looks like an NIS server to the clients. There is also a version of NIS+ available for 4.X systems; this provides another option for ensuring the compatibility of network information services during the transition to Solaris 2.x or any time that you have both Solaris 2.x and SunOS 4.X systems.

A full description of NIS+ would require a complete book and, indeed such a book exists and is included in the summary at the end of this chapter. In this chapter, we will provide some general descriptions and advice on making choices concerning your NIS+ configuration.

13.2   Structure of the NIS+ Namespace

To understand how information is organized in NIS+, you don't have to go any further than your present file system. Hierarchical in nature, the directory tree that you have known since your earliest days with UNIX is much like the namespace of NIS+. At the root of this structure, you have the organization itself. Most organizations, whether they are on the Internet or not, will adopt the high-order naming conventions of DNS, and the root domains will have names like `BigBucks.com`, while departments will have names like `Sales.Big-Bucks.com`. Unlike the structure of your file system, NIS+ names go from the specific to the general (or small to large) as we move from left to right. NIS+ names contain dots rather than slashes. A final dot is often mandatory as it indicates a fully qualified name. A simple diagram of an NIS+ namespace (partial) is illustrated in Fig. 13.1.

At the root of the organizational NIS+ namespace is the root-master server. There is only one root-master server and it services the root domain. Since domains can exist at each level in the NIS+ namespace, master servers can also

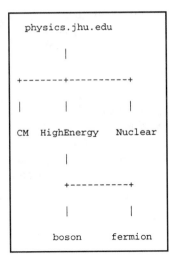

```
physics.jhu.edu

        |

+-------+----------+

|       |          |

CM   HighEnergy   Nuclear

        |

   +----------+

   |          |

  boson     fermion
```

Figure 13.1 NIS+   hierarchical namespace.

exist at each level as well. A *domain* is a collection of the objects that exist within its namespace. In Fig. 13.1, boson and fermion are members of the domain physics.jhu.edu.

13.3 Masters and Replicas

Similar to the master-and-slave server relationship in NIS, NIS+ maintains master and replica servers. There is a single master for each root domain and a master server at each point in the organizational hierarchy that subdomains are created. Although it is not necessary to have more than a single master in the entire organization, larger organizations will no doubt benefit from being able to distribute control to larger and more autonomous divisions within the organization.

13.4 NIS+ Information Propagation

The propagation algorithm used with NIS+ is both efficient and robust. NIS+ masters try to batch updates and send them to replica servers using an approach that manages to keep the replicas in step with the master even though they may be down during some of the updates.

NIS+ changes are stored in several places: on disk, in memory, and in a transaction log. Each update is a copy of the changed object. Timestamps are used to coordinate these updates between the master and replicas. When a master tells the replicas that it is ready to send a batch of changes, the replicas respond with the timestamp of the last changes that they received. With this information, the master is able to send, however, many changes from the transaction log that are needed to bring the replica up to date. The master can clear its update log once all replicas have been successfully updated. There is a resync operation with which a master sends complete information regarding its domain to a replica that is useful if replicas are added or reinstalled. The `nisping` command, on the other hand, causes the replica servers to request changes from the master.

The log files for NIS+ are named after the table that they are mirroring with a `.log` appended. Thus, the log file for the host's file is `hosts.log`. The disk-based copies of NIS+ tables lag the memory-resident copies and the log files on servers receiving these updates. In order to purge the log files and commit the remaining changes to disk, you can use the `nisping -C` command. An example is shown below.

```
boson# nisping -C org_dir
Checkpointing replicas serving directory org_dir.physics.jhu.edu.:
Master server is boson.physics.jhu.edu.
   Last update occurred at Sun Oct 31 01:42:55 1993

Master server is boson.physics.jhu.edu.
checkpoint has been scheduled with boson.physics.jhu.edu..
checkpoint has been scheduled with fermion.physics.jhu.edu..
```

13.5 NIS+ Information Retrieval

When an NIS+ client requires information, it first checks the server for its own domain. If this server cannot supply the needed information, it sends the client information to help it locate the correct server. Over time, the client caches information about various NIS+ servers and is able to locate the network information that it requires fairly efficiently. Experienced administrators can shorten the time that it takes to build up this cache by including additional information in the client's `coldstart` file. This file provides information with which the client begins the search, so that any information provided here reduces the discovery process that the client goes through to build up its cache.

13.6 NIS+ Name Expansion

Simple names in NIS+, like `Mgr`, are expanded to their fully qualified names, like `Mgr.Sales.BigBucks.com.`, by NIS+. The process of name expansion involves searching through the home domain, and then through parent domains until it finds the name or reaches a domain with a two-part name (in this example, `BigBucks.com.`). You can define search paths which alter the order in which this search is conducted or allow the search to descend into domains below parent domains, like `Research.BigBucks.com`, before completing the search. Fully qualified names, those ending with a dot, do not invoke this name expansion. A search path for NIS+ is established through the use of the environment variable `NIS_PATH`. In the `CShell`, you would establish a path with a command like that shown below:

```
setenv NIS_PATH Sales.BigBucks.com.:Research.BigBucks.com.:Mfg.BigBucks.com.
```

13.7   NIS+ Tables

The list of NIS+ tables very closely resembles the maps of NIS. System tables include those listed below.

`hosts`	Host names and addresses
`bootparams`	Parameters (root and swap) for diskless clients
`passwd`	User information
`cred`	Security credentials
`group`	Group definitions
`netgroup`	Netgroup (groups of hosts) definitions
`aliases`	Mail aliases
`timezone`	Timezone information
`networks`	Lists of networks
`netmasks`	Nonstandard netmasks used
`ethers`	Ethernet addresses (required with diskless clients)
`services`	Network services
`protocols`	Network protocols
`rpc`	Remote procedure calls
`auto_home`	Map for automounting home directories
`auto_master`	Master automount map; contains list of maps

Notice the slight change in the Automounter tables. The dots are replaced by underscores to avoid conflict with the dot-separated conventions of the hierarchical naming scheme.

NIS+ is composed of objects and directories. These NIS+ tables are objects in the `org_dir` directory. The structure of NIS+ tables, as you see in outline form in Fig. 13.2, hierarchical in nature since these tables, like the host addresses we discussed above, are part of the overall directory and object structure of NIS+. When we list the contents of the passwd table, we refer to it as `passwd.org_dir` or by its fully qualified name, which in this example is `passwd.org_dir.physics.jhu.edu`.

Just as you can list files in a directory with `ls`, you can list objects in an NIS+ directory with `nisls`. Notice how the command displays the fully qualified table name before displaying its contents. Similarly, the command to display the contents of an NIS+ object is similar to the command used to display a file. We've shown an example of using the `niscat` command below.

```
boson# nisls org_dir
org_dir.physics.jhu.edu.:
```

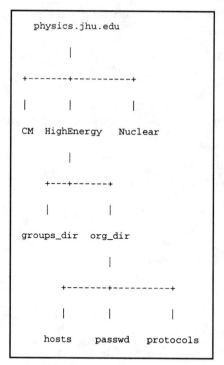

```
   physics.jhu.edu

          |

+-------+----------+

|       |          |

CM  HighEnergy   Nuclear

               |

     +---+------+

     |          |

groups_dir  org_dir

               |

     +-------+----------+

     |       |          |

   hosts   passwd    protocols
```

Figure 13.2 Tables in NIS+ hierarchical namespace.

```
auto_master
auto_home
bootparams
cred
ethers
group
hosts
mail_aliases
sendmailvars
netmasks
netgroup
networks
passwd
protocols
rpc
services
timezone
boson# nisls passwd.org_dir
passwd.org_dir.physics.jhu.edu.
```

```
boson# niscat hosts.org_dir
localhost localhost 127.0.0.1
localhost loghost 127.0.0.1
boson boson 128.220.26.137
gauss gauss 128.220.26.4
flux flux 128.220.26.5
ssc ssc 128.220.26.6
...
```

13.8 NIS+ Security

In NIS+, users and workstations have credentials which determine NIS+ access privileges. Each NIS+ request includes the credentials of the requester. These credentials are subsequently authenticated, or they are not. Depending on the access rights set up for an object, authenticated and unauthenticated requests can be granted or denied. If, for example, a request is authenticated for a group member, but the group is not granted access to the object, the request is denied. On the other hand, an unauthenticated request for an object which gives access to `nobody` will be granted.

NIS+ can run at one of three security levels. Security level 0 involves no examination of credentials. This is "insecure" NIS+ and is used for testing and configuration. Security level 1 accepts either local or DES credentials. Since local credentials can be forged, this security level is generally used only for testing. Security level 2 uses DES only and is the highest security level available in NIS+.

Individual objects in NIS+ have an access matrix which closely resembles that associated with UNIX files. For each category of user—owner, group, world, and nobody—there is an access matrix including fields which represent read, modify, create, and destroy. The hosts' object, for example, may have the following access characteristics.

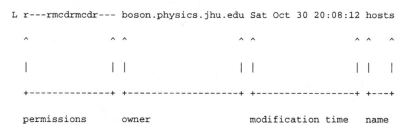

13.9 The Name Service Switch

Name services, as we have been alluding to in this chapter, provide a mapping between host IP numbers and the names that we humans like to use and remember. They also provide the means to manage this information in a distributed fashion so that each name server maintains information about hosts within its domain and knows how to "look up" addresses for hosts outside this domain. Solaris 2.x allows you to select which of several name services you use for what types of network information through use of a configuration file called `/etc/nsswitch.conf`.

The name service switch is external to NIS+, but it allows NIS+ clients to look for information in other places, or in addition to, the NIS+ database. The logic that you establish in this file will determine the order in which naming services are searched for network information. You will likely search NIS+ first, but you can also specify NIS, the `/etc` files, or DNS (but only for hosts, since DNS does not house other types of network information). The name service switch provides a very simple way for you to fold information from several sources into your network information database. If you are using both NIS+ and DNS, for example, configuring your switch file to search both for host information is extremely straightforward.

Each line in the `nsswitch.conf` will look something like this:

```
hosts:      nisplus[NOTFOUND=return] files
  ^           ^        ^             ^          ^

  |           |        |             |          |

mapname     first    status       action     next
            source   after        to         source
                     search       take
```

You can specify a single source or several, and the bracketed test (include the brackets!) is optional. The line

```
hosts: nisplus [NOTFOUND=return] files
```

specifies that NIS+ is to be queried first for hosts. If NIS+ reports that it cannot find them, the search is ended. If NIS+ returns any other status, the search continues. If, therefore, NIS+ is down, returning a status of UNAVAIL, the `/etc` files will be used instead.

The possible statuses that NIS+ can return are

Status	Means
SUCCESS	Entry found
UNAVAIL	No response from NIS+
NOTFOUND	No such entry
TRYAGAIN	Source busy

The actions that can be specified are

Action	Means
return	Stop looking
continue	Try next source

Solaris 2.x provides preconfigured name service switch files for NIS, NIS+, and the `/etc` files. The file `/etc/nsswitch.nisplus` is the configuration file which

includes NIS+ as the first place to look for network information. When this file is copied to `/etc/nsswitch.conf`, the search scenario that it describes is used. The preconfigured switch files for NIS and `/etc` files are called `nss-witch.nis` and `nsswitch.files`.

The default `nsswitch.nisplus` file is pictured in Fig. 13.3. This file specifies that the system should first search for `passwd` and group information in the `/etc` files. For services, protocols, and so on, it should look in NIS+ tables.

```
# /etc/nsswitch.nisplus:
#
# An example file that could be copied over to /etc/nsswitch.conf; it
# uses NIS+ (NIS Version 3) in conjunction with files.
#
# "hosts:" and "services:" in this file are used only if the /etc/netconfig
# file contains "switch.so" as a nametoaddr library for "inet" transports

# the following two lines obviate the "+" entry in /etc/passwd and /etc/group.
passwd: files nisplus
group: files nisplus
# consult/etc "files" only if nisplus is down.
hosts: nisplus [NOTFOUND=return] files

#Uncomment the following line, and comment out the above, to use both DNS and
NIS+
#hosts: nisplus dns [NOTFOUND=return] files
services: nisplus [NOTFOUND=return] files
networks: nisplus [NOTFOUND=return] files
protocols: nisplus [NOTFOUND=return] files
rpc: nisplus [NOTFOUND=return] files
ethers: nisplus [NOTFOUND=return] files
netmasks: nisplus [NOTFOUND=RETURN] files
bootparams: nisplus [NOTFOUND=return] files

publickey: nisplus

netgroup: nisplus

automount: files nisplus
aliases: files nisplus
sendmailvars: files nisplus
```

Figure 13.3   The default `/etc/nsswitch.conf` file.

13.10   NIS+ Commands

As we've already mentioned, the commands of NIS+ are quite similar in function and format to the names of familiar UNIX commands. Taking advantage of this similarity will help you get a head start at understanding how NIS+ works. We will cover each of the commands very briefly in this section.

13.10.1   `nisls`

The `nisls` command is like the UNIX ls command except that it lists objects which belong to an NIS+ directory. As with the `ls` command, you need to have access rights to read a directory's contents. Also like `ls`, the `nisls` command has a number of options to modify its behavior. If you add a -d to an `ls` command, you get a listing of the directory object itself. If you add an -1, you get a long listing complete with permissions. The -g option will display the associated group. Other options include the following:

-L   Follows links and gives information about the linked directory

-M   Gives information only about the master server

-R   Recursively lists directory contents

-m   Display modification time rather than creation time

13.10.2   `niscat`

The `niscat` command is like the UNIX cat. It displays the contents of an NIS+ table the same way a cat displays the contents of a file. With a -h, you get the table header. With -M, you get only information from the master server. With -o, you get object information about the table.

13.10.3   `nischmod`

The NIS+ `nischmod` command, obviously, manipulates the access rights to an NIS+ object. Like the chmod command, it allows you to modify access rights for each group. However, `nischmod` works only with the +- syntax and not with numeric equivalents of the access rights. NIS+ also allows you to change access rights for individual entries in tables by specifying the column name and its value within the command. The second example below illustrates this.

```
boson# nischmod g+rm East.Sales.BigBucks.com.
boson# nischmod g+rm [name=boson],hosts.Sales.BigBucks.com.
```

13.10.4   `nischown`

The `nischown` command works like the chown command. It allows you to change the owner of one or more objects or entries. Like the `nischmod` command, it allows you to change ownership of an object or to specify entries by specifying a column name and the value to match.

```
nischown slee.Research.BigBucks.com. [name=boson],hosts.org_dir.BigBucks.com
```

13.10.5 `nischgrp`

The `nischgrp` command changes the group ownership of objects or table entries. You can also specify a `[column=value]` entry for this command. As with the UNIX `chgrp`, this command requires that you have modify permissions to the object or entry you are changing. The master NIS+ server for the particular domain must also be running.

```
boson# nischgrp admin.pha.jhu.edu.hosts.org_dir.pha.jhu.edu.
```

13.10.6 `nisrm`

The `nisrm` command removes an object provided it is not a directory. To remove a directory requires a `nisrmdir` command. It has an interactive mode, specified with `-i`, and a force option, `-f`, which attempts an `nischmod` and retries the `nisrm` if the first try fails.

13.10.7 `nisrmdir`

The `nisrmdir` command removes an NIS+ directory. Alternately, it can be used to disassociate a replica server from a directory without removing the directory on the master. It also has a force option which allows the command to succeed even if affected replicas are down; these replicas will be updated when they reboot. Examples of each version of the command are shown below.

```
boson% nisrmdir supercollider.physics.jhu.edu.
boson% nisrmdir -s hbar supercollider.physics.jhu.edu.
boson% nisrmdir -f supercollider.physics.jhu.edu.
```

13.10.8 `nismkdir`

The `nismkdir` command creates a directory and designates servers which support it. Unless specific permissions and replicas are specified with this command, the new directory will duplicate the parent directory's values.

13.10.9 `nisgrep` and `nismatch`

The `nisgrep` and `nismatch` commands search the NIS+ tables for matching strings (`nismatch`) or regular expressions (`nisgrep`.) These commands have many options (e.g., `-c` for printing only the count of matching items and `-h` to include column headers). The nisgrep command will search any column. The `nismatch` command is faster, but searches only searchable columns.

```
boson% nismatch name="slee" passwd.org_dir
slee:r/hkgCoCJg/uI:253:100:S. Lee Henry, x7392:/home/eta/slee:/bin/csh:

boson% nisgrep -h name="^slee" passwd.org_dir
# name:passwd:uid:gid:gcos:home:shell:shadow
slee:r/hkgCoCJg/uI:253:100:S. Lee Henry, x7392:/home/eta/slee:/bin/csh:
sleester:HTwRvCLLH9J1Y:111:100:Sandra Leester:/home/eta/sleester:/bin/ksh:
```

13.10.10 nisln

The `nisln` command creates symbolic links between NIS+ table entries and objects. It will link objects to objects, entries to entries, or objects to entries. The `-L` option available with most of the NIS+ commands directs the command to also follow these links. In the example below, we are making a link called `hosts.physics.jhu.edu` that points to `hosts.org_dir.jhu.edu`.

```
boson# nisls hosts.physics.jhu.edu.
hosts.physics.jhu.edu.:Not found.
boson# nisln hosts.org_dir.physics.jhu.edu hosts.physics.jhu.edu
boson# nisls hosts.physics,jhu.edu
hosts.physics.jhu.edu.
```

13.10.11 nispasswd

The `nispasswd` command changes or displays a password in the NIS+ `passwd` table. It can also be used to view or modify aging information for the specified user.

```
boson# nispasswd slee
Changing password for slee on NIS+ server.
New login password:
Re-enter new password:
NIS+ password information changed for slee
```

The credential information for slee will not be changed.

```
User slee must do the following to update his/her
credential information:
Use NEW passwd for login and OLD passwd for keylogin.
Use "chkey -p" to reencrypt the credentials with the
new login passwd.
He/she must keylogin explicitly after his/her next login.
```

13.10.12 nisping

The `nisping` command sends a ping to NIS+ replicas. This causes them to check the master for updates. The `nisping` command, therefore, initiates a checkpointing operation for NIS+ information.

13.10.13 nisaddcred

The `nisaddcred` command creates security credentials for NIS+ principles (hosts and users). These credentials are stored in `cred.org_dir` in the default NIS+ domain or one which is specified.

13.10.14 `nisaddent`

The `nisaddent` command is used to add NIS+ table entries in bulk (as from the `/etc/passwd` file or NIS map) or individually. Depending on the options used, the new entries will override or be merged with existing entries.

13.10.15 `nischttl`

The `nischttl` command changes the time-to-live value of an NIS+ object. When an option expires because the time-to-live has decremented to zero, it is flushed from the cache. Once an object is flushed from the cache, a new copy will be required. Therefore, assigning short time-to-live values for objects which change frequently will help keep them current while assigning longer time-to-live values for objects which are fairly stable will result in more efficient retrievals.

```
boson# nischttl 2d hosts.org_dir.physics.jhu.edu
```

13.10.16 `nisdefaults`

The `nisdefaults` command returns the default values for the NIS+ name returned by calls to the local naming function.

```
boson# nisdefaults
Principal Name: boson.physics.jhu.edu.
Domain Name: physics.jhu.edu.
Host Name: boson.physics.jhu.edu.
Group Name:
Access Rights: —rmcdr--r--
Time to live: 12:00:00
Search Path: physics.jhu.edu.
   jhu.edu.
```

13.10.17 `nisgrpadm`

The `nisgrpadm` command is used to administer groups. It can be used to create, destroy, or list groups or add or delete members. NIS+ groups are represented using a syntax similar to that of NIS+ objects, but they are stored in `groups_dir` namespace rather than the `org_dir` namespace.

Groups can contain explicit members, explicit nonmembers, and groups of members (implicit or recursive). Implicit members belong to another NIS+ group, while recursive members belong to another NIS+ domain. Groups of nonmembers is also possible. Nonmembers are specified by preceding the member name or group name with a minus sign.

```
boson# nisgrpadm -c friends.physics.jhu.edu.
Group "friends.physics.jhu.edu." created.
```

```
boson# nisgrpadm -a friends.physics.jhu.edu jones
Added "jones.physics.jhu.edu." to group "friends.physics.jhu.edu."
boson# nisgrpadm -a friends.physics.jhu.edu -scrooge.physics.jhu.edu.
Added "-scrooge.physics.jhu.edu." to group "friends.physics.jhu.edu."
boson# nisgrpadm -l friends.physics.jhu.edu
Group entry for "friends.physics.jhu.edu." group:
Explicit members:
   jones.physics.jhu.edu.
   slee.physics.jhu.edu.
No implicit members
No recursive members
Explicit nonmembers:
   scrooge.physics.jhu.edu.
No implicit nonmembers
No recursive nonmembers
```

13.10.18 `nissetup`

The `nissetup` command is a script used to set up an NIS+ domain. It creates the `org_dir` and `groups_dir` subdirectories for the NIS+ domain, but does not populate them. The tables can be populated with the `nispopulate` script or with the `nisaddent` commands.

13.10.19 `nisshowcache`

The `nisshowcache` command prints the contents of the per-machine shared-directory cache file. All the hosts using NIS+ on the particular system use this information.

```
boson# nisshowcache
Cold Start Directory:
dir_name:'physics.jhu.educ.'
NisDirCacheEntry[1]:
dir_name:'groups_dir.physics.jhu.edu.'
NisDirCacheEntry[2]:
dir_name:'org_dir.physics.jhu.edu.'
```

13.10.20 `nistbladm`

The `nistbladm` command provides the means to manipulate NIS+ objects. You can create, destroy, or simply list objects with this command. To create a new table, you'll have to assign it a name, a table type (a string you create), and columns.

```
boson# nistbladm -c proj_tbl name=S,a+r,o+m desc=S,a+r projects.physics.jhu.edu.
                 ^ ^        ^   ^        ^    ^   ^
                 | |        |   |        |    |   |
                 | |        |   |        |    |   +---- table name
                 | |        |   |        |    +-------- column attributes
                 | |        |   |        +-------------- column name
                 | |        |   +------------------------ column attributes
                 | |        +---------------------------- column name
                 | +---------------------------------------- table type
```

13.10.21 `nisupdkeys`

The `nisupdkeys` command updates the public keys in an NIS+ directory object.
If the public key for an NIS+ server is changed, it also propagates the changed
keys to all directory objects which reference that server.

13.11 Planning Your NIS+ Installation

Before you take any steps toward setting up NIS+ for your organization, you
should map out the namespace that you want. The root domain should correspond to your organization. It might have a name like `BigBucks.com` or
`Physics.jhu.edu`. You also need to determine which host will act as your
root-domain server and how many root replica servers you want to maintain.
Then you need to decide whether to establish subdomains for fairly independent business units or departments. Each time you set up a domain, you'll need
to determine which set of hosts should be clients of that domain. You will have
clients of your root domain as well as clients of your subdomains.

The number and layout of NIS+ domains that you will create will depend very
heavily on the structure of your organization and the people who will be maintaining this information. Try to avoid creating too many domains, especially if
there will be a lot of interaction between them since this will proliferate the requirement to maintain credentials to support these interactions. Create domains
when there is a clear administrative advantage and when the resultant domain
represents a unit of your organization which is likely to be highly autonomous.

13.12 Setting Up NIS+

The first step in setting up NIS+ is to identify and configure the root-domain
server. Following this, you will need to populate the root domain with the information about your network and set up the root server's clients. Some of the
clients can later be turned into replica servers. Others may be used to serve as
masters of subdomains.

Following setup of your root domain, you may want to set up non–root domains, each composed of domain servers, replicas, and clients. You will need to
populate your NIS+ tables at these levels as well.

In Solaris 2.3 and later, most of the commands needed to set up NIS+ are incorporated into three scripts. These are Bourne shells scripts and are stored in `/usr/lib/nis`.

`nisserver`	Sets up the root master server as well as replica servers
`nispopulate`	Populates the tables from the source that you specify
`nisclient`	Creates credentials for hosts and users; initializes

In addition to these scripts, you'll have to use a few NIS+ commands. Since the scripts will establish default tables and authorizations, you'll have to add any custom tables, and change permissions from the standard where required. You'll also need to add additional people to the `admin` group. If you want your clients to also use DNS to resolve hostnames, you'll need to specifically set this up.

13.13   Setting Up the Root Domain

Once you've selected the name and server for your root domain, you can begin setting up NIS+. To be sure that the configuration scripts are accessible to you add `/usr/lib/nis` to your path with one of the commands listed in Fig. 13.4.

The system is now configured as a root server for domain `physics.jhu.edu`. You can now populate the standard NIS+ tables by using the `nispopulate` or the `/usr/lib/nis/nisaddent` command. The nispopulate command will let you take network information from the `/etc` files or directly from NIS. What works for you will depend on whether you have an NIS master that corresponds one-to-one with the new domain. More than likely, you will only be using a subset of a much larger host and user database, since many existing workstations and users might be appropriately maintained within a subdomain you haven't yet established. In any case, if you can get the information that you want in the appropriate format (e.g., make it look like the `/etc` files), you can use it to populate the new NIS+ tables. In the example shown in Fig. 13.5, we have used all the infor-

```
setenv PATH $PATH:/usr/lib/nis cs.jhu.edu.created
protocols.org_dir.physics.jhu.edu. created
rpc.org_dir.physics.jhu.edu. created
services.org_dir.physics.jhu.edu. created
timezone.org_dir.physics.jhu.edu. created


adding credential for boson.physics.jhu.edu…
Enter login password:
Wrote secret key into /etc/.rootkey


setting NIS+ group admin.physics.jhu.edu…
restarting root server at security level 2…
```

Figure 13.4 Using `nisserver` script.

```
boson#./nispopulate -Y -h eta

NIS+ Domainname :physics.jhu.edu.
YP Domain :physics.jhu.edu
YP Server Hostname :eta

Is this information correct? (Y or N) N

NIS+ Domainname: [+pha.jhu.edu.] physics.jhu.edu
NIS Domainname: [physics.jhu.edu] +pha.jhu.edu
NIS Hostname: [eta]

NIS+ Domainname :physics.jhu.edu.
YP Domain :+pha.jhu.edu
YP Server Hostname :eta

Is this information correct? (Y or N)

This script will populate the following NIS+ tables for domain
physicis.jhu.edu. from the YP maps in domain +pha.jhu.edu:
auto_master auto_home ethers group hosts networks passwd protocols services
rpc netmasks bootparams netgroup aliases

Do you want to continue? (Y or N)

populating auto_master table from +phs.jhu.edu YP domain..s
auto_master table done.

populating auto_master table from +phs.jhu.edu YP domain…
populating auto_home table from +pha.jhu.edu YP domain…
auto_home table done.

populating ethers table from +pha.jhu.edu YP domain…

populating group table from +pha.jhu.edu YP domain…
parse error: no gid (key +)
group table done.

populating hosts table from +pha.jhu.edu YP domain…
parse error: no gid (key +)
group table done.
```

Figure 13.5 Using nispopulate.

```
populating hosts table from +pha.jhu.edu YP domain...u
hosts table done.

Populating the NIS+ credential table for domain physics.jhu.edu.
from hosts table. The passwd used will be nisplus.

dumping hosts table...
loading credential table...
apl-gw.apl.jhu.edu.physics.jhu.edu.:domain of principal 'physics.jhu.edu.'
does not match destination domain''.
Should only add DES credential of principal in its home domain
nisaddcred: unable to create credential.
bo.mrs.jhu.edu.physics.jhu.edu.:domain of principal 'physics.jhu.edu.' does
not match destination domain''.
Should only add DES credential of principal in its home domain
nisaddcred: unable to create credential.

The credential table for domain physics.jhu.edu. has been populated.
populating networks table from +pha.jhu.edu YP domain...
networks table done.

populating passwd table from +pha.jhu.edu. YP domain...
from passwd table. The passwd used will be nisplus.

dumping passwd table...
loading credential table...
nisaddcred: LOCAL credentials with auth_name '6006' already belongs to
'fos.physics.jhu.edu.'.
nisaddcred: LOCAL credentials with auth_name '6006' already belongs to
'fos.physics.jhu.edu.'.

The credential table for domain physics.jhu.edu. has been populated.

populating protocols table from +pha.jhu.edu YP domain...
protocols table done.

populating services table from +pha.jhu.edu YP domain...
services table done.

populating rpc table from +pha.jhu.edu YP domain...
rpc table done.
```

Figure 13.5 (*Continued*).

```
populating netmasks table from +pha.jhu.edu YP domain…
parse error: no mask (key #)
netmasks table done.

populating bootparams table from +pha.jhu.edu YP domain…
bootparams table done.

populating netgroup table from +pha.jhu.edu YP domain…
netgroup table done.

populating aliases table from +pha.jhu.edu YP domain…
aliases table done.

Done!
```

Figure 13.5 *(Continued)*.

mation from the previous NIS domain. Note, however, that hosts in /etc/hosts clearly belonging to another domain are rejected with a message saying that the domain of the principal does not match the destination domain. This will occur with hosts that were specified in your /etc/hosts file or NIS map with fully qualified host addresses, like the name apl-gw.apl.jhu.edu. After the script appends the new domain name, this hostname would become apl-gw.apl.jhu.edu.physics.jhu.edu. Such a host (if it were not a mistake) would not be a client of the root master server.

13.14 Setting Up Root-Domain Clients

Once you've established the root-domain server and populated its tables, you can begin to set up its clients. All the hosts which exist at the root-master level will have the root-domain name as part of their fully qualified name. The workstation hbar, for example, if it becomes a client of the root domain, physics.jhu.edu, will be hbar.physics.jhu.edu.

The root-master server itself is a client of the root domain. However, it is already established as such and has its credentials set up by the time you finish setting it up as the root-master server. For all other clients at this level, use the nisclient script. You must be logged in as superuser on the client you are setting up as an NIS+ client.

To set up additional NIS+ clients, you'll need to know the domain name for the root domain, the password that was created by the nispopulate script (the default is nisplus), the root password of the host you're setting up, and the IP address of the root-master server. Using the nisclient script for clients of non–root domains will require corresponding information for the non–root master. You may want to allow individuals in your organization to set up their own hosts (they will need root access). If so, give them the information shown below, and they will be able to run the script.

```
NIS+ Client:              ———
Client Root Password:     ———
Domain Master Name:       ———
Domain Master IP address: ———
Network Password:         ———
```

You or they will then run the `nisclient` script with a few arguments. The `-i` specifies that the client is being initialized. The `-d` is followed by the domain name. The `-h` is followed by the hostname of the NIS+ server. The command

```
hbar# nisclient -i -d physics.jhu.edu. -h boson
```

will then add the client, `hbar`, to the `physics.jhu.edu` domain, and its fully qualified name will be `hbar.physics.jhu.edu`.

Interactions with the `nisclient` script are shown in Fig. 13.6.

Once you've initialized the client using the `nisclient` script as shown here, the users of the particular client must also be initialized. To do this, all users should log in as themselves and will need the default network password. Using

```
hbar# nisclient -i -d physics.jhu.edu.-h boson

Initializing client hbar for domain "physics.jhu.edu."…
Once initialization is done, you will need to reboot your machine.

Do you want to continue (Y or N) Y

Enter server boson's IP address: 128.220.26.111

setting up the name service switch information…

Please enter the network password that your administrator gave you.
Please enter the Secure-RPC password for root: nisplus (this will not echo)

Please enter the login password for root: whatever (this will not echo)
Wrote secret key into /etc/.rootkey

Client initialization completed!!
Please reboot your machine for changes to take effect.
```

Figure 13.6 Interactions with `nisclient` script.

```
hbar% nisclient -u
Please enter the network password that your administrator gave you.
Please enter the Secure-RPC password for jones:
Please enter the login password for jones:

All users of this NIS+ client must go through this procedure.
```

Figure 13.7 Using nisclient script.

the nisclient script to initialize a user requires only a single argument -u as shown in Fig. 13.7. Here, user jones is initializing herself. She also has to enter the default network password (same as the Secure-RPC password) and her own login password to verify that it is actually she. Make sure the user is logged into a machine in the same domain in which her credentials were created (i.e., the domain in which her password entry was processed by nispopulate).

13.15 Adding Replica Servers

Once a client is set up as an NIS+ client, you can convert it to an NIS+ non–root-domain NIS+ server or a replica for the root master or a non–root-master server. Replicas contain copies of all the NIS+ information maintained by the master server. Non–root masters contain all the information for that portion of the overall NIS+ domain. You can also configure these hosts to be NIS-compatible if needed. However, masters and replicas for the same domain should all be set up the same.

To convert an NIS+ client to an NIS+ server, you will start up the NIS+ daemon, rpc.nisd. You must be logged in as root to do this. Use the -Y option if the master server for that domain supports NIS compatibility. Add a -B option if you are also using DNS. DNS forwarding will allow unresolved hostnames to be processed by DNS.

```
hbar# rpc.nisd
or
hbar# rpc.nisd -Y
or
hbar# rpc.nisd -Y -B
```

To configure this server to start up with these options for NIS and DNS, uncomment the line beginning with EMULYP in the /etc/init.d/rpc file and make it look like the one below. The line below specifies both NIS compatibility and DNS forwarding. When rpc.nisd starts up during a reboot, it will pick up these options from this line.

```
EMULYP="-Y -B"
```

To use DNS forwarding, you must also configure your `/etc/nsswitch` file to include `dns` in the search path for hostnames and set up your `/etc/resolve.conf` and `/etc/boot.named` files. The internet domain name system daemon, `in.named`, needs to be running, but will start automatically at boot time.

13.16   Setting Up Non–Root Domains

To set up an NIS+ client to be an NIS+ replica, you use the `nisserver` script on the root master with a `-M` option to specify that you are setting up a new master server. You also need to specify the new non–root subdomain using the `-d` option and the name of the new master server. An example is shown below.

```
boson: nisserver -M -d highenergy.physics.jhu.edu. -h fermion
```

The new master server will be set up with the same default values of the root-master server. You next need to populate the subdomain on the new master server itself. It is a good idea to have replica servers for subdomains just as it is a good idea to have replicas for the root-master server.

13.17   Setting Up Domain Clients

Setup of an NIS+ client involves several steps. It is necessary to establish its security credentials, add the client to the proper groups, determine which domain it belongs to, and prepare the name service switch settings which define alternatives that it will use in locating network service information.

To install a client for an NIS+ subdomain, you use the same script as you would installing a client in the root domain, but specify the subdomain following the `-d` option in your command.

```
fermion# nisclient -i -d highenergy.physics.jhu.edu. -h hbar
```

13.18   Summary

This chapter has only introduced NIS+ and provided a synopsis of its services and setup scripts. To really understand NIS+, you need to use it. We also recommend several manuals available in AnswerBook, the *NIS+ Quick Start* and the *Administering NIS+ and DNS* guides; see also Rick Ramsey, *All About Administering NIS+,* SunSoft, 1993.

Theory of Operation

14

The Solaris
Kernel

One major change that Solaris 2.x brings is the structure and function of the kernel. Formerly the kernel was a statically linked program image that was stored in the file /vmunix. The structure and implementation of the kernel under Solaris 2.x has changed and now lives as a dynamically linked program stored in /kernel/unix. This module will explore these changes and some of the commands and features available to the system administrator to take advantage of this new structure.

14.1 Kernel Functionality

The traditional UNIX operating system supports the notion that a file has a "place to live" and that a process has a "life." These two notions and the two entities involved, a file and a process, are still central concepts to the Solaris operating system. The purpose of the kernel is to act as a resource manager to control the needs of these two items. The kernel is needed to manage these resources because they are typically limited in supply. Such resources include, but are not limited to, the following:

Memory

Disk drives

Network

Other processes

Some examples of a process requesting a system resource or service are when

- A process will need a file [open() system call] and load the data that is stored there [read() system call].

- A process will communicate with another process or machine via the network [`socket()` or `t_open()` system calls].

- A process will need room in memory to build a table for temporary use [`malloc()` system call].

- A process desires to communicate with another process via shared memory [`shm_at()` system call].

Notice that any request for system services is made through a system call. That is the function of system calls. Anytime a process needs a system service or resource, a system call must be made and the kernel will run on behalf of that process in order to acquire the service or resource. This leads to the first important concept. All processes run in either kernel mode (also known as *system mode*) or in user mode. The transition from user mode to kernel mode is made via the system call (Fig. 14.1) and the transition from kernel to user mode is made on return from the system call. There are only two ways to return from a system call: (1) the service or resource was acquired and the local program may use it or (2) the resource was not available and the system call failed.

Responding to system calls (or service requests) is the first major function of the kernel and is an example of a synchronous activity. It is synchronous because the kernel acted directly as a result of the system call made by the process. The number of system calls can also be used as a measure of how much work the kernel is doing or helping to determine whether the system is being slowed down by too much kernel work. Using the `vmstat` command you can determine how many system calls were made during a certain time period.

When a process is running in user mode, it will use local data, locally mapped in files, and a local stack. In short, the process will have all the resources it needs to continue locally. This is important because if all the resources are available, they can be accessed very quickly compared to accessing kernel resources. For example, a local memory-mapped file can be accessed up to 100 times faster than executing a read or write system call on the same file. The ac-

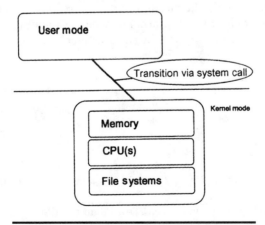

Figure 14.1 Transition from user mode to kernel mode.

tual performance gain depends on many factors, including architecture and network performance, but the comparison is still valid. Later, when threads are discussed, we will discover that a local thread context switch executes three to five times faster than a kernel context switch and faster than the traditional `fork` and `execv` system calls. This is because threads are a local resource, not a kernel resource, and no kernel intervention is required.

When a process is running in kernel mode, it is running on a shared image of the kernel. All other processes running in kernel mode are also using this shared image, and therefore things do not happen as fast. A common example is a group of processes all requesting access to the same disk drive or even the same file. All these processes will be operating in kernel mode, but since there is only one shared kernel and one disk drive, each process will have to wait its turn for access to the file.

The kernel has one other major function besides acting as a resource manager for files and processes (synchronous events). The kernel must respond to interrupts from devices. These interrupts occur because a process requested a service from a particular device, and when the interrupt occurs, the process must be notified that the service is ready. However, the interrupts do not have any knowledge of the source of the request. The request was started by a process, and the kernel is simply notified when the device access is complete. This is an example of an *asynchronous* activity (see Fig. 14.2).

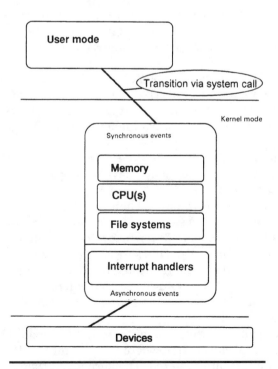

Figure 14.2 Kernel structure: asynchronous versus synchronous activities.

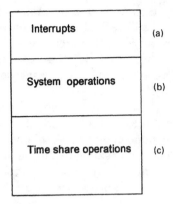

Interrupts	(a)
System operations	(b)
Time share operations	(c)

Figure 14.3 Default scheduling classes.

The picture is now complete. There are basically three major operations that must be regulated by the kernel: processes in user mode, processes in kernel mode, and responses to asynchronous events from hardware devices. In the Solaris 2.x kernel, each of these three modes of operation have a separate *scheduling class*. By default, there are three scheduling classes, timeshare (TS), system (SYS), and the interrupt class (Fig. 14.3).

All processes operating under user mode are in the timeshare scheduling class and are subject to timesharing between the other timeshare processes. In other words, a user mode process is subject to involuntary context switches due to running out of time.

Kernel mode processes are not subject to such timesharing. A kernel mode process will continue to run until it voluntarily gives up the CPU (goes to sleep) or the resource it is seeking to acquire becomes free (return from system call). Additionally, all system mode processes run at higher priority than do all timeshare processes.

To be precise, there is no interrupt scheduling class. The scheduling algorithm, however, responds to all interrupts by guaranteeing that they will run at the highest priority in the system.

Here is an example showing the whole mechanism. A process, running in user mode, will make an `open()` and a `read()` system call. This would happen, for example, if the `cat <files>` command were executed. A request is made to the kernel to fetch the data from a file. This sort of request will typically require access to the disk drive where the requested file lives. One argument to the `read()` call is a buffer where the results of the read will be stored on return from the system call. This buffer is a local resource which can be used when control is returned by the kernel.

By making the `read()` call, the process is put into kernel mode. The kernel must then execute the internal calls to find where the data for the file is located and go to the device where the data is stored. The kernel will then call the appropriate device-specific routines (known as *device drivers*) to initiate the hardware activities to retrieve the data. The time spent doing actual device access is fairly long in computer terms. A typical device (e.g., a disk) is on the order of 15 ms. In that amount of time a CPU running at 40 MHz can run about 6000 instructions! Rather than have the kernel simply spin CPU cycles and wait for the device to complete its work, the kernel will suspend operation of that process and work on something else. This is known as "putting the process to sleep." When the device is completed with its task, it will notify the kernel via an interrupt and the kernel can then wake the sleeping process so it can continue.

Historically, UNIX kernels are not nonpreemptible. This means that when an interrupt is received, the kernel must stop whatever it is doing and respond to the interrupt. The normal response is to wake up the process that initiated the use of the device. The Solaris kernel is fully preemptible. This means that a device driver interrupt routine runs as a separate kernel activity and can be scheduled as a separate entity. Now, when a device interrupt is received, the kernel no longer has to stop what it is doing to service the interrupt. Rather, a separate interrupt thread, running at a very high priority (higher than all system mode processes) will be scheduled and the work of the kernel need not be suspended to deal with the interrupt. However, since the interrupt thread runs at such a high priority, interrupt servicing will still occur very quickly.

In any event, when the interrupt is received, the process requesting the service will be awakened, or put back into runnable mode, and the data will be transferred from the device to the local user address space for use.

14.2   Kernel Structure

One major improvement made moving to Solaris 2.x was the modularization of the kernel. Prior to Solaris 2.x the kernel was a statically linked program that was stored in /vmunix. With Solaris 1.1, which included SunOS 4.1.3, this file was approximately 1.8 Mbytes in size unless kernel configuration had been done. This fairly large program had support for all possible devices regardless of whether they were actually connected to the system. Kernel configuration involved editing a large file in /sys/<architecture>/conf running the config command and then doing a make and reboot.

This process could take a long time and require that the system be rebooted for the changes to take effect. The other drawback of having this large kernel was that it took away memory that could be used for other processes. During the boot sequence, the /vmunix file was read by the boot program. Enough pages of memory were allocated to the kernel and locked out from use by anyone else. If support for devices were still installed, this meant that pages were allocated and locked for use and never used!

Under Solaris 2.x the large /vmunix program has been replaced with a much smaller static core kernel program and a directory of loadable modules. With this model the static core, stored in the file /kernel/unix, is much smaller, about 900 kbytes. This means at boot time only the 900 kbytes of pages are allocated and locked down. These pages are used more efficiently also, since the core kernel in /kernel/unix contains the pages required to run

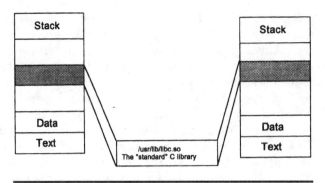

Figure 14.4 Use of shared libraries.

the kernel and no more. In other words, the static core does not contain support for any devices.

The model that is used now is (see Fig. 14.4) very similar to the shared-library model introduced at SunOS 4.1. In the shared or dynamic library model for processes, a process does not link libraries into its virtual-address space when the program is compiled. Rather, a reference to the library and the library call is put into the program. When a particular library call is encountered the library is mapped into the process by the runtime loader (`ld.so`), and the process will continue using the mapped-in library.

There are several benefits to using this model: (1) the actual compiled program is smaller because in developing the program the library was not made part of the program, (2) memory needs were smaller because libraries not used were never called into memory, and (3) the same library could be used by many processes currently running. These improvements saved disk space and reduced the overhead of starting up a process.

The disadvantage of this model is that when a call is encountered for a function not currently loaded, there will be a page fault to load the library. This performance hit was absorbed only by the first process to load a library. Since other processes share the same library, subsequent processes using the same library will use the same memory page.

A model very similar to the shared-library model for processes was used to build the kernel process. When the system boots, the only thing that is loaded is the static core which is stored in the file `/kernel/unix` or the kernel file specified during the boot process (see Fig. 14.5).

File `/kernel/unix` contains only that part of the kernel needed to get started. Parts not included are device drivers, stream modules, scheduling modules, and file system modules. As all these modules are needed, they will be loaded into the kernel address space much as the shared library is loaded into a process address space.

This model for kernel loading has the same advantages as the shared-library model does for individual processes:

- The amount of memory locked out for kernel use will always be exactly the amount needed and no more.

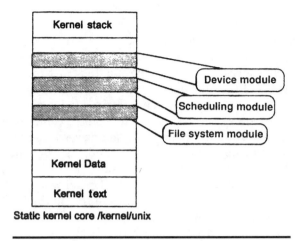

Figure 14.5 Static core and loadable modules.

- Booting is faster because a smaller file /kernel/unix is being loaded.
- Kernel configuration is not needed because /kernel/unix is already the minimum configuration.

The disadvantages are the same as the shared-library model as well. The first time a kernel module is loaded, the process initiating the load will have to wait for the kernel to load that module. This penalty is the same as the penalty paid by the first process that loaded a shared library. This penalty can be avoided by making an appropriate entry in the system configuration file /etc/system. (The /etc/system file is discussed in some detail in a later section.)

14.3 /kernel Directory

The list of modules available for loading is listed in the /kernel directory. Each subdirectory has a collection of similar-type modules. A complete description of each module is too lengthy to list here and changes with each release of the operating system. With Solaris 5.2 there are over 125 loadable modules. The /kernel directory and a brief description of the types of modules in each listing are as follows:

```
listing of /kernel directory
drv         - device drivers
exec        - executable file formats
fs          - file system types
sched       - scheduling classes
strmod      - streams modules
sys         - system calls
misc        - miscellaneous modules (DES, ipc, virtual swap..)
```

14.4   Kernel Tuning Concepts

One purpose of rebuilding the generic kernel supplied with a SunOS 4.x system was to change kernel variables to make system tables larger or to allow a greater number of files or more of a certain type of data structure such as semaphores or other System V IPC (interprocess communication) types.

Tuning kernel variables was done under Solaris 4.x by editing the file `/usr/kvm/sys/conf.common/param.c`. After the `config` command was run, this file was copied into the build directory under name `param.c`. In `param.c` there was a limited set of variables such as `nprocs` and `nfiles` which could be tuned by hand to help optimize system performance. The file `param.c` was edited to reflect the needed changes before the new kernel was created. Lines such as `nprocs=400;` or `ninodes=1000;` would be entered in the file, and then the new kernel was created by issuing the `make` command.

This method of changing kernel parameters required that the system administrator have some knowledge of C programming language syntax. Further, the system would have to be halted and rebooted using the new kernel for the changes to take effect. Rebooting could be avoided, depending on the variable changed by using the kernel debugger `adb` to make your changes. The disadvantage was the need to understand adb, and that the changes would not be documented as they could be by adding comments to the configuration file, `param.c`.

The second issue with changing variables by this method was understanding the effect of making such changes. For example, when `nfiles` was changed, the size of the system open file table (SOFT) was changed. This table determined how many files could be opened at one time for the entire system. This variable would be changed if the error message `File table full` was received. Since this array was a statically allocated part of the kernel, one consequence of making these tables larger was that the kernel itself got larger; the file `/vmunix` grew (see Fig. 14.6).

Other kernel values that were not table sizes were used to optimize performance. Values such as the `tcp` window size would help network throughput, or `ip_forwarding` could be changed to assist with routing. These were still static values that were part of the kernel. In the end, the system administrator had to understand adb, C language, and kernel configuration to effectively tune the kernel. Improper tuning could lead to loss of performance in the event that the kernel table became too large and took memory away from user processes.

14.5   The `/etc/system` File

Under Solaris 2.x, the concepts for tuning the kernel are exactly the same. There is still a list of variables, such as `nproc`, `nfile`, `ufs_ninode`, `maxusers`, and others that can be changed to enhance the performance of the system. There are some important differences, however.

First, kernel variables that used to control the sizes of static tables no longer have the same function. For example, `nprocs` no longer controls that size of the

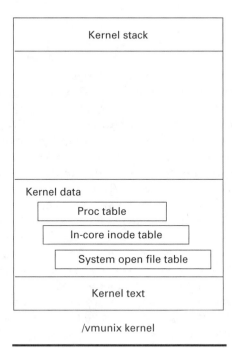

Figure 14.6 File /vmunix and static table allocation.

process table; it is now used as a "high water mark" to indicate that no more processes can be started. The use of a high water mark means that initially there is a very small table or perhaps no table at all. During the operation of the system, the table will dynamically grow as needed up to the size of the high water mark. Attempts to grow the table larger than the high water mark will result in the familiar error messages, such as Proc table full in the case of nprocs.

The philosophy for this is the same as for loadable kernel modules and shared libraries. Resources, in this case a table, are created only as needed and no more. The other advantage is that since no static tables are created as part of the kernel, these sizes or high water marks can be changed using adb, and the system will not have to be rebooted.

The adb method for setting the system variables is the same as that under SunOS 4.x. Use adb to change any kernel variable you need, except when you change a variable that affects a high water mark and not the size of a table; you will not have to reboot the system.

Solaris provides an easier way to change variables if you can accept the requirement of rebooting. Values may be set in a configuration file, and the file will be read when the system is rebooted. The default place to make these changes is the file /etc/system.

To change a value using the /etc/system file, you need to use a line very similar to Bourne shell syntax for setting a variable.

14.6   Other Entries in `/etc/system`

The `/etc/system` file can also be used to improve performance for other system activities. As noted before, the various kernel modules are loaded on demand as they are used by the system. This load will result in a performance penalty for the first process that uses the module. This performance penalty can be avoided by forcing the module to be loaded at boot time regardless of its ultimate usage. The `/etc/system` file is the place to take care of that.

When the `forceload` line is encountered (see Fig. 14.7), the named module will be loaded. The `exclude` line will prevent the named module from being loaded. The `/etc/system` file is read exactly once when the system is booted. Any changes made in the `/etc/system` file will require that the system be rebooted. The only way to make changes to kernel values without a reboot is to use adb. Changes made using adb should also be made in `/etc/system` so that they will be in effect when the system is rebooted.

The line `moddirs: /kernel /usr/kernel` is very similar to using a PATH environmental variable in your shell. It will direct the kernel to search for an alternate directory location when searching for a module to load.

Module loading is accomplished using the `modload`, `modunload`, and `modinfo` commands. If you want to force a particular module to be loaded without rebooting the system, you will need to issue a command such as `modload rfs`.

If you are making major changes to the default `/etc/system` file, you should make a copy of it and modify the copy. You can then ask the kernel to read the modified file at boot time instead of the original. This is done using the `-a` (ask) option on boot. When booting with the `-a` option the loader will ask you which configuration file you wish to read to set up the system.

14.7   Summary

This chapter has examined the basic functionality of the Solaris kernel including process states, the use and function of system calls, transition to and from user mode, the dynamically configured kernel, and the concept of synchronous and asynchronous operations.

```
-------------------------------
#cat /etc/system
forceload: rfs
exclude: rt
moddir /kernel /usr/kernel
set maxusers=64
set ip:ip_forwarding=0
-------------------------------
```

Figure 14.7 Other entries in the `/etc/system` file to forceload a module, set system variables, and use alternate directory search.

For further examination of the topics the following man pages should be read:

```
modload(1), Modunload(1), modinfo(1)
/etc/system(4)
a.out(4), coff(4), elf(4)
intro(2)
```

The AnswerBook also has a good section on real-time programming and real-time factors for system performance.

15

Multithread Architecture

Introduction

All programmers are familiar with a thread of control. A *thread of control* is a sequence of steps to be executed in order to perform a particular task. At any given instant, exactly one instruction is being executed. A thread is synchronous in the sense that the next step to be executed is blocked until the previous instruction or step has been completed.

A traditional UNIX or SunOS process is a program with a single thread of execution. While that thread is running, it has access to and control of its own address space. Previous versions of SunOS did not have threads libraries, but it was still possible to create multiple threads of control. Any program that uses more than one process sharing a common piece of data is a form of multithreading (see Fig. 15.1). Typically, these forms of multithreading used the System V interprocess communication forms of shared memory or message queues. The drawback to this model was that each thread of control was a separate process created by the fork() system call and therefore required kernel intervention to manage the process.

To take advantage of emerging multiprocessor technology, a process should, ideally, have multithreading capability. In other words, there should be multiple threads of control within one process. If the threads of control are within the same process, the kernel does not have to manage each thread and events will be much faster.

This chapter will define terminology, and provide an overview of the multithreaded process architecture which will allow the multiprocessor hardware to run at its full capabilities.

15.1 Benefits of Threads

There are several reasons for developing a threaded application model. First, the model will allow users to take advantage of underlying multiprocessor tech-

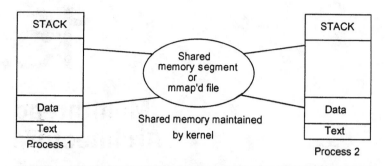

Figure 15.1 Implementing threaded functionality with multiple processes and kernel shared memory.

nology. It is possible to take advantage of more than one processor only if the program or process is broken up into pieces. If there is one thread of control, then only one instruction can be executing at a given moment and only one processor can be used to run that instruction. With multiple threads, there can be many instructions running at a given instant and therefore many processors running on behalf of the process.

There are benefits to be gained from a threaded process even if the computer has only one processor. If a single-threaded process would normally block, waiting for disk I/O, for example, the entire process would be swapped out or put to sleep waiting for the I/O to complete. When the I/O was complete, the process would then have to compete (via the scheduler) for use of the CPU. Each move to the sleep queue or to swap space and back would result in context switches further delaying the process.

If the same process were broken up into various threads of control, each thread would then be independent of the other. When one thread within the process initiated an I/O request, as before, only the single thread would block awaiting completion and another thread from the same process could take over control of the CPU and move the process toward completion. All this would happen without any context switches or moves in and out of the swap area. See the example of threaded execution in Fig. 15.2.

Another motivation for using threads is concurrency. Many applications, especially those with more complex user interfaces can be structured as several

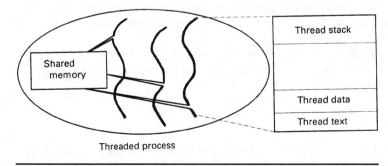

Figure 15.2 Threaded execution.

independent calculations. For example, one thread may parse and deliver command line input, while another thread does the actual computation, while a third may format data for output. Another example may be a window application, such as mailtool. Each button on the `mailtool` panel may represent a thread in the application. A programmer can potentially create thousands of threads with very little impact on system resources because a program will use system resources in proportion to the number of *running* threads and not the total number of threads.

A window server or an application such as `mailtool` are both I/O bound processes. In other words, many threads would exist but be waiting most of the time for I/O to complete or waiting for user input. The other end of the spectrum is a compute bound process. If it were possible to spread out the computations over multiple processors, the entire process would complete much faster.

An example would be a program which does matrix multiplication. A thread would be created to compute each element of the result matrix by multiplying the appropriate operand vectors. Each of these threads could be running on a separate processor. All this would happen transparently to the programmer in the sense that it is not known beforehand how many processors will be available.

15.2   The Threaded Solaris Kernel

In the case of the Solaris 2.x kernel, threading plays a major role. Rather than have a single threaded program as in previous releases, the kernel now is threaded into many pieces which can operate independently on separate processors.

For example, it is no longer necessary to start more `biods` to improve the performance of NFS. Each `biod` is a separate thread, and a new thread will start in response to each NFS request. This means that there are always exactly the number of `biods` running, no more, no less.

Another example is in handling device interrupt requests. In the past, the kernel had to stop what it was doing and service an interrupt by calling the interrupt routine of the device driver for the particular device. Now the interrupt routines are simply scheduled as independent threads running at very high priority, and the kernel will be able to continue work on other tasks.

15.3   Basic Thread Concepts

A *thread of control,* or a *thread,* is a series of instructions that is executed by a program. In traditional UNIX, one process is one thread. With Solaris 2.x, one process may have many threads. Threads have some very important characteristics:

- One thread can execute independently, but may share data with another thread. Data stored in shared memory that is changed by one thread is immediately seen by other threads sharing the same shared memory.

- In general, there is no way to predict the order of execution or completion of the various threads.

- Threads have their own identity and their own priority; each thread and the number of threads is not known by other threads. Each thread has its own address space, program counter, stack, data, and set of registers.

- Threads within one process share system resources such as files. If one thread opens a file, all threads have access to that file.

- Some thread actions may affect other threads. For example, if exit() is called by one thread, all threads associated with a process will exit.

- Some thread actions are independent. Signals, for example, are delivered to and handled by an individual thread, not the entire process.

One very important distinction is the concept of a kernel thread versus an application thread. Remember that the kernel itself is a threaded application. At any given moment, a user application may take an action which will attempt to use one of the threads in the kernel program. This will happen whenever a system call is used, access to a device is needed, or a system resource is required. Kernel threads cannot be created or used directly by the user. Kernel threads are used directly through the system calls and are created by kernel programmers (device driver writers). Applications threads are the type that are available to the user via the threads library (programs linked using -lthread option). Since these are library calls, they are all executed in the user's address space and no kernel intervention is required; thus, they are very fast and use no system resources. The catch is that even when a program is running in user mode, i.e., needs no system resources, it needs the kernel to schedule its execution on a processor. So an interface between the user and the kernel for execution is needed; this interface is called a *lightweight process* (LWP) (see Fig. 15.3).

The thread library schedules runnable threads by allocating an LWP which the scheduler then uses to allocate processor resources. From a user level, an LWP can be thought of as a virtual CPU. (LWPs are discussed in detail later.)

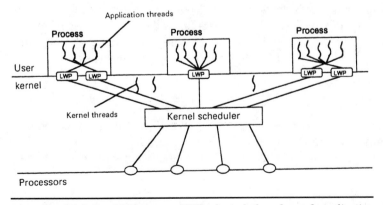

Figure 15.3 Relationship between LWPs, kernel threads, and application threads.

15.4 Thread Synchronization

Threads from the same process share the same address space and therefore may share common data. If one thread tries to write to a variable and another thread attempts to read the variable, the reader cannot determine whether the variable contains valid data. Some means of synchronizing the thread sequence is required to assure data integrity.

The Solaris threads implementation uses a shared-memory model for performing such synchronization. Library calls are made to create synchronization objects or locks. The locks are placed in shared memory (Fig. 15.2) and are maintained by the threads library and are accessible to other threads, even though other threads are invisible to the thread doing the update.

Locks may also be placed in files which have a lifetime beyond that of the creating process. For example, a file may contain database records which can then be mapped [via the mmap() system call] into the local address space and access controlled via synchronization primitives.

15.5 Solaris Synchronization Facilities

The Solaris threads model is implemented using the UNIX international threads interface which is based on the POSIX 1003.4a specification. This specification calls for four different types of synchronization objects to be used for accessing shared data.

Mutex locks

Condition variables

Semaphores

Reader/writer locks

Each type of synchronization object has an associated data structure which is allocated in the local address space and a set of functions used for synchronization. At a minimum, the function set will contain some form of acquire and release operation. In the simplest form, a typical scenario for synchronizing threads will go as follows:

- The shared data to be accessed will contain along with its usual components a synchronization variable s.

- One of potentially many threads will try to access the data by first attempting to "acquire" the synchronization variable, s. If s has been acquired by another thread, then the attempt to acquire will block and wait for s to become available.

- When s becomes available, the synchronization object will be set to some default value to indicate that it is in use. This will have the effect of blocking any other threads attempting to acquire this object.

- When a thread is done using an object it will perform a release function. This is done by setting the variable to some preset value and has the effect of unblocking other requests to access this data.

The key to this entire scenario is the ability to atomically load and store a variable. An atomic operation is one that cannot be interrupted. If the load operation were interrupted, then the synchronization would not be possible. In the SPARC instruction set, such an instruction exists, LDSTUB (load and store unsigned byte). Although the actual library routine, such as mutex_enter(), is many lines of code, when the actual lock is set, the ldstub instruction is used to test and set the actual lock.

15.6   Synchronizing Kernel Thread and Multiprocessor Activity

The kernel has the same problems as any other program when it comes to sharing critical data and synchronizing threads. For example, there could be severe consequences if two threads attempted to update the time-of-day clock at the same time. Most situations such as this can be dealt with in the same fashion as an application thread. The kernel will acquire a lock and not allow other kernel threads to access the data until the current thread has completed its operations. There are some problems unique to the kernel, though, that must be dealt with. For example, the kernel must respond to external hardware interrupts, whereas an application never does. Also, the kernel must access critical data structures that applications never use, such as inodes (index nodes), proc (processor) structures, and user areas. Hardware interrupts result in software being executed (a piece of the device driver) that can update critical data structures just like any other piece of code. The problems occur when there are multiple interrupts or multiple requests to update a data structure to be serviced at one time.

In the traditional single-threaded kernel using a single processor, the problem was fairly straightforward. Each device or each critical kernel task was assigned an interrupt priority. On a SPARC processor, the priorities run from 0 to 15. When an interrupt of level 5, for example, occurred, all interrupts of lower priority would be blocked out by raising the hardware interrupt priority of the processor.

As an example, suppose a process has closed a file and the inode for that file is being updated. The task to update an inode has been assigned an interrupt priority level of 7. This means that all other operations, with lower interrupt priority, would be blocked until the inode update was complete.

In a multiprocessor system, with a multithreaded kernel, this scheme would not work. If the priority were raised on one processor, the thread would simply run on another processor where the priority was lower. Therefore, another method for synchronization must be used.

There are several ways to implement the synchronization needed for the threads. One is the master-slave relationship (Fig. 15.4) among the processors. In this scheme, one CPU is dedicated to the kernel and has the task of making

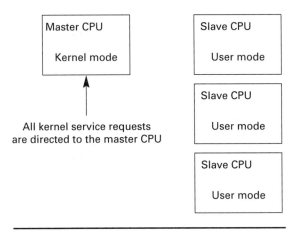

Figure 15.4 Master-slave multiprocessor architecture.

sure that no data is accessed out of order. In this scenario, all interrupts would be delivered to the master processor and all critical kernel tasks would run on the master processor and the original scheme described above would still work. The advantage to this is the simplicity of the design. The disadvantage is that it requires a dedicated processor which may end up being idle most of the time.

Another solution is to use shared memory and locks. When a piece of data is to be shared, a lock will be allocated and used to control access to the data.

Continuing with the example above, the inode data structure itself will contain a lock. Any task requesting an update to that inode must first acquire the lock associated with the inode. The advantage of this method is that no dedicated processor is required and better use of the hardware is achieved since the task can run on any processor.

This is the method used by SunOS 5.x. Each of the kernel threads can run on any processor independent of all the other threads, and critical pieces of data are protected via the synchronization methods described above.

15.7 Summary

The concept of threads and threaded programming techniques is presented as an extension of currently existing programming models as a means to take advantage of emerging hardware technology. The various pieces of a threaded program must be protected by using the various synchronization techniques such as mutexes and semaphores. Threaded programming techniques need to be understood in order to best utilize the Solaris kernel and network features.

For further information the intro(3) manual page should be consulted for general information about library calls relating to threads. There is also an excellent section on threads presented in the AnswerBook.

16

Scheduling

Introduction

The introduction of Solaris 2.x brings major changes to the process scheduling and control algorithms of the operating system. One of the major new features of scheduling in Solaris 2.x is the bounded dispatch behavior for designated processes or even a class of processes. In order to achieve bounded dispatch behavior, more commonly referred to as *real-time behavior,* the kernel was designed to be fully preemptive. With the advent of preemptive kernel processing, the possibility of deadlock or severe performance degradation exists because of priority inversion. This module will discuss the features of bounded dispatch scheduling, the preemptive kernel, scheduling classes, symmetric versus asymmetric multiprocessing, and the table-driven scheduling in Solaris 2.x along with guidelines and commands for using real-time processes.

16.1 Definitions

Before a discussion of scheduling can be meaningful, it is important to fully understand some of the features and terms of the Solaris processing environment.

16.1.1. SMP versus ASMP

The first topic is asymmetric multiprocessing versus symmetric multiprocessing. In a multiprocessor environment, there are some choices to be made as to how to execute the operating system when it is in kernel mode or processing system requests. This topic was discussed in Chap. 15 but is worth reviewing again.

One solution to running the kernel in a multiprocessor (MP) environment is to dedicate one processor to the task of handling system requests, such as I/O and management of system resources. In this case, one of the processors is designated the master (see master-slave CPU arrangement in Fig. 15.4). The master processor is responsible for all system requests while all other processors manipulate user functions. This sort of processing arrangement is known as *asymmetric multiprocessing* (ASMP) because the kernel always runs as stand-alone and there is no concurrency or symmetry in the kernel.

There is a variation of the master processor scenario where the kernel still runs as standalone, but the kernel is not dedicated to a particular processor. If, at any moment in time, there are no system requests pending, all processors will be running in user mode. When any process makes a system request, the kernel will begin operation on that processor and continue until all system requests are done and then release the processor for use in user mode.

Since the kernel is still run as a standalone process, this variation is still considered asymmetric. It is more efficient, however, because there is not a processor set aside for dedicated use. This variation is exactly the way Solaris 4.1.2 and Solaris 4.1.3 handle multiple processors.

The major drawback to the asymmetric model is that performance suffers when there is a large number of system requests. It will be particularly true when there is a large number of I/O bound processes. The advantage is that this model is easy to implement because there is no preemption of the kernel and no need to protect critical data structures.

At the other end of the spectrum from ASMP is symmetric multiprocessing (SMP). In the SMP model, the kernel is split up into pieces or, in the case of Solaris 2.x, threads. Each thread is an independent flow of control which can perform a specific function. Each one of these threads can operate on any of the available processors. Thus the kernel, or at least a piece of the kernel, can operate concurrently or symmetrically on more than one processor at a time. The more threads that are available to run independently, the more "symmetric" the kernel. Solaris 2.x is a highly symmetric operating system with more than 150 threads available to run concurrently in the system. See Fig. 16.1.)

16.1.2 Real-time versus bounded dispatch latency

Another issue affecting scheduling, specifically real-time scheduling, is that of preemption—or, more to the point, a preemptible kernel. *Preemption* is the ability of one process to take over control of a processor while another process is running. The problem with preemption is that a process can be in any state when the preemption occurs. If the process is in the middle of updating a critical data structure which is shared, the consequences could be dire.

In earlier releases of Solaris, kernel preemption could occur only when a process was running in user mode and the preempting process had a higher priority. Since all the data being used by a user mode process are local, i.e., not

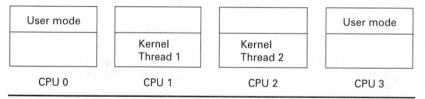

Figure 16.1 Symmetric multiprocessor.

shared kernel data, preemption became reasonably straightforward for user mode processes. Problems with preemption occur when one tries to preempt the kernel in the middle of a critical section of code.

With earlier releases of Solaris, kernel interruption, not preemption, was possible. This meant that while the kernel was running, a process could request temporary use of the processor and then control returned to the kernel. Typically, such kernel interruption occurred when a device interrupted from the hardware.

This scenario becomes an obstruction to real-time performance in UNIX in general and Solaris specifically. If a process tries to preempt a processor where the kernel is running, the process is delayed until the kernel has completed its task. In a real-time system it is necessary to gain control of the CPU, or one of the CPUs, without delay. The only way to accomplish such a response is to design a preemptible kernel.

In Solaris 2.x, the kernel is fully preemptible. This means that any process needing use of a processor, with appropriate permissions and priority, can gain almost immediate control of the processor. The problem with preempting the kernel is the same as preempting an ordinary process; specifically the kernel may be in the process of doing a critical operation that cannot be disturbed.

In order to be completely accurate, then, the Solaris kernel is defined as fully preemptible with several nonpreemption points. A *nonpreemption point* is a point where the kernel cannot be preempted and thus cause a delay to a process attempting access. However, these nonpreemption points are small in number and designed to execute very quickly. Because of the existence of these nonpreemption points, Solaris scheduling cannot guarantee real-time access to a processor. Rather, it guarantees access within a bounded period of time.

The period of time a process may have to wait because it attempted access during a nonpreemption point is called *latency*. The starting up of a process is called *dispatching* in Solaris 2.x; hence the term *bounded dispatch latency* is used rather than real-time. This means that a process designated as *real-time* is guaranteed to gain access to a processor in a bounded period of time. This period of time varies on different architectures but is typically on the order of 1 to 2 ms.

There is one other problem with real-time performance in Solaris. The virtual model used by Solaris does not guarantee that the page which is needed by the process is going to be loaded in memory. If the page needed is not loaded then the process may gain access to a CPU only to wait for the page fault to be processed thus defeating the purpose of having a real-time priority.

Prior to Solaris 4.1 there was no way to guarantee that a particular page was loaded. After 4.1 and included in 2.x is the `mlock()` system call. The `mlock()` system call can take an address range and lock the relevant pages in memory. The pages are also marked so they are not subject to the usual page-out criteria.

16.2 Fundamental Scheduling Concepts

As the next generation of software applications develop, there is increased demand for time-critical applications to have control over their scheduling behavior. Applications such as virtual reality and multimedia will be divided into schedulable pieces, some of which require real-time access while other pieces will not. One goal of the Solaris 2.x environment is to provide a standard interface to the programmer which allows such mixed-mode scheduling behavior.

With this goal in mind, two features have been included in Solaris 2.x that are available to the programmer for manipulating the scheduling behavior of processes:

- Deterministic scheduling
- Standard system call interfaces

Deterministic scheduling means that the kernel will schedule tasks based on priority and scheduling class. In Solaris the basic entity to be scheduled is a thread. The programmer will be able to decide the initial priority of a thread as well as the scheduling class that the thread will belong to. Once a thread has entered a class, its behavior is well defined, that is, deterministic, because of a dispatch table associated with that particular class. The makeup of the dispatch table is also configurable by the user or system administrator. The table will determine whether a thread will be time-sliced, how long the time-slice will be, and what the new priority will be if the time-slice expires.

The standard system call interface provided for these manipulations is `priocntl()`, which can be used to change scheduling class as well as set priority within the class. The table that will be followed to determine priority changes through the lifetime of the process is manipulated by `dispadmin(1m)`.

16.3   Scheduling Implementation

Scheduling in Solaris is built on the internal architecture of a process, namely, the threads and lightweight process structures that compose a process. At any given moment during the running of the system there is a set of runnable threads which are stored in a systemwide dispatch queue. The *dispatch queue* is an array of threads which are ordered according to their priority.

Each thread has associated with it information for accessing files, user credentials, and signal context and other information. The kernel itself consists of a set of threads which are responsible for a multitude of tasks including paging, swapping, and servicing STREAMS requests. There is an idle thread which will be selected for execution whenever there is no other runnable thread available. The idle thread will be switched out whenever any other thread becomes runnable.

Threads interact using the synchronization objects discussed in Chap. 15: mutex locks, condition variables, counting semaphores, and reader/writer locks.

In addition to user threads and kernel threads, there are interrupt threads which technically are kernel threads. The difference between a kernel thread and an interrupt thread is that all interrupt threads run at higher priority than do all system or kernel threads. Interrupt threads are created when a device interrupt occurs and are destroyed when the interrupt processing is complete.

Since threads have enough information in the thread local stack to be self-contained, it is possible for interrupt threads to be blocked using the same synchronization objects as other threads. Also, interrupt threads will be bound to the processor to which the interrupt was delivered and will not migrate to another processor. This characteristic is called *processor affinity*. All other threads have no processor affinity and will move from processor to processor as needed to complete processing.

16.4 Priority

Associated with each thread is a priority. The priority is initially assigned based on application parameters and potential command-line options. The priority is used to index into the array of dispatch queues. One dispatch queue is a linked list of runnable threads which have the same dispatch priority. The scheduler will look at an array of such dispatch queues and select the first thread on the first nonempty dispatch queue (as shown in Fig. 16.2).

Typically, a new thread or a thread just completing its time-slice will be added to the end of the list of the appropriate dispatch queue. Threads will be taken from the front of the list and put into execution. Thus a round-robin algorithm is implemented among threads on the same queue, namely, of the same priority.

If a thread is waiting on a synchronization object (e.g., a mutex lock), it will not be found on one of the dispatch queues; rather it will be found on a sleep queue, also known as a *turnstile*. One sleep queue is a linked list of threads waiting on the same object. The linked listed is ordered according to dispatch priority. Thus when a synchronization object becomes available, the highest priority thread waiting for it will run first.

16.5 Attributes

Solaris 2.x is delivered with three different scheduling classes:

- Timeshare (TS)
- System (SYS)
- Real-time (RT)

Each of these scheduling classes is a separate kernel module which is loaded as needed. Unless specific programs have been started with real-time priority,

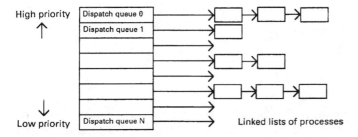

Figure 16.2 Dispatch queues.

only the TS and the SYS scheduling classes are loaded at boot time. These kernel modules can be found in `/kernel/sched/ts` and `/kernel/sched/sys`.

Attributes for each class are determined by the class-specific functions provided in each scheduling module. Certain attributes are determined by general rules for scheduling. For example, one rule says that the higher the priority value, the higher the priority of that thread. (If you are familiar with SunOS 4.x, you will note this is reversed from those releases where the lower the priority value, the higher the priority of the process.) On the other hand, a scheduling class is free to decide on the range of priorities used by that class or even if threads in that class will time-slice. A thread will initially inherit the class of process that created the thread and any class specific data within the parent. A thread may change the class using the `priocntl()` system call.

The timeshare class is the most widely used class for scheduling. All user-mode (non-real-time) threads will run in the TS class. The timeshare class uses a time-slice method for sharing the processor(s). In other words, a thread will run only for a designated period of time before it is switched out to allow another thread to run. The time-slice, by default, will vary from 40 to 200 ms. The length of the time-slice changes according to the priority, which changes every time a context switch occurs. The default can be changed by updating the dispatch table with the `dispadmin(1M)` command. The TS class uses this round-robin scheduling method to ensure all user level threads get a chance to run.

The SYS class is set up to run kernel threads. Threads running in the SYS class have a fixed priority and are not time-sliced. This means that once a thread is put into the SYS class at a specific priority, the thread will run until it is blocked, preempted, or completed. A user may not move a user thread to the SYS class; however, user-level threads will be automatically moved to the SYS class on execution of a system call. Since there is no time-slicing in the SYS class, there is no dispatch table to manipulate.

The real-time (RT) scheduling class is also a fixed-priority scheduling class which *does* do time-slicing. Real-time threads are scheduled on the basis only of their priorities. Once a thread has been put into the RT class at a specific priority, the priority will remain the same. The thread will run for the time period indicated by the RT dispatch table and then check to see if it is the highest-priority thread. If so, the thread will continue to run for another time-slice.

Interrupt threads are not a scheduling class but receive special handling. Interrupt threads are guaranteed to be the highest-priority thread running in the system. This means that if a scheduling class is loaded dynamically, interrupt thread priorities will automatically be recomputed.

The ranges and the global priorities are shown in Fig. 16.3 for each of the classes described above.

16.6   Scheduling

Up to this point we have described the elements and the attributes of the elements involved in scheduling. Before we can describe the scheduling model, we need to make some assumptions about the scheduling system.

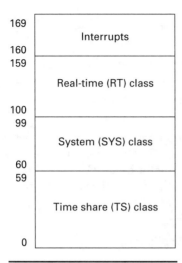

Figure 16.3 Scheduling classes and default priorities.

- The synchronization objects used by threads are contained in global shared memory available to all threads and all processors.
- Threads are in exactly one of three states: blocked, runnable, or executing.

Blocked threads are stored in turnstiles (sleep queues), and runnable threads are stored in the dispatch queue (run queues) (see Fig. 16.4).

Keeping in mind the priority discussion from the previous section, the scheduling model is fairly straightforward. A runnable thread will be dispatched, that is, assigned to a processor and begin executing, if it has a higher priority

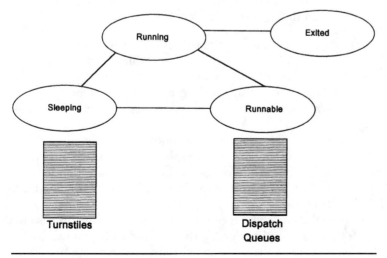

Figure 16.4 Process state model.

than some thread currently executing on a processor. There are some things to note in this model.

- Interrupt threads will always have the highest priority and will preempt all other threads except higher-priority interrupt threads.

- If there are no runnable threads in the dispatch queues, then the processor(s) will run the idle thread.

- The kernel will always select the highest priority runnable thread. This means that if a higher-priority thread, T1, for example, becomes runnable while another thread, say, T2, is waiting for dispatch, T2 will not be the next thread dispatched. The lower priority thread is effectively "preempted" while on the dispatch queue.

16.7   Basic Guidelines for Running Real-Time Applications

From an administrator's perspective, a process must have three conditions present to gain real-time response from the scheduling system:

- The process must be running in the RT scheduling class as described above. This can be done from the command line when the process is started with the priocntl(1) command or programmatically with the priocntl(2) system call.

- All the pages of the processes virtual-memory address space must be locked down. This is done programmatically with the mctl(2) system call or the mlock(3) library call. This will assure the process is not delayed because of page faults.

- The process must be statically linked when compiled. This is done using the -N option to the C-compiler command. Optionally, an environmental variable, LD_BIND_NOW, may be set non-NULL, and this will force all the shared library pages to be faulted in at process startup time.

Once these conditions are true, the process will gain access to a CPU within a bounded period of time, typically less than 5 ms. This time is compared to several hundred milliseconds for timeshare processes. Once a process in the RT class is running, it will continue to run as long as it is the highest-priority runnable process. This statement has two major implications for overall system performance.

First, a real-time process (or thread) is not guaranteed to be the highest-priority process in the system. There may be other real-time processes with higher priority within the RT class, or there may be another class with higher priority than all RT processes. Also, interrupt threads will always have higher priority than will RT class threads.

Second, there are several things which could make the real-time process not runnable. As with all threaded applications, a thread, and thus potentially the entire process, may be blocked waiting for synchronization objects to become available.

These concepts lead to the following general guidelines for running real-time processes:

- Overall system performance degrades if a real-time process performs synchronous I/O, i.e., the process blocks waiting for the completion of an I/O request.

- When starting multiple real-time processes, only one can be the highest priority. Therefore, other real-time processes may suffer from CPU starvation.

- Interrupt processing does not favor real-time processes. In other words, an interrupt for a device controlled by a real-time process is not done ahead of an interrupt for a device controlled by a timeshare process.

- Use of shared libraries can save large amounts of memory. The tradeoff is that the library usage could cause a page fault when used. Real-time processes can use shared libraries *and* avoid the page faults by setting the LD_BIND_NOW environmental variable to non-NULL. The tradeoff here is an increase in process startup time.

16.8   Runaway Real-Time Processes

If a real-time process is stuck in a loop or some other runaway condition, the system can stop or degrade to the point where the system appears to be stopped. There is no easy way to regain control of the system because the process will not respond to control-C or any other signals such as SIGKILL. The kernel variable rt_abort has been added to the kernel for the purpose of regaining control of the kernel in such instances. To gain access to this variable when the system is stopped, halt the system with the L1-A keys and set the rt_abort value to nonzero (see Fig. 16.5).

Setting rt_abort has the effect of changing the currently running RT class process to the TS class with a priority of 0. This process may now be killed or stopped in the usual manner using kill(1).

16.9   Use of dispadmin(1M) to Control Scheduling

As was noted before, scheduling in Solaris 2.x is table-driven. This means that a scheduling class and initial priority have been established for a particular process, all other scheduling parameters, such as time-slice, and priority after a

```
Use the L1-A keys to halt the system
to PROM Monitor level

ok rt_abort 1
ok rt_abort=0
```

Figure 16.5   Steps to stop a runaway real-time process.

```
# dispadmin -1
TS SYS
# dispadmin -c TS -g > /tmp/tc_table
# vi /tmp/ts_table
        Make changes as needed
# dispadmin -c TS -s /tmp/ts_table
```

Figure 16.6 Commands to change timeshare dispatch table.

wakeup, are all determined by looking at a class-specific table which outlines those features. Each scheduling class has such a table which can be modified by using the dispadmin(1M) command (see Fig. 16.6). The easiest way to change the table value is to redirect the output of the -g option to a file. Edit the new file to reflect the changes you want and then use the -s option to read the new values into the system.

The values and meaning for the real-time and timeshare dispatch tables are on manual pages rt_dptbl(4) and ts_dptbl(4). In the real-time class, the table is simple with only two values: the priority and the time-slice (see Fig. 16.7).

The timeshare class dispatch table (see Fig. 16.8) is more complex. Each priority level has six entries:

priority The dispatch priority.

quantum   The number of CPU ticks this process will be allowed before being switched out (remember 100 ticks per second).

tqexp   The new priority of this process the next time it runs if it used all its time-slice this time. This will generally be lower and has the effect of preventing CPU hogs from remaining at a high priority.

slpret   This is the priority a process will be assigned when it becomes runnable after having been done. This is generally higher and has the effect of preventing CPU starvation.

maxwait   This is the maximum number of ticks a process will wait before it gets its full time quantum.

lwait   If a process has waited maxwait and not used its allocated quantum, it will receive the lwait priority. This also has the effect of trying to prevent CPU starvation.

A close look at the default TS table will reveal that higher priorities have shorter time quantums while lower priorities have a large quantum. This generally means that CPU-intensive, noninteractive processes will end up with lower priorities while user-intensive processes will have a higher priority. Since user-intensive processes are sleeping most of the time, anyway, this seems to be an equitable system.

16.10 Summary

The Solaris kernel introduces a much richer set of functions for control of process priority and lifetime. The kernel is fully preemptible, which allows for

```
# dispadmin -c RT -g
# Real time Dispatcher Configuration
RES=1000

# TIME QUANTUM   PRIORITY LEVEL
# (rt_quantum)
        1000          #        0
        1000          #        1
        1000          #        2
        1000          #        3
        1000          #        4
        1000          #        5
        1000          #        6
        1000          #        7
        1000          #        8
        1000          #        9
        800           #       10
        800           #       11
        800           #       12
        800           #       13
        800           #       14
        800           #       15
        800           #       16
        800           #       17
        800           #       18
        800           #       19
        600           #       20
        600           #       21
        600           #       22
        600           #       23
        600           #       24
        600           #       25
        600           #       26
        600           #       27
        600           #       28
        600           #       29
        400           #       30
        400           #       31
        400           #       32
        400           #       33
        400           #       34
        400           #       35
        400           #       36
        400           #       37
        400           #       38
        400           #       39
        200           #       40
        200           #       41
        200           #       42
        200           #       43
        200           #       44
        200           #       45
        200           #       46
        200           #       47
        200           #       48
        200           #       49
        100           #       50
        100           #       51
        100           #       52
        100           #       53
        100           #       54
        100           #       55
        100           #       56
        100           #       57
        100           #       58
        100           #       59
```

Figure 16.7 Sample real-time dispatch table.

```
# Time Sharing Dispatcher Configuration
RES=1000

# ts_quantum  ts_tqexp  ts_slpret  ts_maxwait  ts_lwait  PRIORITY  LEVEL
      200         0        59          0          50         #        0
      200         0        59          0          50         #        1
      200         0        59          0          50         #        2
      200         0        59          0          50         #        3
      200         0        59          0          50         #        4
      200         0        59          0          50         #        5
      200         0        59          0          50         #        6
      200         0        59          0          50         #        7
      200         0        59          0          50         #        8
      200         0        59          0          50         #        9
      160         0        59          0          51         #       10
      160         1        59          0          51         #       11
      160         2        59          0          51         #       12
      160         3        59          0          51         #       13
      160         4        59          0          51         #       14
      160         5        59          0          51         #       15
      160         6        59          0          51         #       16
      160         7        59          0          51         #       17
      160         8        59          0          51         #       18
      160         9        59          0          51         #       19
      120        10        59          0          52         #       20
      120        11        59          0          52         #       21
      120        12        59          0          52         #       22
      120        13        59          0          52         #       23
      120        14        59          0          52         #       24
      120        15        59          0          52         #       25
      120        16        59          0          52         #       26
      120        17        59          0          52         #       27
      120        18        59          0          52         #       28
      120        19        59          0          52         #       29
       80        20        59          0          53         #       30
       80        21        59          0          53         #       31
       80        22        59          0          53         #       32
       80        23        59          0          53         #       33
       80        24        59          0          53         #       34
       80        25        59          0          54         #       35
       80        26        59          0          54         #       36
       80        27        59          0          54         #       37
       80        28        59          0          54         #       38
       80        29        59          0          54         #       39
       40        30        59          0          55         #       40
       40        31        59          0          55         #       41
       40        32        59          0          55         #       42
       40        33        59          0          55         #       43
       40        34        59          0          55         #       44
       40        35        59          0          56         #       45
       40        36        59          0          57         #       46
       40        37        59          0          58         #       47
       40        38        59          0          58         #       48
       40        39        59          0          58         #       49
       40        40        59          0          59         #       50
       40        41        59          0          59         #       51
       40        42        59          0          59         #       52
      .40        43        59          0          59         #       53
      .40        44        59          0          59         #       54
      .40        45        59          0          59         #       55
      .40        46        59          0          59         #       56
      .40        47        59          0          59         #       57
      .40        48        59          0          59         #       58
      .40        49        59          0          59         #       59
```

Figure 16.8   Default TS dispatch table.

real-time processing; or, in the case of threaded programs, some real-time threads and some timeshare threads. Each scheduling class has its own characteristics, and for the RT and TS classes, tables to define the behavior of a process within the class.

For further information, consult the following manual pages:

```
dispadmin(1M)
priocntl(1)
priocntl(2)
mctl(2)
mlock(3)
```

The AnswerBook has a section on real-time programming considerations which includes pointers on how to stop a runaway real-time process and overall system performance considerations when using real-time programming.

Recently, there have been some changes associated with Solaris 2.3. Most important from an administrator's perspective are changes to the time-share dispatch table. The largest time slice is now 20 ticks instead of 100. The intent remains the same, and the table from earlier releases will work under 2.3. Khanna, Sebree, and Zolnowsky [1] present a very good discussion of the Solaris scheduling model.

Reference

1. Sandeep Khanna, Michael Sebree, and John Zolnowsky, "Realtime Scheduling in SunOS 5.0," SunSoft, Inc.

17

File System Internals

Introduction to File Systems

SunOS 5.x supports three basic types of file systems, disk-based, distributed, and pseudo–file systems. Disk-based file systems are stored on physical media such as a hard-disk drive, floppy-disk drive, or CD ROM. Each type of media has its own format. Currently, SunOS 5.x supports three different types of disk-based file systems:

UFS. UNIX File System. Sun bases this file system on the Berkeley Software Distribution (BSD) 4.2 Fast File system. Some extensions have been added since it was first used by Sun in SunOS Release 4.0. These changes and extensions are discussed below.

hsfs. High Sierra File System. Hsfs is typically used on CD ROM and supports Rock Ridge extensions. Hsfs provides all the UFS semantics except writability and links.

pcfs. Personal computer file system. As the name implies, pcfs file systems support reading and writing of MS DOS formatted disks.

SunOS also supports the notion of a distributed file system. A distributed file system is one that can be shared via the network to appear as if it were local to your workstation. Commands and files to administer distributed file systems have been consolidated into the directory `/etc/dfs` for the most part. The intent is that a user or administrator will not have to learn a new set of commands and files for each new distributed file system type. Currently SunOS supports two distributed file system types:

NFS. Network file system. This is the default distributed file system type used by SunOS 5.x. It is virtually unchanged from previous releases of nfs.

RFS.   Remote file system. RFS has been the default distributed file system type for AT&T UNIX implementations for a long time. Conceptually, it is the same as NFS in that files or file systems can be shared via the network to appear local to a given workstation. There, however, are two significant differences from NFS. First, RFS supports the notion of domains. This feature allows an RFS file system to be shared among a restricted group of users or workstations. Also, RFS supports the sharing of physical devices by sharing the block or character device file. In this way, a shared tape drive, for example, can appear local to your workstation.

A *pseudo*–file system is used to gain access to kernel-specific information using the UFS style of filenames and system calls without using any additional disk space. In other words, it provides access to files in the usual manner without using any disk space. Typically, this is accomplished using the virtual-memory (VM) resources of the kernel or swap space. SunOS 5.x supports the following pseudo–file systems:

tmpfs.   Temporary file system. Tmpfs is a memory-based file system which uses the structure of the VM system rather than a dedicated piece of physical memory. Normally, the `/tmp` directory is mounted at boot time as type tmpfs. This version of tmpfs is the same as previous releases of tmpfs.[4]

proc.   Process file system. The proc file system is new to SunOS 5.x but has been part of System V, Release 4 (SVR4) for some time and is implemented in SunOS the same as SVR4 systems. Its purpose is to provide an interface for debugging and to provide an interface to gain access to more general process information. The proc file system is discussed in more detail by McKusick and Leffler.[1]

lofs.   Loopback file system. Lofs is used to create a virtual file system which is a copy of another file system or to overlay an existing file system. For example, `/usr` may be a read-only file system, but we may want to write on `/usr/local` (assuming `/usr/local` is not a separate partition). The administrator may use lofs to mount `/usr/local` to another mount point as read/write to gain access without making all `/usr` read/write.

Several other pseudo–file systems are derived from the SVR4 world. These files systems do not have a visible interface to the user and are used by programmers and will not be discussed at length here.

`fifofs`.   First-in first-out (FIFO) file system entries are made when named pipes or anonymous pipes are used. This is an improvement over previous releases in that one piece of common code is used for both types of pipes. Therefore, the kernel level code to execute this is reduced.

`fdfs`.   File descriptor(fd) file systems allow access to files using a file name space. There are three entries that use fdfs: `/dev/stdin`, `/dev/stdout`, and `/dev/stderr`. These entries correspond to `/dev/fd/0`, `/dev/fd/1`, and `/dev/fd/2`.

`namefs`.   The name file system is used primarily by the STREAMS interface for files. Namefs will allow the mounting of any file descriptor on top of any filename. For example, mounting a filename on top of /dev/console has the effect of redirecting console output to the named file.

The remainder of this chapter will make a close examination of the most commonly used file system in SunOS, the BSD 4.3 Fast File System and take a look at the virtual swap mechanism.

17.1 The BSD Disk-Based File System

The basic SunOS 5.x file system is a modification of the file system released with BSD at Release 4.2. This has been the standard for all releases of SunOS since the release of SunOS 4.0. The default disk-based file system in SunOS is known as the *Fat Fast File System* (FFFS) and has System V enhancements. In order to understand the adjectives *fat* and *fast,* it is necessary to compare the current disk geometry with the original that was based on the AT&T disk model.

The disk-drive geometry developed by AT&T places exactly one file system on each partition of the disk. The specific layout and contents of the file system are contained in a data structure called the *superblock.* Among other things, the superblock contains a count of the number of files, a count of the number of data blocks, and a pointer to the list of data blocks not currently in use.

The contents of the file system are a set of files and a data structure containing the basic parameters for files called *inodes* (index node). The directory entry for a file contains a number which is an index into the table of inodes for this file system. The inode contains many items, including some time stamps, the size of the file, file permissions, the type of the file, and most importantly, a list of addresses which represent the location of the data blocks containing the actual data within the file (see Fig. 17.1).

One thing to note is that the name of the file is *not* one of the items stored in an inode. The only place the inode number and the filename are connected is in the directory file. This means that if the directory entry is deleted, there is no way to retrieve the file because there is no way to find the correct inode!

The traditional (AT&T) file system is laid out with one superblock, a table of inodes, and a table of data blocks. The data blocks range in size (by powers of 2)

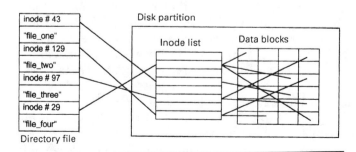

Figure 17.1 Directory–inode relationship.

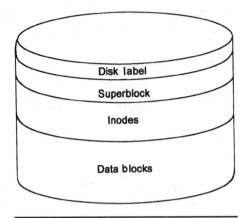

Figure 17.2 AT&T disk layout.

from 512 to 2048 bytes. There must also be space for a disk label and a boot program in the first 8 kbytes of the disk. This leads to the layout shown in Fig. 17.2.

The layout shown in Fig. 17.2 has several disadvantages. The first is the small size of the data block. For large files, this requires many searches to the disk in order to fetch all the data for one file. Next, the layout of the data blocks is not efficient. Over time, data blocks for one file will be spread out all over the partition as the file grows. This means seek times grow also. The same is true for inodes. As a directory grows, the inodes representing the files in that directory are spread out and seek time increases for certain directory operations. Last, since there is only one copy of the superblock, there is the potential for catastrophic loss of the contents of a file system if the superblock is damaged.

With use of the AT&T layout, performance degrades rapidly as the size and number of files increase. One way to restore performance is to dump the file system, reformat the disk, and then restore the contents. This will rearrange the inode and data blocks in an efficient manner, but the problem will reappear as files and directories grow.

Work at Berkeley has led to a better disk geometry.[1] The new layout calls for a disk partition to be divided into cylinder groups. A cylinder group is a group of consecutive cylinders on the disk. By default, on Sun file systems, a cylinder group is 16 cylinders, although the number of cylinders per cylinder group is an option to be used with the mkfs command. Within each cylinder group there is a redundant copy of the superblock, a set of inodes, and a set of data blocks. In order to keep each cylinder group manageable, there is also a cylinder group summary structure which has the location of free inodes and free data blocks (see Fig. 17.3).

The method for where to place new data blocks and new inodes is also changed from the original. All the data blocks for one file will be kept within the same cylinder group (if possible) and all the inodes for the same directory will be kept within the same cylinder group (if possible). These improvements will greatly reduce seek time for files and prevent file data blocks from becom-

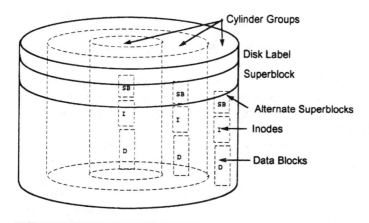

Cylinder Groups

Disk Label

Superblock

Alternate Superblocks

Inodes

Data Blocks

Figure 17.3 BSD FFS file system layout.

ing spread out on the disk. The default data-block size was increased from 1 to 8 kbytes. This means fewer data blocks to fetch for a large file.

The drawback to using large data blocks is that small files will waste space by using an entire data block. The new file system will prevent that by allowing a data block to be divided up into fragments which are typically 1 kbyte within an 8-kbyte data block.

It should be noted that the default data-block size and the default fragment size was established when the file system was created with the newfs(1M) or mkfs(1M) command. With the large data blocks and the small fragments, the new file system receives the speed improvements attributable to a large block and the space efficiency from the smaller fragments.

These improvements have been designed to use a much larger bandwidth of the available disk transfer rate, and further the performance does not degrade over time. Hence the adjective fast file system. What about the *fat* part? With Sun's original implementation of the file system, there was a calculation done with the newfs(1m) command to determine the number of inodes that would be allocated for each cylinder group. The default was to allocate one inode per every 2 kbytes of data. This calculation was made and the smaller of the calculation, and 2048 was used as the number of inodes per cylinder group. This number of inodes could lead to a problem if there were a large number of small files. The file system would run out of inodes before the file system was full.

In SunOS 4.1, the calculation for the number of inodes was not truncated at 2048 and the number of inodes per cylinder group grew. Now there are many more inodes than should ever be needed; hence the adjective *fat* file system.

17.2   System V Enhancements and EFT

With the release of SunOS 5.x, the basic FFFS remains the same. This means all SunOS 5.x file systems are compatible with SunOS 4.x file systems. The only exception to this is in the case of SunOS releases prior to 4.1. Prior to

SunOS 4.1 the file systems were not fat, and attempts to mount 5.x file systems on releases prior to 4.1 will not work correctly.

There has also been a small change to the disk label in order to make SunOS file systems completely compliant with the System V standards. This additional information is called the *volume table of contents* (VTOC). The VTOC is a 512-byte sector in the label that contains a volume name, partition tags, and partition flags to identify permissions for a particular partition. The values are explained more fully in Chap. 4.

Also, added to SunOS 5.x file systems are extended fundamental types (EFTs). These values are used for major and minor numbers on devices and for user IDs. In the past major and minor device numbers were expressed as one 16-bit word, 8 bits for the major number and 8 bits for the minor number. This meant that the largest major number for a device was 255. As the potential number of devices has also grown, the need for a larger possible value for major and minor numbers has grown. Now the major and minor number for a device is expressed as one 32-bit number: 18 bits for the major number and 14 bits for the minor number. This means the largest value for a major device number is now 256 kbytes and the minor device number can range up to 16 kbytes. Also expanded is the value for a user identifier (UID). In the past, 16 bits were allowed for UID or a maximum of 64 kbytes. Now the UID uses 32 bits for a maximum 4-Gbyte value.

Generally speaking, these changes to the label in the VTOC and EFT for devices and UID, do not affect compatibility of 4.x and 5.x file systems. The VTOC is not used by 4.x, so if it is set by a 5.x system, the file system is still mountable and the VTOC will be ignored. If EFTs are used, they will be truncated when using earlier releases. The only issue for compatibility is the changes introduced for the *fat* part of the file system. The increase in the number of inodes means the file system will not be backward-compatible to 4.0 systems. Figure 17.4 summarizes the compatibility issues for SunOS disk-based file systems.

17.3   Virtual Swap Implementation

The current implementation of the SunOS virtual-memory subsystems uses the concept of mapping physical object, namely pages of physical memory are mapped into the virtual address space of an individual process (see Fig. 17.5). Common examples of objects that are mapped are files, shared libraries, and

	Export		
Mount	5.x	4.1	4.0
5.x	OK	OK	OK
4.1	OK*	OK	OK
4.0	No	No	OK

*EFTs may be truncated.

Figure 17.4   File system compatibility.

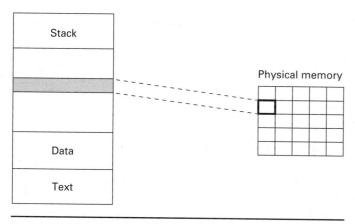

Figure 17.5 Mapping a physical page to virtual memory.

device nodes. Typically, the mapping occurs when the `mmap()` system call is encountered.

In the case of a file or a shared library, the object being mapped has an identity in the file system, i.e., a filename like `/usr/lib/libc.so` or `/kernel/unix`. However, not all objects mapped have such an identity. Since these objects have no name in the file system, they are known as *anonymous memory* or more commonly, `swap`.

When a process begins execution, it is known that some amount of swap space or anonymous memory will be required, although the exact amount is not known. Under the current system of VM, when a process is started it will reserve the maximum number of pages it may need from available swap space. This will assure the process that sufficient swap space is available before running the process. These reservations decrease the amount of swap space available to other processes.

An analogy would be a restaurant. You call the restaurant and make a reservation for 20 people for dinner. The head waiter would then set aside 20 seats and make them unavailable for other prospective patrons. What happens if you arrive at the restaurant with only 12 people? The remaining 8 seats cannot be used because reservations have been denied based on 20 people arriving so the eight seats are wasted.

The problem is the same for a process reserving swap space. What if your process does not use all the pages of anonymous memory it has reserved? As it turns out, this is exactly what does happen! About one-third of the reservations made are never used. This means a new process may not be able to start because it cannot make a reservation even though there is space that may never be used.

One solution to the problem is, of course, to make the restaurant (the swap partition) larger. Another solution is to make the restaurant (available swap) *appear* larger. This is the concept of *virtual swap* (or a virtual restaurant!).[2] When a request for a reservation arrives, the system will count as available pages of swap, in addition to swap partitions and files designated as swap, pages of memory not currently in use.

In the restaurant analogy, it is like saying there are seats in the kitchen if needed, but we are counting on the fact that some people who made reservations will not show up and the kitchen seats will not be needed.

17.4   Performance and Swap Partition Size

The objective of introducing virtual swap was primarily to reduce the need for very large swap partitions and to take advantage of I/O subsystems hardware during paging and swapping operations. The performance objective was to *not reduce* overall system performance.

The problem with making too small a swap partition is that physical memory will be full of anonymous pages which cannot be freed for use by processes. In the virtual restaurant, this is analogous to clogging up the kitchen with customers and not having room for the cooks to prepare new meals. Performance benchmarks showed that, depending on the workload, swap partitions as small as 20 percent of the size of main memory showed very small performance slowdowns on standard benchmarks.

However, if you read the documentation for SunOS 5.x, it is recommended that the size of the swap partition be sized at three times the size of main memory. This is reinforced by the `suninstall` program, which will select default sizes for swap at three times main memory. The reason for this size selection is that the standard benchmarks do not account for the unusual demands placed on swap caused by pseudo–file systems such as `proc`. Remember, *virtual* does not mean *infinite*. Processes can still fail because of lack of swap space even with virtual swap in use.

An important point to note is that the use of virtual swap is transparent to the user and administrator. There is no way to turn off this feature or to force swapping to be done to memory pages rather than disk pages. The only way to examine how many pages of swap are currently in use is with the `swap -1` command. The intent is twofold: first, to make more efficient use of swap by delaying the allocation of pages until needed rather than when they are reserved; and second, to allow the swap partition to be a little smaller than the old swap mechanism demanded.

The real answer to sizing swap is to experiment with your typical workloads to see if there are performance gains or losses when changing the size of swap partitions.

17.5   Summary

This chapter examined the basic terminology, types, and mechanisms used by the Solaris file system. There have been some changes to the file system layout since SunOS 4.x including VTOC and EFTs. These items are incorporated into the *format* which correctly reads and writes these data structures. Also discussed was the concept of virtual swap and pseudo–file systems such as `/proc`.

For further examination of these topics you should consult the following man pages and AnswerBook search entries:

```
fsck(1M)
mkfs(1M)
newfs(1M)
format(1M)
swap(1M)
vfstab(4)
fs_ufs(4)
mount(1M)
```

References

1. Joy McKusick, Fabray Leffler, "A Fast File System for UNIX," Computer Systems Research Group, University of California, Berkeley, 1984.
2. Howard Chartock and Peter Snyder, "Virutal Swap Space in SunOS," 1990, Sun Microsystems Inc.
3. L. W. McVoy and S. R Kleiman, "Expert-like Performance from a UNIX File System," 1991, Sun Microsystems Inc.
4. Peter Snyder, "tmpfs": A Virtual Memory File System," 1991, Sun Microsystems Inc.
5. Roger Faulkner (Sun Microsystems Inc.) and Ron Gomes (AT&T Bell Laboratories), "The Process File System and Process Model in UNIX System V," 1991.

18

Solaris
Networking

Introduction

Solaris 2.x still uses the basic networking model provided by Sun and is based on the OSI/ISO seven-layer architecture. However, there have been many changes to the underlying implementation of the networking model. Some of the changes include:

- Streams-based network device drivers
- TLI programmatic interface to transport layer programming
- Transport-independent remote procedure calls
- IP multicasting
- Kerberos authentication
- Network parameter tuning

This module will explore these changes within SunOS 5.x.

18.1 Networking Technology

The basic architecture used by SunOS for networking is the Open Systems Interconnect (OSI)/International Standard Organization (ISO) seven-layer model (Fig. 18.1). This model is well described by Comer* in particular as well as many others, and the discussion here will focus on how the model was implemented by Sun instead of the functionality of the model.

---

*Douglas E. Comer, "Internetworking with TCP/IP," in *Principles, Protocols, and Architecture,* vol. 1, Prentice-Hall, Englewood Cliffs, N.J., 1991.

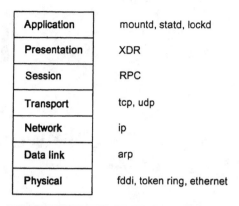

Application	mountd, statd, lockd
Presentation	XDR
Session	RPC
Transport	tcp, udp
Network	ip
Data link	arp
Physical	fddi, token ring, ethernet

Figure 18.1   SunOS network implementation.

Layer 1: physical layer.   This layer is concerned with the actual media for transfer of information such as twisted-pair, fiberoptic, fddi, token ring, and Ethernet.

Layer 2: data-link layer.   In Sun implementations, the data-link and physical layers are included on the Ethernet card. Sun uses ARP and ICMP protocols at this layer.

Layer 3: network layer.   This layer deals with the routing of network message to the networks or deciding if a message is addressed to this particular host. Protocols used to perform this function at this layer are IP (Internet Protocol) IGMP and RIP.

Layer 4: transport layer.   The transport layer is concerned with the transport mechanism of the network traffic. The basic choices for Ethernet are connection oriented protocols such as TCP or connectionless protocols such as UDP. X.25 is a connection-oriented protocol that may be used at this layer also.

Layer 5: session layer.   The session layer deals with things such as waiting for responses to messages and network acknowledgments (ACK). This is generally taken care of by a programmatic interface. In the case of SunOS the interface is remote procedure calls (RPCs).

Layer 6: presentation layer.   The function of the presentation layer is to present the data to the network interfaces in a machine-independent fashion. We do not want to have to deal with big-endian or little-endian issues at the lower levels of networking. Both ends of a networking conversation must agree on the format of the data. SunOS provides external data representation (XDR) as both a set of library calls and a standard for network data representation.

Layer 7: application layer.   The application layer is the interface to the user. Tools such as `mountd`, `lockd`, and `statd` are implemented on top of the other six layers of the network model.

The most important thing to note about the model is that it is exactly that, a model. Not all applications are built using the model. Programs such as ftp, telnet, and smtp do not use the model in a strict layered fashion. Rather, the functionality of the layers are built into the program. Some programs do not start directly at the top layer. Many programmers choose to interface directly with the transport layer, for example, by using the transport-layer interface (TLI) on System V machines or the sockets interface on BSD machines. The notion is that the more a program sticks to the layered approach the more portable it will be across network implementations.

Another notion, that the layered approach may be more efficient, is probably not the case. As a network message passes through each layer, there is more work to be done and skipping some of the layers may actually improve performance.

18.2   Network Driver Implementation

A discussion of the SunOS implementation of networking will begin at the device driver level. In SunOS 5.x the network device driver has been changed and is implemented as a streams-based device driver. Streams-based drivers were supported under SunOS 4.x but not widely used and in particular were not used to implement the network device driver. Before examining the network driver the next section will examine the UNIX STREAMS interface in general.

18.3   What is a STREAM?

The UNIX STREAMS interface is a set of tools used primarily in the development of UNIX communications services. Historically, STREAMS was used to aid development of terminal interfaces. The original idea was that instead of developing a new driver for every type of terminal being made, there would be a standard raw interface. A user (or programmer) could connect to this raw device via a "stream" and then modify the flow of information into the stream by using streams modules which were "pushed" into the stream flow. The original idea of using a stream-based driver to work with terminals has been expanded to include any communication service, most notably network interfaces.

The STREAMS package provided with System V–compliant operating systems consists of a set of system calls, kernel routines, and kernel resources. A streams device driver is a special case of a character-based device driver. A stream is constructed by linking a stream head and a stream driver with zero or more modules between the stream head and the stream driver (see Fig. 18.2). The stream head is the end of the stream closest to the user process.

All system calls made by the user that interface with the stream are processed by the stream head. The initial construction of the stream between the stream head and the driver occurs when the open() system call is made.

Between the stream head and the raw device is a two-way flow of information, consisting of an "upstream" path and a "downstream" path, if you will. Into this flow of data, a user may push modules, which will massage the flow of data received by the raw device.

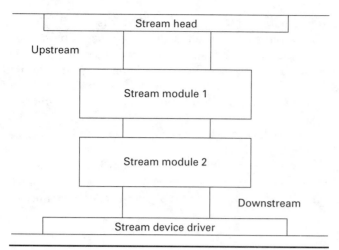

Figure 18.2   Construction of stream.

A stream module represents a "black box" that massages the data as it travels upstream or downstream. A stream module is user written and contains a set of well-defined routines and stands alone from other stream modules. One module may be part of more than one stream at a time, and one stream may have many modules inserted in its data path. Modules are pushed into the stream with the ioctl() system call.

Communication between modules pushed onto the stream is handled by the kernel and is transparent to the user. By using the ioctl() system call a programmer may send information to a particular module such as a signal. Again, such delivery of messages and message handling is taken care of by the kernel STREAMS package.

18.4   Streams and the Network Interface

The advantages of using a stream-based driver for the network interface can now be shown (see Fig. 18.3). By default, TCP and IP protocols are used with Sun network equipment. In the STREAMS-based driver this configuration would look as shown in Fig. 18.3.

The action of configuring the network interface could be made to occur at boot time by using a utility called autopush, which reads a configuration file that defines the modules to be pushed onto a particular stream device. Default network modules and devices are listed in the file /etc/netconfig. By using this scheme, it is easy to see how the basic network architecture can be changed simply by pushing a different protocol module onto the network stream, X.25, for example.

18.5   Transport-Independent RPC

In order to achieve the modularity that is required by the STREAMS protocol, it was necessary to make the other layers of the network model more modular

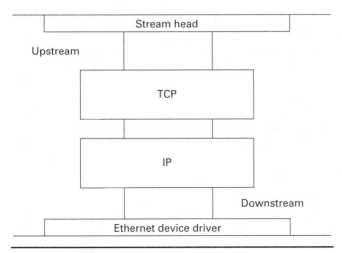

Figure 18.3 Network stream model.

as well. The modules discussed in the previous sections were transport-layer (layer 4) modules, TCP, UDP, and the network-layer (layer 3) module, IP. Since it is not known beforehand which transport modules will be pushed onto the network stream, the session layer (layer 5) module must pass messages to the transport layer without regard to the type of transport.

This concept is the basis for transport-independent remote procedure calls (TI-RPCs). RPC calls no longer specify the specific type of transport to be used, but rather specify the characteristics of the transport to be used. Characteristics such as connection-oriented protocol, connectionless protocol, or connection oriented with orderly release are used in lieu of TCP or UDP.

These properties of network transport are then passed to an intermediate layer whose function is to perform network or transport selection and then pass the message to the transport protocol module. For this mechanism to work, any and all transport modules must be prepared to accept a standard format message. This standard format message is specified by the Transport Provider Interface (TPI). The TPI specification is a standard part of SVR4, and all transport providers must adhere to this specification. At the other end of the transport module there is a similar situation. There must be a standard way to pass the transport data to the network layers. This standard format is specified by the Data-Link Provider Interface (DLPI). The DLPI defines how a user of the data-link services interacts with the provider using STREAMS messages.

18.6 Transport Layer Interface (TLI) Programming

The Transport-Layer Interface (TLI) is the preferred way to establish communications endpoints across the network in System V UNIX. TLI was first used in System V Release 3 as an alternative to the sockets interface provided by Berkeley UNIX implementations.

TLI is functionally equivalent to sockets, but TLI attempts to more closely align with the ISO seven-layer networking model. The TLI functions are included in the network services library, and programs must be linked with the -lnsl option when compiling network programs. This means that the TLI functions are library calls and not system calls. These functions are written to be the interface between the transport user and the transport provider, or in ISO terminology, between layers 5 and 4.

Using TLI is very similar to socket programming in that it uses the client-server architecture, and each endpoint must know and understand its particular role in the architecture. Figure 18.4 lists basic socket system calls and the equivalent TLI library call to perform the same role.

18.7   IP Multicasting

Solaris 2.0 is the first release of SunOS to support IP multicasting. *Multicasting* is a feature that allows messages to be sent to more than one, but not all, hosts on the network. Sending to all hosts is the traditional broadcast which has been supported at all previous releases of SunOS.

The benefits of multicasting fall into two general areas. The first is performance. It is more efficient to send a message to a group of receivers than to have to repeat the same unicast message to a list of hosts. Second, messages can be sent to a service instead of to a system. Some examples where multicasting might be useful include:

- A radio transmitter may send audio packets to subscribing systems.
- Database programs could send updates to a list of servers.
- Multicast could be used to find the location of the nearest service provider. This would eliminate the need to provide the service on each and every subnetwork.

Multicast addressing is implemented using a well-known class D internet address. For SunOS the default multicast address is 244.0.0.0. SunOS provides the means to implement multicast routing. From the perspective of the sending application, this means that the TLI or socket layer is passed the multicast address and all relevant parties will receive the message.

```
Sockets     TLI
-------     ----
socket()    t_open()      to create an endpoint
bind()      t_bind()      to bind an address to the endpoint
accept()    t_listen()    to wait for connection request and make
            t-accept()      the connection
read()      t_rcv()       to receive data
write()     t_snd()       to send data
connect()   t_connect()   to make connection request
```

Figure 18.4   Socket calls versus TLI calls.

18.8 Kerberos Authentication

Kerberos is a network authentication scheme developed at MIT as part of Project Athena. The intent is to provide a public-domain secure networking option for systems. In Solaris 2.x, a subset of the Kerberos Version 4 software is included, so that Solaris systems may use the services of a Kerberos domain. The entire Kerberos software package from MIT includes the following:

- Applications library
- Encryption library
- Database library
- Database administration utilities
- Authentication server
- Database propagation software
- User programs
- Applications based on Kerberos authentication

The Solaris distribution provides the applications library and one application, NFS, which allow use of Kerberos authentication. The applications library takes the form of an option to the RPC programming interface. Solaris 2.x also provides the client side utilities to administer the client side of a Kerberos application.

The most common use of Kerberos will be as an option to mounting and sharing file systems. For example,

```
# mount -F nfs -o kerberos station1:/usr/secure /usr/secure
# share -F nfs -o kerberos /usr/secure
```

To use the Kerberos library, use the -lkrb option on the command line when compiling. In order to use the Kerberos option for sharing and mounting, the kerbd daemon must be running.

18.9 Network Parameter Tuning

With the advent of the STREAMS model for network implementation, there are a number of modules available which may have parameters that can be changed to enhance performance. Some of these modules are listed below:

- /dev/arp
- /dev/icmp
- /dev/tcp
- /dev/udp
- /dev/ip

- /dev/le

- /dev/ie

In the past, specific values and variables have been available for changing through the adb utility. With Solaris 2.x there is a new utility designed for use with network driver modules, ndd(1M). This is a get-and-set utility used to change a particular value for a network protocol. This section is not intended to define the hundreds of variables used by the drivers, but to show how the ndd utility is used and to provide some examples. The ndd utility gets and sets selected parameters from the selected driver. The basic form of the command is

```
ndd [-set] [network module] [parameter] [value]
# ndd -set /dev/ip ip_forwarding 0
```

If no module name is given, the user will be prompted for a module to work with. The user can then view the list of values by entering a ?; the output will show the values and which values are writable (see Fig. 18.5).

Another method for tuning a network variable is to use the /etc/system file. An entry in the /etc/system file such as set ip:ip_forwarding=0 will ac-

```
# ndd
module to query ? /dev/ip
name to get/set ? ?
?                                        (read only)
ip_ill_status                           (read only)
ip_ipif_status                          (read only)
ip_ire_status                           (read only)
ip_rput_pullups                         (read and write)
ip_forwarding                           (read and write)
ip_respond_to_address_mask              (read and write)
ip_respond_to_echo_broadcast            (read and write)
ip_respond_to_timestamp                 (read and write)
ip_respond_to_timestamp_broadcast       (read and write)
ip_send_redirects                       (read and write)
ip_forward_directed_broadcasts          (read and write)
ip_debug                                (read and write)
ip_mrtdebug                             (read and write)
ip_ire_cleanup_interval                 (read and write)
ip_ire_flush_interval                   (read and write)
ip_ire_redirect_interval                (read and write)
ip_def_ttl                              (read and write)
ip_forward_src_routed                   (read and write)
ip_wroff_extra                          (read and write)
ip_cksum_choice                         (read and write)
ip_local_cksum                          (read and write)
ip_ire_pathmtu_interval                 (read and write)
ip_icmp_return_data_bytes               (read and write)
ip_send_source_quench                   (read and write)
ip_path_mtu_discovery                   (read and write)
ip_ignore_delete_time                   (read and write)
name to get/set ? ip forwarding
value ? 0
name to get/set ?
```

Figure 18.5 Sample ndd session.

complish the same as the above `ndd` session. Since the list of values and modules which are available for tuning in this fashion are likely to change from release to release, care should be taken not to depend on this tool too much.

18.10 Summary

This chapter examines the new features of the Solaris 2.x networking model including stream construction, transport-independent RPC, TLI programming, IP layer multicasting, Kerberos network authentication, and tuning of network parameters using `ndd`. These features allow a more robust use of the network facilities and fine-tuning for best efficiency.

For further reference the following man pages and AnswerBook entries should be consulted:

```
The Network Services Library (/usr/lib/libnsl.so) intro(3)
ndd(1M)
kerberos(1)
kerbd(1M)
rpcgen(1)
xdr(3N)
```

Since this chapter is not intended to be a network programming session, the section regarding the functions of the various network layers was intentionally thin. One definitive source for more information is *UNIX Network Programming.**

---

* Richard Stevens, *UNIX Network Programming,* Prentice-Hall, Englewood Cliffs, N.J., 1990.

Index

ABOUT THE AUTHORS

S. LEE HENRY writes a column on Sun system administration for
SunExpert, a monthly magazine for the Sun workstation user's
community. She is a manager of computer and network services at
Johns Hopkins University, and is on the Board of Directors of the
Sun User Group.

JOHN R. GRAHAM has been teaching courses for Sun Educational
Services, both as a Sun employee and as a private consultant. He is
an expert on SunOS internals, network management, and systems
administration.

ABOUT THE SERIES

The J. Ranade Workstation Series is McGraw-Hill's primary vehicle
for providing workstation professionals with timely concepts,
solutions, and applications.

Jay Ranade, Series Editor and best-selling computer author, is a
Senior Systems Architect and Assistant V.P. at Merrill Lynch. Jay
Ranade is also Series Editor in Chief of the J. Ranade IBM and DEC
Series and Series Advisor to the McGraw-Hill Series on Computer
Communications.